14th March

Still Travelling

To Ann. on your 60th
birthday !
Hope it is a good read.
Love,
Sue, Tony, Paul
& Trish
x x x

STILL TRAVELLING

My Life as a Leyland Brother and Beyond

Mal Leyland MBE

ALLEN&UNWIN

SYDNEY · MELBOURNE · AUCKLAND · LONDON

First published in 2015

Allen & Unwin
83 Alexander Street
Crows Nest NSW 2065
Australia
Phone: (61 2) 8425 0100
Email: info@allenandunwin.com
Web: www.allenandunwin.com

Cataloguing-in-Publication details are available
from the National Library of Australia
www.trove.nla.gov.au

ISBN 978 1 74331 871 3

Set in 13.5/17.5 pt Bembo by Midland Typesetters, Australia
Printed and bound in Australia by Griffin Press

10 9 8 7 6 5 4 3 2 1

*To Laraine for her unconditional love and support,
especially when I was obsessed with my own ambitions
and had a not-so-easy-to-live-with attitude.*

Foreword

Like most of my generation, I first heard about the Leyland Brothers when their terrific documentary, *Down the Darling*, aired on Channel Nine in 1964. This was the first time a group of young adventurers had gone on an extraordinary adventure, produced a documentary and managed to sell it to a television station. Until then, documentaries hardly ever appeared on commercial television and the ones that screened on the ABC were produced in-house.

After that, everyone was talking about the Leyland Brothers—well, everyone in adventure circles. I was a young 20 year old Rover Scout and it certainly motivated me to see what I could do. It wasn't long after that—in December of that year—that I headed by yacht to Balls Pyramid, the tallest sea spire in the world, in my first attempt at climbing it.

In 1966 the Leyland Brothers made probably their most famous documentary—*Wheels Across a Wilderness*. The film traced their remarkable journey across the continent from Steep Point, the westernmost point of Australia to the easternmost point, Cape Byron at Byron Bay. And remember, they had to forge their own track; this was well before the oil companies had driven bulldozer cuts across the Simpson Desert. This crossing was an extraordinary achievement for all kinds of reasons, but especially because the four-wheel-drives of those days simply weren't built to cope with the Australian desert. Their Land Rovers broke down regularly with broken differentials and axles, but these dramas made the story even better.

Of course, these days hundreds of people cross the Simpson Desert each year and dozens of them carry a bottle of Indian Ocean water, in the Leyland tradition, from Steep Point to Cape Byron. But back then, it was just not done.

Mike and Mal Leyland were to experience great success. Sell-out crowds of thousands lined up to see screenings of *Wheels Across a Wilderness* in cinemas, church halls and schools across Australia, with queues often stretching down the street. The brothers were forced to learn very quickly about the nature of the film industry, where people tried to take advantage of them. Despite this huge amounts of cash flowed in, making them very wealthy for a time, and allowing them to pay off their homes as well as invest in properties.

Success followed success with the airing of their famous television series, *Ask the Leyland Brothers* which screened in front of Australian audiences for sixteen years. Everyone remembers the famous song, *Travel all over the country side, Ask the Leyland Brothers.*

I first met Mal when I needed some advice on documentary filmmaking. I had made a number of documentaries in the traditional way, using 16mm colour negative film and incurring huge costs. Each documentary actually lost money. I asked industry professionals in Sydney, 'How come the Leyland Brothers can make a living from this? They seem to be doing quite well.' But the industry at that time looked down their noses at the Leylands, and called them amateurish. I said, 'Why do you call them amateurish? These people are making money, while you need huge government subsidies.'

So I rang Mal and explained I was looking for a more effective way of making documentaries, and he invited me to his home. There he explained to me how they had changed over from expensive 16mm professional film to making their films out of Super8 home movie film. It was a brilliant concept and, as you will read in the book, they were so good at it that for many years Channel Nine didn't even know that they were doing this.

At this time I was planning my solo helicopter flight around the world and I needed to know how to document this on film myself. I said to Mal, 'How do you do those beautiful point-of-view shots, looking at you as you are walking along talking and climbing up and down hills? Do you have one of those expensive camera mounts/ steady-cam units?' He said, 'No, Dick, I simply hold the camera out like this at the end of my arm and talk to it.'

Yes, it was as simple as that and I used it extensively on the three documentaries I made of my world flight.

On the day we visited in 1980 it was announced that both Mal and Mike had received New Year's Honours and become Members of the British Empire (MBEs). I remember saying to their father, 'You must be very proud', and he looked at me and burst into tears. As a 'Ten Pound Pom' he had brought his family out from England, and now he had lived to see his two sons become two of the most famous Australians of their time.

I played a small part in helping the Leylands change from Channel Nine to Channel Seven. I was shocked when I discovered that they were being paid such a small amount by Nine and I knew they were worth a lot more. I didn't actually think they would change networks—I thought they would stick with Nine and receive about four times what they had previously been paid, but they did move to Channel Seven for three years before returning to Channel Nine for an even higher amount. Mal tells us that the contract with Channel Nine stipulated that their productions had to be 'amateurish and folksy'—and that's what we loved.

But Mal and Laraine's life has been one of extremes, of exhilarating triumphs and some terrible disasters. I remember the day, on the first of January 1980, when Pip and I called in to their beautiful waterfront home on Wallis Lake near Forster. But I also remember the last time I saw Mal and Laraine, when they were living in a house partially made from a shipping container under almost subsistence conditions on marginal land in the wilderness slightly to the west of the Great Dividing Range.

Mal and Mike were brothers working productively together until they aspired to become theme park operators and created Leyland Brothers World. You will read the sad story of this brave idea and how it turned from being profitable at a time of reasonable interest rates to a complete catastrophe, in which they lost all their millions when interest rates rose to 28 percent, an almost unimaginable amount at the present time. They were paying almost one million dollars a year in interest.

You will read how the pressure of the collapse of Leyland Brothers World led to a total break-up between the brothers. They did not speak to each other for many, many years and to me one of the saddest passages in this book is when Mal receives a visit from Margaret (Mike's second wife) and sees her with an old man behind her whom Mal doesn't recognise. When they draw closer, Mal realises it is his brother, Mike.

When the Leylands went into bankruptcy, the television stations turned on Mal and Laraine, who had to endure current affairs programs attacking them. From being multi-millionaires, the two of them plunged into running a tiny film processing lab, and selling their clothes and other personal items at markets in order to have enough food to eat.

I read *Still Travelling* from beginning to end in one go. At times it is deeply moving; but above all, it is an incredible love story. Mal's first girlfriend, Laraine, became his wife, and more than forty years later they are still married.

They have certainly honoured their marriage vows of staying together for better and for worse.

This is a great Aussie story that will appeal to anyone who enjoyed the Leyland Brothers' shows and watched as their lives careened through the good and the bad times. I simply couldn't put it down.

Dick Smith
November 2014

Contents

Preface

Farewell Brother

My brother Mike died on the 14th September 2009, ten days after his sixty-eighth birthday. At his funeral I sat in the crowded chapel, while a large group spilled out onto the lawns to hear the proceedings over loudspeakers.

As I stared at the polished wooden coffin with my brother's first cinecamera perched on top, next to his felt hat, I reflected on the early days of our extraordinary life together: the childhood that set the strong brotherly bond between us and led to a remarkable partnership that, in spite of our often vocal and sometimes bitter differences, endured for 45 years.

Some of our expeditions were great adventures fraught with hazards. On a number of occasions, we depended on each other to survive. Our connection was locked in place forever. Thinking back over our time as brothers, business partners and good mates, I knew it was unique. Mike was special, but now I had to say goodbye, mate.

Farewell, my brother.

1

A Telegram to the Prime Minister of Australia

It was so bitterly cold that the water had frozen solid. This slippery, glass-like surface made the oddest of battlefields, yet lined up in neat ranks along opposite sides were soldiers standing in rigid defensive poses. These armies were equally matched, as was their stance. One was dressed in green, the other in red.

It was early in the morning, the beginning of winter in 1948. My brother Mike and I were silently watching and shivering while pressed up against the brick wall at the back of our home. A thick heavy fog swirled through the apple trees further down the garden and there was almost no noise. Our wide young eyes stayed glued to the scene on the ice.

'Nothing seems to be happening,' I whispered to my brother.

'Keep quiet!' he said. 'Just watch. It will take a little while.'

There wasn't the slightest movement except the very slow sideways tilting of a few soldiers. Then it happened quickly. Soldiers fell where they stood. Forward, backward or sideways as their warm feet melted through the ice. A cheer went up from Mike when a green soldier plopped into the black depths of the water. One of the opposing army joined him in his icy grave, and I too gave out a hearty cheer. This stand-off continued until only three red soldiers were left standing.

'My side wins,' declared Mike as he snatched them up.

We plunged our small hands into the rectangular tank of frozen drinking water to retrieve our brave lead soldiers. It was almost too deep for my arm and the water was bone chilling. Then we took our toys inside and placed them in front of the open coal fire to heat them up, so we could take them outside in about half an hour for another battle.

This unusual game is one of my earliest memories of a childhood that began in Hitchin, Hertfordshire, England, on the 2nd October 1944. Britain was at war, and apart from my mother and father, three-year-old brother and a few relatives, no one was in any way excited by my birth.

I started school at the age of four and on the first day was led off to school by Mike. He was supposed to look after me and I was to wait for him to show me the way home. Kindergarten children were let loose earlier than the bigger children, so I simply walked home without waiting for Mike. This worried the hell out of Mike and Mum, but after their lecture I never did it again. My brother and I travelled almost everywhere together for the next 40 years.

My family lived in the middle of a row of brick houses with walled back gardens. I shared an upstairs bedroom with my brother, and next to my bed I had a small window that afforded a view over the paved courtyard separating our house from the one next door. I could see beyond this area into the apple trees of our garden and spent many hours surveying the little, limited world I knew.

Up the far end of our row of houses, we had a neighbour who was a bit of a gardener and had his own chickens. He was a kindly old gent who gave Mike and me rides in his wheelbarrow. One day he handed me an egg to take to my mother; this was a great responsibility, for eggs were scarce. I proudly walked home, the fragile cargo cradled in my hands. This was a long journey for one so little and had many obstacles to overcome: muddy puddles, the cat which almost tripped me and rain that had become a heavy downpour by the time I reached the back door.

I scaled the two stone steps but couldn't make Mum hear my shouts. When I raised my hand and gave a good loud knock, I dropped the prize, which splattered on the top step. I was so worried about wasting such a valuable item that I just stood there howling. When Mum opened the door and was confronted by my red face streaming with tears, she picked me up and gave me a huge hug instead of the hiding I was so sure I deserved. I can still see the tenderness in her eyes as she comforted me and took me inside.

These early years were as carefree as could be—but my cosy world was about to change dramatically.

•

It was evening and my family was travelling back from Liverpool by train after visiting my grandmother. Steel wheels rolled over steel rails with a rhythmic clackety-clack, and lights flashed intermittently through the carriage windows. The stomach pain I'd been experiencing for the last hour had become intense. I was curled forward, gazing down at my shiny brown shoes and attempting to endure the discomfort.

'I have that pain again in the belly, Mummy,' I uttered in a weak voice.

The response came from my father: 'So what's he been eating?'

I was taken to sit on the rocking loo of the train, but nothing happened. No diarrhoea or vomiting. The pain persisted. We were travelling in a crowded carriage and my antics caused a good deal of embarrassment to my family. Eventually the pain died down, and by the time we got home I was considered fine and sent to bed.

By the middle of the night the demons were in my stomach again and the only relief I could get was to lie across a lounge chair. In the morning Mum called the doctor. He declared I had a burst appendix and I was rushed to hospital in an ambulance with the siren screaming. At the age of five I found the whole experience terrifying: it was obvious to me that I was being punished because I'd caused so much trouble on the train. I had no idea how serious my condition was.

Once at the hospital my fears grew even greater as a frightening black mask was forced over my mouth and nose. I fought back but there were too many of them in their white coats. The men took my struggle as a sign of defiance and strapped me down with leather binds and buckles. I was then wheeled along a dingy corridor, my head spinning. The faces of those men were very grim and I fell unconscious in a state of absolute anxiety.

When I awoke after the operation, I found myself behind glass like a fish in a tank, my bed the only one in the room. It wasn't long before my mother, father and brother appeared on the other side of the glass. Mum's eyes were tearful, and all I wanted to do was hug her and be home.

My father said, 'This is all we need. Now we'll miss the ship and never get to Australia.' These words are the first recollection I have of any reference to Australia. It turned out we were about to leave England forever: the reason we'd travelled to Liverpool was to farewell my grandmother.

My father had been in the RAF prior to the war, and as a gunner and electrical fitter spent most of the war in Canada training younger men for the fighting back home. During this visit he'd been introduced to a new way of living; compared to what he'd left behind in England, Canada was a classless society. Dad would often tell us how, as a young apprentice electrician converting gas lighting to electricity, he'd hated visiting the homes of the wealthy because he and his fellow workers were forced to use the tradesman's entrance. He had no time for the aristocracy and even less time for anyone who wanted to be part of it.

After the war, desperately wanting to get out of England, my father applied for a post as a peanut plantation manager in Africa. He also applied to migrate to Australia under an assisted passage scheme costing only a token £10. Dad was interviewed several times for the African position, and for a time it was down to him and one other applicant.

Impatient, my father sent a telegram to Prime Minister Robert Menzies. A few weeks later a response came informing him that his family had been accepted and the details of the passage were to be sorted out at Australia House in London. Dad then received news that he could have the plantation job. He declined, of course, which is just as well, as we later heard that the family who did go were killed during an uprising a few years later. I reckon we were destined for Australia.

On the 4th of May 1950, two weeks after my appendix operation, I was considered well enough to make the ride directly from hospital to the dock at Tilbury, London, to board the Orient Line ship *Otranto*. As the ambulance pulled up, I stared at the ship. Its massive steel plates made a long curved wall alongside the wooden dock. I could hardly believe that any ship could be this big.

The launch was an amazingly festive occasion. Thousands of people were gathered on the dock. As the ship pulled slowly away, a brass band played 'Auld Lang Syne'.

Almost everyone was crying and hundreds of coloured streamers were thrown from the ship to the shore. People on both ends of the streamers clung to them until they stretched to their limits and broke. As if an umbilical cord had been severed, our crowded ship of emotional souls was thus set free from Mother England. We were headed Down Under, wherever and whatever that was. For the next six weeks we were to see foreign lands and endless oceans.

We had no sooner left than a call went out over the loudspeaker system for Mr Ivan Leyland to report to the purser's office immediately. Within minutes my father found himself being addressed by the Australian captain of the ship. 'Let's get one thing clear, Mr Leyland,' he said. 'On this voyage you will be treated like any other passenger. Just because you sent a telegram to my prime minister, that doesn't mean you get any special treatment on my ship!'

Dad was quick to agree that this was how it should be, then returned to tell us all about how he'd been dressed down by the captain. He was sure of one thing, though: the telegram had done the trick.

Our cabin, No. 645/8, was a tiny room on E deck. My bunk was only just long enough for me, and so close to the ceiling that rolling over involved dodging a large hot steam pipe. It was wrapped in cloth lagging, but still generated a lot of heat and made gurgling sounds all day and night. The cabin felt like a sauna but we were glad to be under way, and Dad seemed delighted that England was at last behind us.

Life on board ship for me was extremely limited as I was under doctor's orders not to engage in any physical activity for at least six weeks. I was a scrawny, skeleton-like figure with a sallow complexion. Mike restricted his activities too, mostly out of sympathy and a sense of duty to me. Every day was dictated by a routine of set meals at strict sitting times. Otherwise my brother and I aimlessly wandered about the decks with our parents, watching the other children running around and playing games.

For me this was the beginning of a boyhood of relative isolation. I certainly felt like an outsider among the other children on board. Most people interpreted my quiet nature as that of a boy so afraid to mix in that I was too shy for my own good. In reality I'd suddenly lost the security of our cosy home back in Hitchin. We'd left behind our apple trees, our comfortable hearth and the swish of my mother's skirts as she moved around the kitchen. All these familiar things had gone, but they slipped into a special place in my mind. Many years later, I would go back to England and visit my hometown, awakening some of those memories.

On the *Otranto* I felt that my world had been torn apart. My brother was my only friend. At least he was still there, I told myself, even if everything else had changed around me. I didn't fully understand what was happening, and in my own somewhat perverse way, I figured it must all be my fault. If only I hadn't had that stomach ache on the train!

•

About five weeks after leaving England, with a stopover in India, we made landfall in Australia at Fremantle. A large number of passengers disembarked, and since we were there for several days my family went ashore and for the first time walked on Australian soil.

The main thing I recall about Fremantle is the moment when we stopped to gaze into the window of a chocolate shop. There, before our wide eyes, was the most amazing array of chocolates we had ever seen. In England we'd never experienced much in the way of chocolate because that was one of the most difficult things to acquire as a result of war shortages. Mike and I pressed our little faces hard against the glass and stared in awe.

'You can have anything you want in the shop,' Dad announced.

Mike chose a huge chocolate bear, so then I wanted one too. In the next few days, as our ship made its way across the Great Australian Bight to Melbourne, the two of us munched away on our bears. I don't remember getting ill from overindulging, but I do remember savouring each small mouthful. *Australia may not be so bad after all!*

More passengers disembarked when we reached Melbourne, but the majority of the ship's human cargo went on to Sydney where my family made our final walk down the gangway. It was the 9th of June 1950. We had arrived at our final destination in Australia. So where were the fields of wheat and the kangaroos? We'd been shown pictures of these on the ship, but there wasn't a roo in sight, let alone a grain of wheat. Had we been conned?

After a long train journey north from Sydney to the Newcastle suburb of Waratah, we gazed up at a brick block of eight flats. Surrounding the entrance was a curved facade that led to a small hallway and a flight of concrete steps. As we headed up to what was to be our dwelling place for the next few months, the noise of our progress echoed around the barren walls of the stairwell. Compared to the home we'd left behind, this was like a concrete tomb.

Albert and Ada Basford lived in the flat, friends of our parents from England. In order to migrate to Australia under the assisted passage scheme it was necessary to have a sponsor, meaning that somebody who'd already migrated to the country would vouch for the family and recommend them. In the event that the immigrant did not have a job or anywhere to live, the sponsor took on the additional responsibility of providing housing until some more permanent accommodation could be found.

Settling into our new life would require a lot of adjustment. We'd only been shown sunny pictures of the country and were instantly disillusioned. In June 1950 the Hunter Valley experienced a massive deluge that continued for weeks on end. So much rain fell, both night and day, that most of the valley was flooded and towns such as Maitland were completely inundated. The devastating floods of the 1950s have since become the yardstick by which all floods in the Hunter Valley are measured.

After the rains had stopped we finally had the chance to go shopping down the street. I was clutching my mother's hand and, judging by the stares we received from the Australian children, we must have looked every bit the pommy immigrants we were. We paused in the street while Mum spoke to a passer-by, probably asking for directions. At the end of the conversation, the Australian woman said a friendly 'Hooray' as she walked away. Mum responded by yelling out, 'Hip hip!' This caused the woman and several onlookers to burst out laughing.

When Mum later relayed this incident to Ada Basford, she discovered 'Hooray' was the parting equivalent of the greeting 'G'day'. They might speak English in Australia, but we soon realised they also spoke Australian.

•

I was enrolled in the local infant school while Mike went to the primary school. My first day was an amazing eye-opener. Because I was very shy and quiet, I made no impact whatsoever; at least, that's what I thought until we stopped for little lunch. I'd just eaten and was leaning up against a brick wall, in the shade of one of the buildings, when I was approached by a group of about six boys.

'Hoggsy wants to bash you up,' declared one of them.

I eyed the group, who had formed a semicircle around me. 'All right,' I said, wanting to seem agreeable.

'The pommy bastard's pretty game!' the boy yelled to his mates.

I must have looked really puzzled. 'What,' I said, 'do you mean by "bash up"?'

A sinister expression of understanding flashed across the boy's face. 'Hoggsy's bashed up a Russian, a wog, a

Greek, a German and a Frog, but he's never had a chance to bash up a pommy bastard,' he said.

'What is a pommy bastard?' I asked.

'You are, you stupid idiot.'

'I don't understand.'

'He doesn't understand,' the boy echoed in a mocking attempt to mimic my accent. The other boys all began to laugh. From the back of the group, one tall and heavily built boy stepped forward and stood right in front of my face. 'This is Hoggsy,' the spokesman said to me.

'Come on pommy, let's have a go!' Hoggsy said, raising his fists as if he were a boxer. It was only at this point that I understood the meaning of 'bash up'.

'I'm not fighting anyone,' I declared in a small, frightened voice.

A bell rang, signalling that it was time for us to return to class. The crowd dissipated quickly, while Hoggsy's bigmouth spokesman called back to me, 'He'll get you next time, pommy!' I ran to join the line of children for my class, literally saved by the bell. My vocabulary of Australian words had expanded to include 'bash up' and 'pommy bastard'.

From that first day onwards, my lunchbreaks became a struggle to escape Hoggsy and his gang's attempts to get me involved in a fight. I discovered that if I took up positions in the playground that were in plain view of supervising teachers, Hoggsy never attempted to harass me.

Life in the classroom was easier. In the infant school, classes were co-educational. There was one rather nice-looking girl with golden curls, Wendy, who said that I could be her boyfriend. To a shy boy, six years of age, this sounded like a really good idea. We would hold hands when standing in line before we set off to march to our classroom to the strains of 'Colonel Bogey' over the loudspeaker system. One day Wendy turned to me and said, 'We'll get married one day.' Of course I agreed.

Because I was shy and my brother was three years older than me, I looked to him for leadership. Everything he did, I wanted to do; every idea he had, I wanted to have. I was my brother's shadow. When I told him about Wendy, and that I was going to marry her, Mike was quick to tell me that we should have nothing at all to do with girls. 'I hate them,' he said.

'Why?' I asked.

'I just do, that's all.'

The next day at school I told Wendy I wasn't going to marry her and she wasn't my girlfriend anymore. She was very upset and so was I, but I knew this must be the right thing to do, because Mike had said so.

•

We were still living with the Basfords, which made the evenings the worst part of our day. Albert Basford was a really tall man with a bellowing voice who had little time for my brother and me. He was either shouting at us to go to our room and be quiet, or telling us graphic, terrifying stories of his experiences in the war.

The only good times at the Basfords' flat were when Mike and I got to listen to the wireless. Once a week the quiz show *Pick a Box* came on, and we would lie on the carpet in front of the big wooden wireless set. Bob Dyer, the host, made all sorts of jokes and asked fascinating questions. My brother and I thought it was really funny whenever somebody picked the box with the feather in it. Occasionally we were allowed to listen to the wireless on other nights, as long as we didn't make any noise. We liked *Police File*, but my favourite show was *Night Beat with Randy Stone*. He was a newspaper reporter and always had an interesting tale to tell.

At school I'd become quite good at dodging Hoggsy and his gang. The only real danger area was the toilet block, which was located at the far end of the playground, well away from the supervising teachers. One day at the end of our lunchbreak, I couldn't hold on any longer and had to go. I emerged to find Hoggsy and company waiting for me.

'Come on, you pommy bastard!' Hoggsy shouted into my face.

'I'm not fighting you,' I replied politely as I started to walk away.

Without warning he smashed his closed fist into my face. I fell backward onto the ground and within seconds Hoggsy was wrestling me in the gravel. I had no idea how to defend myself and simply became a punching bag for the big bully. A large crowd gathered around the two of us. The chant went out: 'Fight, fight, fight!'

Then the school bell rang and the crowd dissipated. Hoggsy and his mates were the last to leave but made a clean getaway. I was struggling to my feet when two teachers rushed towards me and one grabbed me by the scruff of my neck. I was hurried off to the headmistress's office.

I waited for ages before I was ushered in. The room seemed enormous. The headmistress was a large woman who stood facing me with her legs wide apart, an imposing silhouette against the bright sunlight that came through the window behind her. She was holding two of the big long rulers that she always carried with her on her rounds.

After saying nothing for quite a while, she bent over and looked straight into my face. 'What do you have to say for yourself?'

'Nothing, Miss.'

'Nothing, is it? Well, this is something!' she bellowed as she started whacking the calves of my legs with her rulers.

At the first belt, I flinched and screamed out. On the second and third, I clenched my teeth. By the fourth, tears were trickling down my small face.

'You migrant children are the worst kind,' she said at the end of the punishment. 'Let that be a lesson to you. I don't want to see you in here again for fighting. Now return to your class immediately.'

I hobbled back in agony. Luckily my class teacher was a kind lady who took great pity on me when she saw the large red welts on my legs. She also questioned me as to why I'd been fighting, but a friend had warned me that I'd be in bigger trouble with Hoggsy if I ever revealed what he was up to, so I refused to tell her anything.

From then on Hoggsy never gave me any trouble and even spoke to me in a friendly manner. By taking my punishment and not dobbing him in, I had inadvertently acquired a degree of respect from him and his kind.

2

Discovering Film, Photography and Adventure

Keen to move out of our temporary accommodation, Dad used nearly all his savings to pay 'key money' so that he could rent a house in Broadmeadow, the next suburb over. This was great news! Mike and I were still at the local school, but we no longer had to live with the Basfords and now had our own good-sized bedroom. There was a corner store just down the road, a huge empty paddock at the back of our large block of land, and a small airfield for light planes about half a kilometre away.

We soon met two boys who lived a few doors down, Clive and Len Croft. Clive was one year younger than Mike and Len was the same age as me. The four of us became great friends, as did our parents.

One day we boys decided to play cowboys and indians, and we needed to make weapons. We constructed bows from small saplings, but how to make arrows? The empty paddock had plenty of wild bamboo growing in it, and we quickly discovered that the young shoots could be made into arrow shafts. We made arrowheads from small pieces of bitumen from the road surface that had gone sticky in the summer heat. We rolled small balls of bitumen and attached them to the ends of our shafts, then shaped them into authentic-looking arrowheads.

Our little group became almost inseparable. We were together every day after school and nearly every weekend. Most of our time was spent in the paddock shooting arrows at all sorts of things, exploring a huge stormwater channel, and walking up to the airfield to watch the planes taking off and landing. We learnt which were which, from Tiger Moths to Chipmunks.

Only a couple of kilometres away were the horse-trotting track and showgrounds. The 'trots', as everyone called them, were very popular, and occasionally my whole family went along. The best times, however, were when the four of us boys would sneak down to the trots on Friday nights.

Children weren't allowed to go in unaccompanied by an adult, so we would wait until most of the races were over, then climb the corrugated iron fence and drop over the other side. We then wandered about in the dark shadows under the grandstand and exposed wooden seats to collect empty drink bottles discarded by the punters. The big lemonade bottles were worth sixpence and the Coke bottles, tuppence.

The only problem was some bigger boys tried to tell us to bugger off as this was their patch. They caught us quite a few times and confiscated our booty, but we kept going and avoided them often enough to make it worthwhile. We took the bottles to the corner shop and cashed them in for sweets, or should I say lollies, as our Australian friends corrected us.

•

Dad had found a job in real estate and there was soon enough money for us to move from our rented house into our own home. Our family had become so close with the Crofts that they moved with us, and we all ended up in a brand-new estate at Hillsborough, near Charlestown on the outskirts of Newcastle. When we moved into our two adjacent houses, there were only a few others in the entire estate. The blocks of land were narrow and deep, and we were surrounded by bush. We had so much country to explore!

The weekends were spent knocking about the bush, climbing trees, scrambling over rocks, crossing creeks, identifying the native birds and generally having a great childhood. By then we were getting lots of ideas out of books on how to make things. We built a cubbyhouse using leftover materials from the new homes being constructed on the estate, and even wired it up with a torch battery and small light globes. We hung big swinging ropes from trees and drew a map of the surrounding bushland that showed all its features.

Most Saturday afternoons we'd walk the few kilometres to Charlestown and catch the movie matinee. When the cinema started showing horror films at night, we'd make the walk in the dark. One night we saw the movie *Them*, which features ants big enough to fill the stormwater drains of New York City. I thought it was really scary and all the way home I kept imagining ants the size of cars lurking in the gloom. This was the beginning of a youth spent watching many movies and studying how they were made.

Of course, moving so far from Waratah meant attending a new school. I had to catch the bus from the top of our road to New Lambton Primary. The school system was oversupplied with students because of the post-war baby boom and there were insufficient classrooms, so about 45 of us were accommodated in a storage area underneath one of the buildings. It was open on two sides with wire mesh security fencing; when we experienced inclement weather, tarpaulins were dropped down to keep the rain and wind out. It was very cold during the winter.

Because my academic achievements had been so poor at my previous school, I was sharing this dingy classroom with all the other low achievers. We were known as the no-hopers in Class 4F and spent most of the time throwing balls of screwed-up paper at each other and generally making life near impossible for the teacher, an old retired bloke who'd been brought in to deal with the unexpected number of kids. He, however, did not believe in using the cane and somehow managed to muddle through.

While this was going on, builders were frantically constructing four new classrooms. Eventually the big day came when we moved into one of them. It was like moving from a dungeon to a palace!

•

Great as it was living at the Hillsborough estate, it didn't last long. Dad announced that we were moving to Wallsend. This became a pattern: he would take clients out to find a suitable house, but if he couldn't do that he'd sell them the one we were living in. Finding friends in each new suburb was always a challenge, so Mike and I were each other's best mate.

In Wallsend the school was co-educational. My teacher, Mr Laurie, said that I could choose any of the empty seats in the classroom. I selected the only one that wasn't next to a girl, which meant I was sitting on my own at a desk for two. This proved to be a fortuitous decision, as I could better listen to the teacher and found myself tuning in for the first time in my life. In just one year, Mr Lawrie single-handedly turned me around from being the child who'd always come last in the class to one who came second. He had the happy ability of making everything we had to learn a fascinating exercise in discovery.

Once he took our class on a walk through the playground to a tree festooned with chrysalises and some very fat caterpillars. Over the next few weeks we kept a close eye on these creatures, learning how the chrysalis is an enclosed cocoon in which a butterfly forms. We also took several of them into the classroom and waited until the butterflies emerged. I was absolutely enthralled and greatly helped along by the detailed drawings that Mr Laurie put on the blackboard. This lesson in natural history was where my lifelong interest in animals and wildlife began.

Unfortunately, being scrawny, pommy and academically inclined had consequences. At the end of each day it became a battle to get through the bullies and find my way home without being pummelled.

•

Television had just been introduced to Australia, and Dad paid a lot to install an antenna and a receiver. We could pick up a snowy picture from Sydney, but only on a good night. Mike and I found ourselves watching all kinds of programmes, including the early works of David Attenborough. His *Zoo Quest* series featured exotic places throughout the world where animals were being captured for the London Zoo. We found the Komodo dragons of Indonesia particularly impressive, and were glued to these shows even when we could only listen because the picture was so fuzzy.

A good friend of our father's, Col Beck, had a 16mm movie camera and filmed his trips catching marlin around the Great Barrier Reef. He also owned a couple of ex-army jeeps and used to head into the Barrington Tops Ranges using little more than goat tracks. Sometimes on Friday evenings we'd go to his house for dinner and a film night. We would watch his home movies completely enthralled. Mike started saving up his pocket money to buy home movie-making books and magazines.

In 1956 the Olympic Games were coming to Melbourne, and a number of companies and personalities agreed to pay for tickets to be won by young Australians. Coca-Cola ran a drawing competition to sponsor about twelve lucky winners. Mike was pretty good at art and drew up a comic strip featuring a young boy encouraged to mow his mother's lawn in order to receive a glass of Coke. Another drawing competition was sponsored by a radio star, Smoky Dawson, whose programme Mike and I had been listening to every week. We wrote down the entire contents of an episode and Mike then drew it out as a comic strip.

My brother couldn't get his entries into the mail quick enough. To everyone's surprise, he won both tickets! Although he wanted to give me one, the competition judges decided that this wouldn't be fair to the other applicants. Instead Mike accepted a cash compensation. He used this money to buy 16mm movie film, while Dad coughed up for a camera. My brother was away in Melbourne for a couple of weeks and managed to capture heaps of events on just four rolls of film.

While Mike's obsession with movie-making grew, I became much more interested in still photography. The local barber was an enthusiastic photographer who regularly bought monthly photographic magazines, as well as *National Geographic* and *Life*. He kept these in the waiting area where I would consume them before my turn in the chair. I'd frequently let people jump the queue until I finished reading an interesting article. Until then I'd never been keen on going to the barber's, so Mum must have wondered why I suddenly wanted my hair trimmed every two weeks.

The barber, like most in his profession, enjoyed a good yarn. When he realised that I was hoping to be a photographer, we spent a lot of time chatting about different ideas and techniques. He had a beautiful German camera and I just had Dad's old box camera, but I dreamt of working for *National Geographic* or *Life*. I scrutinised their pages and believed their standard to be the best in the world.

After lots of broad hints, my parents bought me a home-processing kit for Christmas. I used the bathroom as a darkroom by blocking out the windows with bits of old plywood and stuffing towels around the crack at the bottom of the door. I made what they call 'contact prints', meaning that the image was the same size as the negative. To get a glaze on the surface of each print, they needed to be placed on a spotlessly clean piece of glass, all the water and air bubbles squeezed out, then left to dry overnight. In the morning, the pictures were easily removed with a nice glossy finish.

I didn't have a spare piece of glass, so I'd place them on top of Mum's glass-topped dining table and onto the shaving-cabinet mirror in the bathroom. Unfortunately they didn't always come off the glass properly, and when this happened it was impossible to save them.

'Malcolm, get this rubbish off the mirror!' Dad would call out first thing in the morning. He wasn't too impressed when he couldn't see himself because of the torn remains of half a dozen prints.

Soon I realised that what I really needed was an enlarger, which is similar to a projector and mounted on a vertical column. The negative is placed inside and projected onto a piece of photographically sensitised paper, allowing the production of pictures of any size provided they fit into the developing trays. Unfortunately enlargers were expensive: there was no way I was ever going to buy one from my pocket money of two shillings a week to mow the lawns and wash the car.

Faced with this problem, I embarked upon my first business venture at the age of eleven. Using a toy printing kit—small rubber letters that were placed onto grooves on a block of wood then pressed into an ink pad, I produced a number of flyers and distributed them into the letterboxes of our neighbourhood. I used Dad's phone number for customers to call and waited until business came rolling in.

Malcolm Leyland's Printing Service was never going to be a threat to the processing opportunities offered by pharmacies in the main street, but I did get enough business to make some money. I was often up late in my bathroom/darkroom and the last to bed in our household, sneaking in sometimes as late as 1 a.m.

I needed £20 to buy the enlarger, and at the end of one year I'd managed to make £10. Even though I doubt they understood what it was for, my parents generously donated £10 as a Christmas present.

•

At the end of the year when Mike left school to become an apprentice sign-writer, I moved on to high school at Cooks Hill. Because I spent most evenings in my make-shift darkroom, I would use the morning bus rides to scribble down my homework. Of course, my academic performance suffered.

Mike continued to make home movies and I took an interest in the idea of adding soundtracks. Our parents bought me a tape recorder so I could give this a try, and I remember once using Mum's Mixmaster to simulate the sound of speedboat motors for a holiday movie Mike had made in Queensland. I soon discovered another use for the tape recorder.

By then I'd made a couple of new friends at school. One was David Price who, unlike me, almost always got good marks. When I ran out of time to do homework, I'd ring him up and he would read out his assignments. I recorded this by placing the microphone over the telephone earpiece, then played it back slowly and rewrote it with plenty of changes so the teacher couldn't identify it as a copy. I didn't consider this to be cheating, just saving time!

Although my interest in photography made me neglect my studies, I did have favourite subjects: technical drawing, English and science. I found physics the most interesting but also enjoyed chemistry. My least favourite subject was physical education and I remained a tall, skinny weakling.

One rainy morning I was wandering across the play-ground to class when one of the school's biggest bullies came up behind me and kicked my school port out of my hand. It was a hand-me-down from Mike and had a broken lock on one side. It crashed to the ground heavily, burst open and spilled my books into a large puddle.

I wheeled around and something snapped in my brain. Adrenaline took hold of me. Without hesitation I grabbed the bully, who was two years older than me, and dragged him down towards the wooden weather shelter. There I smashed his head into a steel post until blood was streaming from his nose and scalp. About a hundred boys had gathered around, chanting, 'Fight, fight, fight!' I wanted to drown the mongrel, so I dragged him to the hand basins and held his head under water. My anger gave me a fearless, unstoppable strength.

Then David yelled out, warning me that the teachers were coming. I dropped the big bully to the ground. David had saved my books and packed them back in my bag, which he handed me. Most of the students were already lined up in orderly ranks. The rain had turned from a drizzle to a downpour, meaning that my soaking at the hand basins didn't make me stand out. I quickly joined our class line. Those left behind in the weather shed were being quizzed by the teachers when an ambulance screamed to a halt with sirens blaring.

The headmaster addressed us from his wooden rostrum. 'A boy has just been seriously injured in the weather shed. We need to know who inflicted these injuries.'

I was shaking in my boots. To this day I don't know where the energy came from for me to overpower the big bully. I suppose the pent-up anger from years of being the bullies' favourite whipping boy all came rushing out that morning and the poor sod copped the lot.

The headmaster stood there holding an umbrella and staring down at us for what seemed like an hour. The rain continued to soak us as teachers walked up and down our ranks, eyeing everyone carefully.

'If you come forward now,' the headmaster said, 'it will be easier in the long run. The police will be making an investigation.'

Crikey, I thought, *it doesn't get much worse than that!* To my amazement, nobody stepped forward and named me. The teachers didn't give me a second glance: I was a quiet student, never involved in this kind of thing, and seemingly unable to overpower the victim.

The police did come, however all investigations came to nothing because the code of silence was absolute. Meanwhile, my new reputation quickly spread throughout the school. It was several months before the big bully returned, a much subdued personality. He and his group of friends treated me with respect.

One afternoon a group of us were getting wet in the drizzling rain as we waited for the bus outside school. The street was lined with terraced houses and some had shallow, covered entrances with just enough room for one person. A boy in my year called Keith Davey had managed to get there early and secure a dry spot. Then a heavily built boy came up to him, grabbed him by the shirt collar and pulled him out into the rain. I told the bully to let Keith get back in again.

'Who's going to stop me? *You?*' he asked, eyeing my spindly form.

'Yes, if you insist,' I responded confidently.

Just then one of the well-known bullies in the school rushed up, grabbed his friend's arm and pulled him back into the rain. 'You don't argue with him,' he advised his mate, and both left peacefully.

Keith moved to one end of his dry spot and invited me to join him. It was a tight squeeze. Sometimes it pays to have a reputation, even if it's undeserved. Keith and I became great friends from then on.

•

Mike was going well with his apprenticeship and used his weekends to do foreign-order signs at home in Dad's garage. This way he accumulated enough money to buy another camera and film, as well as a 16mm sound projector. He was also kind enough to buy me my first still camera that had proper adjustments on the lens: an early Minolta that used 35mm film. I was delighted to no longer need Dad's box camera.

As a very active member of the Wallsend RSL, Dad had access to the movies that the club hired for screening on Sunday nights. He would bring them home on Saturdays and we'd have a movie session with all of my parents' friends and some of the neighbours. Mike and I studied the movies carefully and compared editing techniques to those in books he'd bought.

About this time Dad had a client with a cinema for sale: a small operation at Nords Wharf on Lake Macquarie. Cinemas weren't going too well at the time because of television's huge popularity. This particular cinema was equipped with 16mm projectors, unlike the 35mm ones in town. It cost about £400 and because Dad was aware of how keenly we wanted to be in the film business, he loaned the money to Mike.

This venture was strictly my brother's but that didn't stop me from going every Saturday and Sunday night to help out. Mike created all the advertising posters at home, and we'd run around after each show pulling down last week's and sticking up next week's. Our takings certainly weren't high: the most we ever took was £13, ten shillings and sixpence.

Dad included sufficient funds in his loan for Mike to buy an old Vauxhall. We filled the boot with the projectors and carried the portable screen on the roof. During the week we would pick up Keith, get into town and view the latest movies.

•

After the intermediate certificate examinations I moved on to Newcastle Technical High School and Keith went to Newcastle Boys. We kept in touch by going to the movies during the week and bush-bashing up tracks on the weekends in the Vauxhall, my brother at the wheel.

I'd decided to complete the leaving certificate exams, although I was a little uncertain about what I really wanted to do: I just needed to pass so that I could enter university. I had no bully problems at this school but I found the work quite difficult, although I enjoyed literature classes and was one of the few boys who actually liked Shakespeare's works.

I was spending a lot of time in the school library and discovered a whole section of books on adventures all over the world. Stories of expeditions into Africa, the Amazon and other exciting places. The best book I read was the story of the Kon-Tiki expedition by Thor Heyerdahl. It is a marvellous true-life account about a group of men who built a balsawood raft and crossed the Pacific Ocean in an attempt to prove that the Polynesian islanders originated from South America.

I didn't just have my nose in books, however. I'd always been a skinny kid and now that I'd reached my full height of 6 feet and 1.5 inches, I felt it was necessary to put on a few pounds, increase my chest size and get a bit fitter. I started on a Canadian Air Force training programme known as the 5BX Plan. This simple set of exercises is supposed to make anybody fit enough for military service and although I certainly got fitter, my appearance didn't noticeably change.

My PE teacher took great delight in trying to get me to be part of his football team and other forms of sport in which I had no interest. One day he announced that we were all going to do push-ups together. 'Leyland, this includes you!' he yelled.

About 50 of us lined up, facing the teacher. He went down and we all went down. A chant went out. One, two, three, four . . . At ten, half a dozen boys had dropped out. The counting continued and boys dropped off quickly. At 25 there were only six of us left, including the teacher. The class was clapping with each push-up. Everyone was slowing down. I knew I had him. By 40, it was just him and me. The class shouted out the numbers as we slowly approached 60.

Then the teacher stopped. 'Enough, Leyland,' he gasped. 'You've proved your point.'

He never again insisted that I try football, but he did pull me aside and ask, 'How did you do that?' I told him all about my fitness programme and he shook his head, then laughed. We got on famously from then on.

•

Life at home had taken a downward turn. A credit squeeze was on, so very few people could borrow finance to buy houses. Dad's income had run out because it came from commissions on sales. He quickly got into big debt and triple-mortgaged our house in order to have spending money.

Within weeks Dad took out a loan from a friend and bought a leasehold on a shop in Holmesville, one of the outer suburbs not far from West Wallsend. This general store sold almost everything, including wheat for chicken feed, petrol, groceries, fruit and vegetables, corned meat, sausages and cheeses. On top of all that, it was a post office and a bank branch.

I would arrive home from school after two bus rides, or one and a half hours of travel. The chores then started. In the storeroom I weighed up bags of sugar and packs of potatoes. Many customers placed orders with Mum and I'd make them up into cardboard boxes for home-delivery. This was a job I eagerly took on because I was learning to drive.

I was highly conscious that these were desperate times for my family. Then I failed the final exams and didn't get the leaving certificate. Two more percentage points in history and I would have. No university for me! I felt I should never have completed those two years at school: I'd not only failed the exams but also failed the family by placing an additional financial burden on my parents. I was extremely depressed about this, but Mum assured me that it didn't matter. All I wanted was to find a job.

•

December 1961 was life-changing for me. I'd decided that photography would probably be the best way for me to earn a living. Mike's annual holidays were due so I put looking for a job on hold for a few weeks so we could go away for an excursion to the outback. We decided to follow in the footsteps of the late Charles Chauvel.

In 1958, Chauvel had made a thirteen-part television series called *Australian Walkabout* for the BBC. He and his wife, Elsa, had set out from Sydney and travelled right through Central Australia. Mike and I planned to repli-cate their journey using a second-hand Land Rover. Keith was our travelling companion.

Australia was experiencing a severe drought at the time. We were staggered to see how dry and desolate the country was. Skinny, desperate sheep on the verge of collapse were a common sight alongside the red dusty roads. Wind pumps driven by a gentle desert breeze produced a grinding noise all night, but it was the moaning and groaning of starving sheep that kept us awake at most of our camps.

According to the book based on Chauvel's series, *Walkabout*, once we reached a town called William Creek we should turn off to the Anna Creek cattle station, then head west. William Creek turned out to be no more than a pub. According to the service station road map we carried, there was no track, but undaunted we headed west and arrived at Anna Creek. The station appeared to be abandoned which isn't surprising, considering it was the middle of summer. An elderly Aboriginal woman emerged from one of the small buildings and walked across the dry dusty quadrangle between the outer buildings.

'Which way to Coober Pedy?' we yelled from the open window of the Land Rover.

She looked at us for a few seconds, then pointed to wheel tracks wending between two buildings. 'This way little way,' she called back, then turned on her heel and disappeared inside.

'Well,' I said to Mike and Keith, 'it's headed in a westerly direction, so that must be it.' We all agreed.

Soon we were driving along a rough track that became even less defined the further we went but it seemed to take us in roughly the right direction, so we continued on.

It eventually became obvious, even to us three idiots, that we were probably on the wrong road. By then we'd stopped off at several earthen dams. The real problem was that we had only just enough fuel to reach Coober Pedy with a small amount to spare. We had used half of our fuel and there was no more track ahead of us: we'd reached the last water bore on what was probably a bore maintenance track.

'Do we go on or do we go back?' asked Mike.

'I reckon we go on,' I suggested, as I pointed at the map. 'We've been travelling in a mostly western direction, therefore we must be here. Going back is about 60 miles and it should be the same to go on, so we may as well. What do you reckon?'

A short discussion followed, then we all agreed that going on was the best course of action. Guided by our Boy Scout compass, Mike kept driving west. The country was studded with thousands of gibbers the size of cricket balls that smashed into the underside of our vehicle for hours.

We ran out of daylight and camped. Even though it was the middle of summer, the night was freezing cold and a wind whistled across the open plain. We were hopelessly lost and only a quarter of our fuel remained, but going back was no longer an option.

That night we sat around the hurricane lamp, lost in our private thoughts. Keith wrote in his diary, Mike made a few notes and I decided to write a letter to my mother. I starting off by telling her that if she was reading this it had either been found on my dead body or I'd survived the ordeal and mailed it to her. I detailed the highlights of our trip so far and concluded by saying that if this letter had been found on me, I didn't want her to be too concerned because I'd died doing what I wanted and had no regrets. I can't imagine how devastating it would be for a mother to receive a letter like that from her seventeen-year-old son.

Next morning the horizon to the west was just as grim as it had been the night before: a featureless desert beneath a cloudless sky of hazy blue. The wind was still whisking tiny clouds of dust into the air, creating a pink tinge that blurred the line between land and sky. We kept watching the compass, stopping every now and then to climb onto the bonnet in order to scan the barren vista for landmarks, then move on cautiously in first gear.

Finally, late in the afternoon, we spotted a shimmering mirage around what appeared to be low hills on the horizon. We estimated the distance as about 16 kilometres. The road map indicated that Coober Pedy was on high ground. Could this be it?

Buoyed by this thought, we pressed on for a few kilometres when we came across a fence running north–south. To our great joy there was a track alongside the fence. Our biggest dilemma now was whether we should turn north or south: we took a guess and headed north.

After only a few minutes we came to a gate and were relieved to see a real graded road running along the other side of the fence. We passed through the gate and continued north, confident that we were now on the main road from Port Augusta that would lead to Coober Pedy. From there we had a clearly marked road to our goal, Ayers Rock.

3

Doing the Daily

The attractive secretary was a few years older than me. Her well-groomed brown hair was cut to a 'sensible' length, and she was dressed and made-up immaculately.

'I'm afraid he's too busy to see you,' she explained. 'There's no point in waiting.'

'That's all right,' I responded. 'I have plenty of time.'

'It could be all afternoon.'

'I'll still wait,' I insisted, grabbing a chair and plonking myself onto it.

'Suit yourself, but I can't guarantee that he'll have time to see you at all.'

I smiled back with what I hoped was a good impression of an innocent puppy. She returned to her notebook and started typing. I was clutching my envelope, looking as nonchalant as possible, but in truth I was far from relaxed.

I glanced at the dark oak door with *Editor* emblazoned upon it in gold leaf.

My strategy was simple. Everyone needs to go to the toilet eventually, so all I had to do was wait until she left. I used this time to rehearse what I was going to say, and to watch as copyboys and very busy journalists rushed in and out of the editor's office. Each would knock firmly on the door and wait for a single-word command from the other side: 'Come!'

My patience finally paid off. The secretary stood and disappeared from the waiting area. From my observations, I knew that no one but the editor would be in the room. I cautiously approached his door and rapped three times.

'Come!'

My legs went to jelly, perspiration ran down the back of my neck and I strode into the room doing my best imper-sonation of someone who had every right to do so. My mind went blank as my carefully rehearsed speech evaporated.

Seated before me at a huge oak desk strewn with sheets of paper was a commanding man who looked about the same age as my father. His dark-rimmed glasses matched his black hair.

He glanced up from his work. 'Who are you?' he demanded.

'I'm your new cadet photographer,' I uttered in a quiv-ering voice, as I opened my large envelope and started to cast my 20 by 25 centimetre photographic prints onto his desk like oversized playing cards.

'Cadet? What cadet?' he roared.

He picked up the prints and stacked them into a neat

pile. I noticed that he took the time to have a good look at each photograph.

'Malcolm Leyland, Sir,' I quivered, 'and I heard you're looking for a new cadet photographer.' A small part of my rehearsed speech returned, enabling me to finish with, 'So look no further.'

The scowl on his face turned to a wry smile, but only for a split second.

'Well, Malcolm . . . What was it?' he asked, unable to remember my surname.

'Leyland, Sir,' I responded, and he wrote my full name on the back of one of my precious prints.

'Phone number?'

I gave him my home phone number.

'Right.' He hesitated for a second. 'Malcolm,' he said, 'I'm putting the first edition together here so never burst in on me like that again.'

Again! Now that sounded promising.

He held my prints in his hand and then asked, 'Did you take these yourself?'

'Yes,' I replied meekly.

'Did you process and print them?'

'Yes, Sir. In my mother's bathroom.'

He looked me up and down, scribbled a note that I couldn't read from my side of the desk, and shoved the full set of prints into his desk drawer. Would I ever see them again?

'You know it's just possible, young feller, that you might have what it takes to be a press photographer.' He paused for effect, and then added, 'One day. Now get out!'

I closed the door gently behind me, smiled at the secretary, and walked briskly out of the Newcastle Herald and Sun building on Bolton Street to catch the 90-minute bus ride home.

When I finally arrived, Mum handed me a note. It was a request for me to phone the paper and speak to their senior photographer, a Mr Milton Merrilees.

Had my uncharacteristically brazen actions worked, or had I burnt my bridges before I even started to cross them?

Mr Merrilees told me to meet him in the second-floor photographic department at ten the next morning.

I got up early, took the long bus ride, walked nervously up Bolton Street and arrived at the appointed time. To my great relief, I was now subjected to a proper job interview, during which I was given a chance to handle a press camera and to demonstrate how I could make a print in the darkroom.

I'd been in the building for just over an hour when things got busy and I was dismissed. I left clutching the precious photographs that I'd left with the editor the day before. During the course of my interview I'd discovered that he was a highly skilled amateur photographer and a member of the Newcastle Photographic Society. Apparently he was impressed with my pictures, even if the audacious manner of my gaining his attention had been unconventional.

By the time I arrived home, Mum had a new message instructing me to please phone the *Newcastle Sun*.

It's difficult to express how excited I was to hear I'd been successful and was to start as a first-year cadet on

Monday morning. Had I been capable of it, I would have done cartwheels down the street. The first three months would be a trial. If I proved to be suitable for the work, I had a four-year cadetship ahead of me.

Monday was the 26th of January 1962, the Australia Day public holiday is when I discovered that journalists and photographers worked on whatever day they were rostered on—whether it fell on a public holiday or not. I couldn't have cared less. I had my dream job. My forebodings of failure dissolved into thin air.

•

With my addition to the team, the *Newcastle Sun* had four photographers. Milton Merrilees, who had interviewed me, would be my immediate boss. He was a great all-rounder and a technical perfectionist.

Part of a photographer's job, it turned out, was to drive journalists to various assignments. I didn't mind this because it meant I had my own parking space within the building, but obviously I needed a car. Dad came to my rescue by selling me his Vauxhall for £85, and then lending me another £25 to have the motor done up. I now owed Dad £110, which I would have to pay off gradually from my wages. Another part of my job was learning how to mix up all the chemicals, keeping the darkroom clean, and accounting for the use of all films and printing paper. I was given a large camera, which took 13 by 10 centimetre sheets of film. Under instructions from Mr Merrilees, I loaded and reloaded the magazines in the pitch black of the darkroom until I could have done it in my sleep.

I was also given a box of 100 sheets of film and told to wander about town and shoot anything I wanted to. We had no light meters, so I was expected to learn how to judge the light and adjust the settings accordingly.

'You must do this over and over until it becomes second nature,' Mr Merrilees said. 'In the world of press photography, you don't have time to muck around with the settings. Just keep taking pictures and processing them until you get it right.'

I felt guilty using up all those materials. I was using large amounts of printing paper in the darkroom too, so I could learn how to make a good print quickly.

'You need to be able to walk in from a job and walk out of the darkroom with a satisfactory print within three minutes when you really have to,' explained my mentor.

This meant that the photograph was dripping wet; but when it was a rush job, that didn't matter. It could still be used.

•

At the time it was almost mandatory that page three of an afternoon tabloid newspaper should be adorned with a glamorous girl. I was expected to supply some of these pictures. For a shy boy who had no experience with girls, this was a daunting task.

In my third week I was sent off by the news editor to scour the beaches for a page three girl. If I was successful, this was to be my first picture printed in the paper. After half an hour I returned to the darkroom to process the result.

'What do you call this?' demanded the news editor as he studied the print I'd just handed him.

'It's a picture of a girl on the beach, Sir.'

'I can see that, Malcolm. How old is she?'

I produced my notebook and read the information, 'She is three years old and she made that sandcastle herself. I was pretty lucky to get that shot really. There weren't any other girls on the beach today, Sir. It *is* rather cold.'

I didn't need to get a telegram to receive the message that this wasn't exactly what he had in mind for a page three girl. I was preparing myself for a dressing-down when the editor walked into the room. He spotted the picture and said, 'Is this your work, Malcolm?'

'Yes, Sir,' I quickly replied. 'Not a lot of people on the beach this morning.'

He picked up the photograph, walked briskly out of the office and into his own.

The first edition came off the presses at about 12.30 p.m. Copyboys would run along the corridors delivering one to every desk. When our copy landed in front of me, there on the front page, taking up four columns, was my picture of the three-year-old girl making her sandcastle.

Crikey! My first picture ever to be printed in a newspaper, and it ended up on page one. I was over the moon.

Knowing how shy I was with girls, Mr Merrilees said with a wry smile 'Congratulations. You've not only got your first picture published in the paper, Malcolm, but you've also broken two records.'

'What records?'

'You've been here less than three weeks and already had a picture published. No one has achieved that before. I also reckon it's the first time the *Sun* has published a girly shot on the beach of anyone so young. You've established a new standard, young man.'

I have to admit, it felt good. From that day on I went to full roster, working three weeks on day shift and the fourth on night shift, which was from four in the afternoon until midnight. I had a heck of a lot to learn, but my career was now underway. I was an enthusiastic pupil and loving it.

•

In the next few months I went out with the senior photographers, learning different skills from each of them. We covered a huge variety of work, from breaking news to social gatherings and weddings at the weekends.

Mike had completed his five-year apprenticeship as a sign-writer and landed a job at the new television broadcaster in Newcastle, NBN Channel 3. He was the only film cameraman shooting for the evening news, so we often turned up at the same event and soon became news rivals.

Gradually, with lots of encouragement from my mentors, I was getting more appropriate results from my girly shots, but I was not yet producing what could be called *glamour* pictures. I was still rather shy.

Meanwhile, I found sports pictures boring, especially at the football. The large cameras we used were cumbersome because we had just one lens and the focus was so critical. The idea was to set the lens at 8 metres, and then run up and down the sidelines hoping for someone to dive for a try. With luck I could anticipate when this was about to occur and attempt to capture a shot that might—with luck—be in focus. I reckon we ran more than the players, while often wasting lots of film with little to show for it.

One weekend when covering a football game, I left my press camera in the car and used my own 35mm camera with a long lens attached. I captured some great shots and never needed to run around like an idiot.

The sports editor called me down to his office to congratulate me on the photos, but I was then called to the editor's office. He was looking at the back page, which featured one of my football shots. 'Great work at the game,' he commented casually. 'How did you get them?'

'Oh! The usual way. Running up and down the sidelines.'

'No you didn't, Malcolm.'

I glanced up, looking perplexed.

'I was there at the match,' he said, 'and saw you using your own camera.'

'Ah, well . . . the pics were good though, weren't they?'

'Yes, we already established that. But you must use the equipment we supply and not your own, understand?'

'Yes, Sir. But surely it's time to invest in a good 35mm camera like a Nikon with a decent set of lenses?'

'Sorry, but the powers-that-be reckon the quality isn't good enough from the small film. Now go, and don't use your own equipment again.'

What a joke. The newspaper produced pictures with 75 little dots of ink to the inch, which is vastly inferior to the resolution of 35mm film. Still, he was the boss—so back to running along the sidelines for me.

•

'Grab your gear and get down to the water police wharf immediately!' instructed the news editor. 'There's a bomb stuck in the harbour dredge.'

I ran, arriving breathless and in time to leap onto the police launch seconds before it pulled away from the wharf.

As we approached the dredge I could see army personnel moving about on the stern. We scrambled on board just as a burly sergeant yelled out, 'No one gets on or off this vessel until I say so . . . And that includes you lot!' he added, pointing to a second load of journalists and TV cameramen arriving on another launch.

An unexploded cannon shell from a Japanese submarine, which had been fired into the harbour during World War II, was now stuck in the suction head of the dredge. The army disposal experts were studying a manual on how to disarm it.

I then realised that I was the only photographer on board.

One of the soldiers grabbed the manual and a box of tools, and set off to the front of the vessel, where the suction head was located.

I addressed the sergeant. 'If that thing explodes, how much damage will it do?'

'Quite a lot. In fact, I don't think any one of us will survive without some injury. I want everyone to stay exactly where they are.'

'If that's the case,' I asked, 'then it wouldn't make much difference where I was, would it?'

'Perhaps not. Why?'

'With your permission, I'd like to go into the suction head with your man and get some photos.'

He studied me for just a second, giving me the once-over. 'It's your funeral, sonny. Take it slowly and if the corporal doesn't want you there, you have to come straight back. Got it?'

'Yes, Sir.'

To get to the suction head I had to crawl through a long muddy pipe on my stomach, pushing my camera in front of me. Finally I reached the head, which was slightly bigger than the boot of a car. The corporal was examining the bomb. It looked huge: about a metre long and a quarter of a metre in diameter. It was caked with rust. I asked if I could stay while he disarmed the shell.

'You got a death wish or something?' he asked.

'No, but I figured if this thing goes off we're all done for anyway, so I may as well do what I get paid for.'

'All right, but you can't use a flash, okay?'

I nodded and took my first shot of him leaning over the deadly cargo and studying the manual. Eventually he started scraping away flakes of rust to expose a number stamped in the metal. He studied this and referred back to the book. It was shockingly hot in the tomb-like steel suction head, which hung out over the water like some giant arm. Since a child I had suffered from claustrophobia but in the excitement of the moment, with adrenaline pumping through my system, my fear took a back seat. I was concentrating on my work and in spite of the danger, loving it.

'Have you got anything we can use?' came a voice from down below.

I glanced through a crack and saw a launch circling slowly below. On board was Alan James, one of my workmates.

'Yes,' I called back, 'but I can't leave here now.'

'Chuck the film down. You got a spare?'

'Okay, sure—and yes, I've got three magazines altogether.' I checked my watch. We had 20 minutes till the first edition. I let the exposed film drop about 8 metres and Alan caught it. The boat sped off.

In time, the corporal scraped away enough rusty flakes to expose a circular shape surrounded by screws. He squirted all kinds of oily liquid onto the screws and began working on them.

'Have you ever dealt with one of these before?' I asked.

'Nope. This is my first.'

Oh shit. That was not what I wanted to hear.

'I just have to hope this book is right,' he added with a sinister grin.

He gently removed the screws one by one. Amazingly, after all that time in the water, they came free easily.

After another half hour passed, I heard Alan's voice call up. 'Got any more?'

Soon a second magazine of film was falling from the suction head, to be caught and whisked off to the office.

The corporal spoke, 'I'm about to remove the detonator. It's like a cylinder inside this thing and has about a quarter of an inch of clearance. It's magnetised, so I have to pull it out smoothly and carefully. If I touch the side, the last thing we'll hear will be a small click—then an enormous explosion will vaporise us in a split second. You ready for this?'

'Yes,' I responded shakily. I set the focus on my camera.

He began slowly to pull the detonator out. I took my shot and the shutter went *click*. The normally almost-inaudible shutter sounded like a gunshot.

'Shit! Don't do that!' he pleaded.

'Sorry,' I whispered sheepishly.

Perspiration was pouring out of both of us. He resumed the delicate operation.

Within about ten seconds, he triumphantly removed the detonator. My next shot was of him with a huge grin on his face, holding it above the shell. Then my last magazine went through the crack to the boat below. It sped off.

At the newspaper office, the editor greeted me while holding up all three editions. My shots were featured on their front pages along with huge headlines; each edition published an upgraded episode in the saga. The final front page was my picture of the triumphant corporal, and it took up all seven columns. This was my proudest moment as a press photographer.

'Well done, my boy,' the editor said sincerely. 'But you realise that you don't get paid to take that kind of risk, don't you?'

'Yes, but not taking risks would be a bit dull, wouldn't it?'

•

One night on my way home from the office, I came upon a car. It was a Morris Minor, and I found it upside down and perfectly balanced on top of a traffic dome. It looked like some oversized insect with its wheels clawing at the night air. The driver, a young girl, was unharmed but quite shaken by the accident. I took a shot with the flash and made a note of the details, before returning to the darkroom; I then left both the story and the picture on the news editor's desk.

Next day, when I turned up for the night beat, I grabbed a copy of the paper—but my picture could not be found.

'How come you didn't use the car shot?' I asked. 'I thought it was a cracker.'

'Interesting, yes,' came the reply. 'But no one's dead, so no story.'

How cynical can you get?

On another occasion I was driving with Milton Merrilees when we came across a car accident. This time a badly mangled vehicle was perched halfway up a tree. The ambulance was there as well as the police. We piled out of the car and Mr Merrilees said, 'You do this one—I'll watch.'

I took a classic storytelling image: a distraught woman was being helped up the embankment to the ambulance, tears streaming down her face, with her car in the tree behind her. The looks I received from the ambulance officers, as they helped her in and left the scene, could have killed.

'Take another shot of the car,' instructed Mr Merrilees.

'Why? I've already got a better one.'

'Just do it, all right?'

While driving back to the office, I asked why he'd wanted the second shot.

'I was talking to the ambulance men,' he said. 'That woman's husband was driving the car and his dead body had been removed from the wreck just before we got there. Think about it. She's now suffering the greatest trauma of her life and, if your photo goes into the paper, it will be worse for her.'

'Yes, but isn't that what we get paid to do? To get good news shots?'

'Of course, but remember it will be tomorrow's fish and chips wrapper. She doesn't deserve to have her anguish all over the paper like that. If we'd arrived five minutes later, she wouldn't have been there at all.'

Back in the darkroom I processed both shots and printed them up. I studied them carefully. The first, featuring the woman and the ambulance men, was good enough to win a prize, and Mr Merrilees agreed. In the end I burnt both the print and the negative, and handed in the shot of the wreck.

I was beginning to question my sense of ethics. Was I cut out for the newspaper business?

The final episode that made me question what I was turning into occurred when I travelled out with a journalist to an old mineshaft near Holmesville, where a small white cat had fallen in and was 6 metres or so from the surface. The journo rounded up two children—a girl about seven and her younger brother—then got them to peer into the shaft and look forlorn. The cat was supposed to be theirs, but they'd never seen it before. It meowed pitifully all the time we were there.

It was a quiet news day, so the story ran front page, including a shot of the cat taken with the flash on full power, and another of the two pathetic faces staring into the shaft.

The phone rang hot with sympathetic calls, and late that afternoon my brother Mike went to the shaft and filmed the same children for the NBN evening news. By now the children were claiming that the cat was definitely theirs. They were obviously enjoying the limelight.

Next day the *Newcastle Morning Herald* ran a follow-up story, announcing that members of the mines rescue squad were going to get the cat out mid-morning, just in time for us to follow through with another tear-jerker. I couldn't believe it. This was a total beat-up, but off we went to cover the 'rescue'.

When we arrived, the squad members were getting ready to go down. They dropped a rope ladder in and a man started the descent. I got a good shot of him slipping over the edge. When he was a couple of metres down, he began to cough and splutter—then he lost his grip and fell to the bottom. Remarkably, he missed the damned cat, but he was badly injured.

It turned out that there was a pocket of bad air in a band about halfway down the shaft. He'd momentarily lost consciousness and collapsed. The next man to go in was all rigged up with a breathing apparatus and now it had turned into a real rescue.

That afternoon we ran a picture of the children 'reunited' with the cat, and another of the injured man being brought up from the shaft.

'What a great story,' declared the journalist. 'We kept it going for two days.'

I was disgusted. If I stayed in this job, I realised, I ran the risk of becoming as cynically merciless as the journos I worked with, and that wasn't something I was comfortable with. I needed a change.

4

Hungry for Adventure

Adventure is having a hell of a time 500 kilometres away. A thousand kilometres away is twice as adventurous. Based on this principle, if I wanted to live a life of adventure, I needed to travel. Having consumed since childhood almost every adventure travel book I could get my hands on, I was hungry to get on with it.

Mike and I believed we were adventurers without a quest. Together with Keith Davey, my best friend from high school, we'd been spending a lot of our spare time at weekends planning to do something special. Our first, almost disastrous, effort to drive to Ayers Rock in Mike's Land Rover had not only taught us a few valuable lessons, but also whetted our appetite for more. We all had a single-minded determination to become modern-day explorers and to capture our exploits on film.

We needed to do something no one had done before, but what?

At first we settled on the idea of saving up enough money to buy a yacht and sail around the world: our intention was to film our travels and sell it to television.

It soon became obvious that we had no hope of buying an ocean-going yacht, so we lowered our ambitions. We decided to get a smaller boat and take it down the full length of the longest river in Australia. Our research indicated that this was the Darling. After months of research, we discovered that no vessel had undertaken such a voyage before. (In recent times the rivers of inland Australia have been re-defined and the Darling has been incorporated into the Murray–Darling system. By this definition, the Darling has been demoted to second place by the Murray. In 1963 it was named in all the encyclopaedias as the longest river in Australia.)

The Darling is the slowest-flowing river in the world. Less than 2 per cent of its headwaters reach the Murray and finally the sea in South Australia. Some of the old paddle-steamers had plied the Darling when it acted as an inland highway, but none had voyaged along its full length.

We bought hundreds of metres of black-and-white 16mm film. As our funds would only go so far, we printed letterheads that made our 'Darling River Expedition' seem like a reality and mailed requests to boat manufacturers, seeking the loan of a 4-metre boat for six weeks—then we waited. To our amazement, our first choice, Quintrex, responded positively.

So it was time to get a motor. When Scott Outboards came in on this one, we were all but ready.

I arranged to take my four weeks' annual leave, Mike organised four weeks' leave from the TV station, and Keith resigned from his job as a sales assistant. We loaded our equipment, including the boat, onto a railway goods train in Newcastle and sent it on its way to Mungindi. We followed by passenger train.

Mungindi, on the New South Wales–Queensland border, is the point where the Darling changes its name to the Macintyre. Our intention was to travel the 2250 kilometres down the length of the Darling and finish in Victoria. Should be a snap in four weeks, right? Well, ignorance is bliss.

•

We were disappointed when we looked down from the bridge at Mungindi to see a muddy trench choked with fallen trees and sticks. It had a barely discernible flow and was less than a metre deep. *This can't be right!* Radio reports had indicated a depth of a metre. Enough, we'd thought.

After a few enquiries around town we discovered there was a weir downstream from the bridge, and that was where the river heights were taken.

So we organised a flatbed truck and some willing helpers to cart our stuff to a launching point just downstream from the weir. Here the river looked more promising. We had a nice long reach of water with beautiful river gums on both banks. They almost met in the middle, speckling the river with shafts of sunlight.

We crammed our mountain of equipment into the little boat, started the engine and set off. It was the 3rd of March 1963. Only 2250 kilometres to go.

We were elated—but not for long. We'd only travelled several metres when, with a violent jolt, the outboard flew from my hands and blasted out of the water, roaring wildly.

It turned out we'd hit a submerged log and snapped a shear pin. This small metal pin, about 3 millimetres in diameter, passes through the propeller and the drive shaft. It's designed to break if a solid object is struck, saving the engine and gearbox from damage. We replaced the pin, but only after consulting the operating manual.

Our second attempt to get going was more successful; although, by the end of the first day, we'd sheered another of our ten pins.

The river was heavily choked with snags, causing us to spend almost as much time dodging them as moving forward. This far upstream, the river is little more than a muddy shallow gutter as the bottom of a huge trench. It was a navigational nightmare. Ripples on the surface warned us of hazards just out of sight. In an effort to keep the weight down, we'd decided not to carry oars. No oars in a boat! How stupid can you get? So, using a long stick, we probed the murky water until, after no more than a few kilometres, we made our first camp on the banks of the Darling. We pitched our tent by stretching a rope between two trees.

We never gave ourselves nicknames. We stuck with Mike, Keith and Mal. If we had adopted nicknames, we should have been called 'Naive', 'Green' and 'Innocent', or perhaps, collectively, 'The Three Stooges'. Keith and I were only eighteen years old and Mike was twenty-one. What's more, we were city slickers facing a steep learning curve, and so far our expedition had been a comedy of errors.

As well as breaking those shear pins, we'd almost impaled Keith on a protruding branch; scraped the bottom of the boat on countless submerged logs; scratched and chipped the boat's gleaming new paint job; and forgotten to buy kerosene for the hurricane lamp. As an encore, Mike had managed to tread on a snake while stepping onto the bank. Both he and the snake moved with lightning speed in opposite directions. The red-bellied reptile slithered away beneath some shrubs and Mike leapt back into the boat.

We'd also run into the first of many rock bars: a term we used to describe submerged rocks covered with little water. All three of us had needed to climb into the cloudy flow and push and shove the vessel forward.

However, at least we'd developed many of the skills needed for the marathon ahead. In spite of the day's mishaps, we felt very pleased with ourselves.

Then, at sunset, mosquitoes descended on us in their thousands. They'd obviously never had such young and innocent flesh to feast upon before. There were too many to swat. At this rate, we joked, we'd all need a blood transfusion before morning!

Then Keith remembered the citronella. This sticky oil is very effective at keeping insects at bay, but its odour is foul. We crawled into our sleeping bags itching with bites and stinking of the stuff, yet still excited by the prospect of the adventure yet to come.

In the morning we were greeted by a glorious sunny sky. We felt fine. It could only get better, couldn't it?

•

Applying the lessons from the first day, we soon developed a routine to tackle the alternating moods of the river. Around one bend, a lovely stretch of water reflecting gnarled river gums eased our progress and lifted our spirits. Then, without warning, the propeller would crunch into a rock bar or log, and our enthusiasm would evaporate in an instant.

We struggled with the boat in the shallows; we pushed and pulled it over sharp rocks; we hacked our way through countless fallen logs with our terribly blunt axe, then used the block and tackle to drag our heavily laden beast across them. We were slowly whittling away at the huge task we'd set ourselves.

One time we collided with a submerged log and shattered the blades off the propeller. Luckily we had a spare. Always foremost in our minds was the task of capturing it all on film. Each of us could use the cinecamera so we, in turn, took shots of each other. It was necessary to take wide shots to show the setting we were struggling in. This often involved setting up the tripod on the bank, starting the clockwork driven camera and running back to not only show all three of us, but also to provide the extra manpower to move the boat through the entanglement of obstacles.

I used every opportunity to take photographs and of course the extra waiting around by the other two expedition members provided a much-needed rest.

Our bodies were taking a beating. Our shins became covered with cuts and bruises. The block and tackle broke, and the heavy wooden block smashed into my foot, so I couldn't walk for half a day. When we were in the water pushing, lifting and shoving the boat, freshwater shrimp would attack the abrasions on our legs, giving us the nightmarish sensation of being eaten alive.

Our tempers frayed and we began to shout at one another. It was a good thing there were three of us: not only did we need the extra manpower to lift and drag, but also three people in a tight situation created a dynamic that kept each of us from killing another. We each depended on each other to succeed and we all knew it. Today it would be called bonding but whatever it should be called, slowly we evolved into a team respecting each other and reliant on each other. Any one of us could have given up, but failure was never really an option. We were determined to finish what we'd started. Our bonded strength grew with each conquered kilometre. Our main defence against the dire reality of our situation was our sense of humour. When one of us slipped in the mud we would call him a drunken bum or tell him *'This is no time to sit down!'*, or make some other sarcastic comment. It seems childish but it helped to relieve the tensions and provided a much-needed distraction from the physical demands on our bodies. Although it would be an exaggeration to say we laughed our way down the Darling, our sense of humour and youthful enthusiasm lifted our spirits. We laughed at ourselves as much as possible; we were determined not to lose our optimism.

We kept sighting camps and homesteads, and we'd go ashore to make ourselves known to some of the inhabitants. We were surprised to find that most had heard of our voyage on the radio. Our newly acquired friends always turned out to be sympathetic to our objectives, but almost all of them thought we wouldn't make it. Some of the property owners gave us petrol, and on one occasion someone offered to put the boat on a truck and whisk it 80 or so kilometres downstream. We gladly accepted the fuel, but refused the lift. That would be cheating. That would never do.

We were out of condition at the start, but ten days later, when we reached our first town, Collarenebri, our physical fitness was at a peak and we felt ready for the next leg. We'd only covered about a hundred and fifty kilometres—2100 to go. We restocked with food and fuel, and mailed letters home to let everyone know we were still alive. We considered ordering bronze propellers to be sent to the next town, but decided not to. The locals assured us that the river would be easy from here on.

Just past the road bridge that crosses the Darling at Collarenebri is a set of rapids. They took about four exhausting hours to negotiate by pulling, pushing and rocking. We were relieved to see the rapids behind us when more damn rocks turned up! By mid-afternoon we were completely fed up. I didn't have any doubt that if we'd been walking along the banks, we would have made faster progress.

It wasn't all bad. The wildlife was intoxicating: as our small boat passed slowly downstream, lizards scampered up the steep banks, lazy tortoises leapt off sunny perches and birds of all kinds took to the air.

Occasionally we found good open stretches of water, but this was a sign that a huge rock bar was ahead. Then we came to a massive log across the river and decided to try jumping it. I rammed the boat full throttle into the log, leaping over it and crashing down the other side. Buoyed by this new technique, we rammed log after log. Mostly it was successful.

We were breaking shear pins regularly, and soon all our spares ran out. So we used small pieces of fencing wire instead—they seemed to work well enough.

•

Oddly, it wasn't a log jump but an unknown submerged object that brought the expedition to an abrupt halt. We were whisking along a nice open stretch of water when the boat jolted and the motor began to vibrate violently. We'd shattered another propeller: only two of its three blades were left.

With no other option, we idled the motor gently along, knowing that the off-balance vibrations would cause all kinds of trouble in time. Mike and Keith sat on the bow taking soundings with sticks as we crept forward. To make matters worse, it was drizzling rain.

At about five o'clock we decided to camp. It was still miserable and wet. We were slipping around in the mud as we scrambled up the bank to find a suitable spot to pitch our tent.

The weather wasn't any better in the morning and then we hit yet another obstacle, our propeller now reduced to a stump. Things were serious. We hadn't seen a homestead for ages and didn't really know where we were. We had no means of electronic communication and our optimism had left us. What to do?

After several cups of billy tea and lots of discussion, we concluded that we must carry on somehow. We created a long pole from a trimmed tree branch and tried to push our craft along, gondolier-style. Our makeshift pole soon stuck stubbornly in the mud. Back to the drawing board.

Next we rowed using the camp shovel and the frying pan as paddles. It was pretty hopeless, and excruciatingly slow.

Out of desperation we decided to make a new propeller. We considered whittling one out of wood. No! Dumb idea. We settled on using baked-bean cans. The plan was simple: cut the tins into the rough shape of a blade, double them over and wire them to the propeller stump. We completed the illusion by coating the whole thing with a two-part plastic cement: a putty-like substance that needs to harden overnight. We ate the baked beans for our evening meal. In the morning we filed off the rough edges from the cans, gave it a smooth sanding and fitted it to the outboard motor.

To our amazement and delight, it worked!

Well, it sort of worked. At normal speed the motor vibrated violently, because the pitch on the homemade propeller was far too great, so we kept the motor at little more than an idle. No more log jumping. We prodded the water for hidden snags and eased our way downstream. It was still drizzling rain, but our hopes were up a little. After a few kilometres we were so pleased with our repair's success that we allowed ourselves to imagine we could get all the way to Walgett, the next town.

Around eleven, our carefully crafted propeller was chewed to pieces by a submerged snag in the middle of a long stretch of open water. Estimated distance achieved: 20 kilometres.

We'd planned what to do if the boat became immobilised. Keith would stay with the boat in the unlikely event that someone came along, while Mike and I would set off for help with a movie camera, a still camera and a small amount of food.

It was raining heavily as the two of us trudged through the black, slippery mud. Our plan was to walk in an easterly direction, to reach a road we knew followed the river. However, because the river was so winding, with huge sweeping bends, we could be many kilometres from the road.

Suddenly, through the misty air, we spotted the iron roof of a homestead. Tom Cutler was astonished to find two muddy, exhausted and bedraggled characters on his doorstep, especially considering that the road was on black soil; in the rain, no vehicle could move on it. Tom listened intently to our tale of woe as we consumed a cup of steaming hot tea. He couldn't believe we had no oars, but he quickly offered to lend us a pair of his. Then we used his phone to call home.

I was soon ordering two new propellers to be sent to a stock and station agent in Walgett, who would forward them by road to a property on the western side of the river, where the road was better in wet weather. The parcel would get out there on the mail truck.

Tom took us back to our camp in his Land Rover. Keith was surprised to see us so soon!

Before Tom drove off, he told us, 'When you get around a couple of bends you'll see a wind pump on the left. Pull up and come on in for dinner. Our homestead's right on the river.'

What? He must have thought we were a right bunch of fools. All the time his homestead had been just a few minutes downriver. We arrived in time for a hot meal with Tom and his wife.

As we blundered our way down the Darling, the generosity and kindness extended to us by people like Tom was overwhelming. We couldn't have completed our journey without the outback hospitality for which Australia is so well-known. The people of the river gave us their unconditional help and encouragement.

•

Next day, our efforts to row using Tom's oars were a farce. None of us had done this before. I sat in the stern as Keith and Mike pulled on an oar each. We had no rudder, so keeping the boat on course was a nightmare. It was my job to call out instructions: 'More, Mike!' or 'Stop, Keith!' We ran into overhanging limbs, bounced off the muddy banks and weaved all over the place.

After an hour I took an oar to relieve Mike and he moved into the position of 'master' in the stern. Monotonous regularity took over: two hours each on the oars and one on the stern. At the end of the day we had rowed 15 kilometres and were utterly exhausted, our hands raw with blisters. We slept well.

We'd made our camp across the river from Calmundy Station, where the lady of the homestead made us welcome with a cuppa and a chance to use the telephone. We confirmed that everything was in hand. The propellers weren't due for several days, so we could row on to Caloola Station, 16 kilometres downstream.

Progress was agonisingly slow. Our blisters would burst and then quickly be replaced with new ones. The river was often shallow, requiring more pushing and shoving. Rock bars returned and, on our second day after leaving Calmundy, four huge trees completely blocked the river— we had to unload the boat and carry it plus all the gear around these obstacles.

After this mighty effort, our energy levels were so low we could barely bring ourselves to get on with it. We scattered our camping gear at the top of the steep riverbank, then washed our dirty clothes and hung them over the limbs of fallen trees to dry. We set up camp on a flat spot above the bank and collapsed.

We awoke around dawn to the sound of rain once more. Quickly it turned to a deluge. We ran around like chooks with our heads cut off, salvaging the camera equipment and bundling it into the tent. The rain teemed down. Our freshly washed clothes, strung out along the logs, were soon receiving an unnecessary final rinse. The only dry clothes in camp were our pyjamas, and we had them on.

Our total food supply had been reduced to a single tin of spaghetti, left down at the river by the boat. We drew straws to see who would confront the downpour to retrieve our breakfast. Keith, the lucky winner, stripped naked and plodded stoically through the mud down the steep embankment. No way was he going to wet his only dry clothes. Mike and I, relatively dry in the tent, roared with laughter.

We consumed the spaghetti cold, and then accepted that we had no choice but to get back to the task. We descended the treacherous sodden bank to the reality of our expedition. It was almost midday.

The rowing was sapping our energy fast. My hands and back were giving me hell as we rowed with ever-weakening strokes, like worn-out machines. I was ready to give up but would never admit it to the others. The doomsayers had been right—we were mad to attempt the Darling. Our preparation was way off.

More logs, more rock bars and no food. The river now seemed longer than ever. Then, with wild enthusiasm, Keith yelled as he spotted the chimney of Caloola Station on the right-hand bank.

Within minutes we were standing at the homestead doorway with Mrs Elsie Webber smiling affectionately on the other side of the flyscreen door.

'Come on in,' she said. 'I've just cooked dinner.'

We didn't need a second invitation and soon devoured two enormous helpings each of a magnificent curry. While the food was good, the news was great: our bronze propellers had arrived in town and would be coming out on the first mail truck, as soon as the road was passable to traffic.

We ended up staying three days, camping in Elsie's shearing shed and enjoying the pleasant change from the tiny tent.

When our propellers arrived we returned to the voyage invigorated and confident. The river level had risen a bit during our stay, making travel easier.

•

After two more days' travel and a chance to shoot some ducks to supplement our diet, we reached the junction with the Namoi River. More water, better flow. We went up the Namoi to Walgett, where we stocked up with money and groceries. Mike took a short flight in a Tiger Moth biplane to film aerial shots of the Darling. Ahead the river looked so much better. We dared to taste success.

Downstream from the town, the water was wide and deep. We roared along at full throttle, which was an unfamiliar, delirious sensation. Occasionally we still came across fallen trees, but the river was too wide for them to be a problem.

Trees on the banks flew by, birds took to the air and the feel of wind in my hair was intoxicating. This is how we'd imagined the trip would be.

Our complacency shattered with a bone-jarring crash as the motor struck a submerged obstacle and flew out of the water, landing on the rear seat. It was still roaring. I cut the power.

Shit! The motor's cast aluminium mounting had snapped in half. I carried out a temporary repair using fencing wire.

Later one of the two cylinders stopped firing! Now we needed help. Once more we found it with a friendly river property owner who was a bit of a bush mechanic. He worked tirelessly on our motor and had it back together after about five hours, meaning the loss of just one day.

With more caution and lots of luck, our expedition became monotonous. The rest of the river should be a snap, we thought.

At Boorooma Station we had more hospitality lavished on us. Jim Marshall, the owner, had a reputation for throwing uninvited visitors off the place; but he proved most welcoming, even filling our fuel tanks and insisting we owed him nothing.

'Just finish what you started, boys,' he said with a huge grin. 'I admire what you're trying to do. Don't give up. I'll be watching the papers for news of your success.'

So much for reputations. I learnt a valuable lesson: judge people by how you find them and take no notice of what others say.

The expedition was taking longer than planned, but nothing could stop us now. Or could it?

•

With raised spirits we scooted up to the bridge at the town of Brewarrina. We'd travelled 550 kilometres from Mungindi—more than a thousand to go!

We stocked up on supplies and then I telephoned the editor of the *Newcastle Sun*. My four weeks' leave was now into the fifth week, so I explained my predicament. Sympathetic as he was, he gave me an ultimatum: make the effort to get back within a few days, or I wouldn't have a job.

I really wanted my job as a press photographer, but I also felt a strong sense of duty to Mike and Keith. We'd started this thing together, and we should finish it together. I had no doubt that if I gave up I'd regret it for the rest of my life.

I sent a telegram:

HAVE DECIDED TO FINISH THE TRIP. SORRY FOR ANY INCONVENIENCE. MALCOLM.

My dream job was out the window.

Mike's news editor was more understanding than mine and had told him to finish the journey, so we could take as long as we needed.

The routine of travel resumed: good smooth water with occasional rock bars and hardly any snags, and endless wildlife along the banks. The kilometres sped by.

When we reached Bourke, and Mike and I made our way to a general store to restock the basics, the woman behind the counter asked, 'Are you the mob that's going down the river in a boat?'

We nodded, confused.

'Ring the police immediately! Here, use my phone.'

My first thought was of some serious trouble at home; but the sergeant told us he didn't know exactly what it was all about, just that it was something to do with the Australian Journalists Association. The damn union I'd been forced to join.

I called my mother to explain I'd resigned and tell her not to worry. She'd been getting calls from the union rep, demanding that I return. Apparently the AJA had once fought and won a case in the arbitration court when one of its members had been sacked while on leave. If I resigned now, it was embarrassing for them.

Poor buggers! I thought. *What do I care?*

So they tried to blacklist me. I was advised by the AJA that I would never work in any media again. Oddly, for years they sent me reminders to pay my union fees, which continued to increase.

Our expedition was so far removed from the frivolous rubbish of unions and the like we were just enjoying the ride. The river was now a world away from those first three weeks of hard yakka, although I reckon I actually missed it a bit.

•

The last big portage of the trip was when we reached the weir that dams the river at Menindee. From then on it really was a breeze.

We took to boating after sunset. The afterglow from the sun sent amazing red streaks across the sky and illuminated the parade of gum trees on the banks with an eerie blush. When it turned totally dark, we would make our camp by firelight.

At 1.28 p.m. on Thursday the 9th of May 1963, we reached the Murray River. The muddy waters of the Darling mingled with the crystal clear flow of the river like a murky cloud despoiling a perfect sky. We felt a powerful attachment to the muddy, 'ugly river' and its 'dreary banks', as it was described by Charles Sturt, the first European explorer to see it.

We had set ourselves an 'impossible' challenge but in spite of our naivety and lack of funds, had matured together as a team. We slapped each other on the back and inexplicably, starting laughing out loud as the bow of our battered boat crunched into the southern bank of the Murray. We stepped ashore in Victoria.

What now? How should we celebrate?

We did what we'd been doing every day for the last 68 days. We scooped up a billy of water from the river and made a cup of tea. This time, however, it was water from the Murray. No one could ever truly understand the shared experience of that moment. Mike and I bonded in a way that underpinned and strengthened our future together travelling and filmmaking.

There is nothing quite like the feeling of success, and nothing like the first time I experienced it.

5

New Job and New Pursuits

The auditorium was crowded with hundreds of young, enthusiastic would-be filmmakers. Mike and I were on the stage, literally in the spotlight. We were in the third year of making our television series, *Ask the Leyland Brothers*, which was enjoying a weekly audience of roughly three million.

I held the microphone and addressed the graduating students from the Film, Television and Radio School in Sydney. 'I don't want to discourage any of you, but I'm here to tell you that making a film is a lot easier than selling it.' An audible hush rolled through the audience. 'As you all know, having graduated from your filmmaking classes, creating a film is hard enough.'

There had been no one to give us this wisdom 20 years earlier, in 1963, when we returned from our Darling River

Expedition with 3000 metres of exposed film. Editing and selling it would be our next big challenges.

We'd sent all the film to be processed by a laboratory in Sydney, but we couldn't afford to pay the full bill upfront. As money accumulated, we'd send off what we had to the lab owner and he'd return the film to us a bit at a time.

My immediate priority was to process all the still pictures. I pressed Mum's laundry into service as a darkroom and spent weeks using my trusty old enlarger. I began writing freelance stories for magazines and managed to sell quite a few.

I dropped by the Newcastle Herald and Sun office and saw my old workmates. The editor and Mr Merrilees both wished me good luck. Meanwhile, Mike had returned to work the day after we came back from the Darling.

•

I badly needed a proper darkroom, so I went in to NBN with Mike and asked their staff still photographer, Des, if I could use his. I had my own chemicals and photographic paper.

'Sure,' he said, 'as long as it's all right with the boss.'

It was and I installed myself there for a couple of weeks. During this time all sorts of jobs came in and Des was occasionally run off his feet. I stepped in and helped out.

Most of the TV commercials were made using still pictures in those days, so Des had to photograph the products and make prints from them. These were taken to the art department, where graphic artists made up art cards called 'graphics' using the photos and their own drawings. The graphics were returned to Des, who made slides of each one. It was a time-consuming exercise and very precise. Often one commercial would involve ten or twelve slides.

Des's job also involved running the cinefilm processor, which had to be ready all day as film came in. Des mixed the chemicals, made sure they were replenished and put through test strips of film. On top of that he did portraits of TV personalities and took publicity stills.

I ended up spending quite a lot of my time helping out where I could, sometimes staying back late. Often jobs were urgent, because commercials were due to go to air with very short notice.

Then, two weeks after I first walked in to NBN, Des told me he was leaving. He suggested I apply for the job.

I must have looked perplexed. After all, he was a highly qualified man: a Fellow of the Royal Photographic Society in London who had the right to use the letters FRPS after his name. I was only a second-year cadet, I explained to him: 'In fact, I'm not even that. I'm blacklisted by the AJA and I don't have your experience.'

He said that this didn't matter and assured me I could do the job. 'Besides, they don't care about unions in this place,' he told me. 'Ability is all that matters.' He said he'd give me a good reference.

I was overwhelmed by his confidence in me, so I submitted my application to the film department manager.

The very next day I was called into his office for an interview.

'I've looked at your application, Malcolm, and it seems pretty good,' he said. 'Des has highly recommended you.' I listened intently. 'My main concern is: can you do the job? Can you run the film processor?'

I knew he had little knowledge of photographic chemistry, so I decided to rattle off my knowledge of the chemicals involved. The manager tried his best to look as if he understood, but I knew he didn't. His background was in radio.

'Very well,' he finally said, as he added my application to a large pile of others on his desk.

Later that day, he told me I had the job. It was for three months' probation, of course and, if I proved suitable, it would be a full-time permanent position. I was elated.

Bluffing a bit to get the job is all very well, but now came the test. Des was leaving that day, a Friday. I was to start on the Monday. Taking over a full-time senior position with no experienced mentor to turn to . . . scary.

Imagine my surprise when I arrived at work on the Monday morning to find Des in a wheelchair with one leg fully encased in plaster. He'd tripped over some studio equipment on his way out of the building and broken his leg. Since he was technically still employed, he was covered by workers' compensation. He couldn't take up his new job in London for six weeks, so he very kindly opted to hang around for a couple of weeks and nurse me through my settling-in period. Bad luck for Des; good luck for me.

Des taught me all I needed to know about the film processor. I learnt so much from him in those two weeks.

I doubt I could have bluffed my way through without his help.

I couldn't have landed a better job. I was accustomed to working super-fast at the newspaper. This, by comparison, was leisurely. To top it off, I was receiving three times the wage I'd earned as a press photographer; I was treated like a department head and paid as a fully qualified senior.

The photography was mostly product shots for commercials, but I had a fully equipped studio to use when it was warranted. I also had the opportunity to apply all I'd learnt about lighting from my well-thumbed manuals: I had spotlights, floodlights and an array of lighting accessories. The darkroom was fitted out with the best gear and all was new.

Television was still in its early days, and attracting advertising was the big challenge. NBN offered new advertisers free production costs and charged only for the airtime. As a result, the station began to attract more business and I became very busy indeed. Luckily the weekends were free.

•

The big task now was to get our Darling River film sold.

To begin with, Mike and I cut it down to four reels and sent it to the ABC. They rejected it, claiming it would never make a worthwhile programme. This devastating assessment from such a respected broadcaster dented our egos but we were so convinced that our story was worthwhile, we kept reminding ourselves that this was just like another rock bar or fallen tree on the river; an obstacle to be overcome.

We decided to reduce it to two reels and add a soundtrack. We had submitted edited, but silent, film to the ABC and thought that the lack of proper presentation may have reduced our chances of a fair appraisal. Murray Finlay, NBN's newsreader, kindly recorded the narration from a script put together by the station's news editor. I recorded the soundtrack, which now included some music, on a reel-to-reel tape recorder, but it didn't synchronise too well with the film. To keep it running in sync, we needed to stop and start the projector, the short pauses giving the sound a chance to catch up with the picture. This was annoying and crude, but good enough for evaluation purposes. Since the system relied on an intimate knowledge of the film, it wasn't possible to send it off to potential buyers without us there to run it.

Mike and I organised two weeks off work and drove to Sydney with our equipment in the boot. We hawked the film around from one potential buyer to another, and were greeted with a range of disparaging excuses: 'Sorry, haven't got the time'; 'Make an appointment and come back later'; 'Leave it here—I'll look at it soon and send it back.' Of course, there was no way we could do the latter.

In the end we developed a more aggressive approach. First, call and make an appointment. Arrive right on time carrying our projector and tape machine. Plonk it all on the desk of the prospective buyer. Act fast. He mustn't be given time to protest. Draw the blinds. Project it straight onto a wall. Keep talking while setting up. Explain the background to the programme and start the film before he has a chance to chuck us out. If the film is any good, it should hold his attention.

Great technique. Not unlike a door-to-door vacuum cleaner salesman.

Result? Failure!

Despondent, and much lighter in the pocket, we returned to our jobs at NBN.

Was it possible that no one wanted to see our film? Perhaps we were just kidding ourselves.

•

Murray Masterton, who was Mike's boss and the news editor, had great faith in our film. He suggested we call Channel Nine in Sydney and talk to the legendary Bob Raymond, who had launched *Four Corners* on the ABC a few years before and then switched to the Nine Network as executive producer of a similar programme called *Project 64*, the precursor of *60 Minutes*. This one-hour, high-rating show had a prime-time slot on Sunday nights. It was possibly the best we could ever expect.

'No one else even thinks it's worth two bob, including the ABC,' Mike and I told Murray Masterton. 'What makes you imagine Bob will?'

'Nothing to lose, have you?'

So we called and, to our surprise, got straight through to Bob Raymond in his 'special projects' production office. He immediately agreed to a screening and we arranged a time at his editing rooms.

On the appointed day we stepped into a nicely equipped projection room. We lugged all our heavy equipment in and set it up with the tape recorder. Lights out and away we went. Mike and I were nervously glancing at each other as we juggled the projector to keep the sound close to where it should be.

Bob, a large man with a round ruddy face and neatly trimmed goatee, sat in silence for about ten minutes. Then the door swung open and his private secretary came in. She whispered something and they started a low conversation. We stopped the projector.

'Oh! Keep it going. I've got the idea,' he said.

We were horrified, and didn't start up again until their conversation was over. Once more in the dark, we resumed the show. The first reel took about 45 minutes: during that time, Bob left the room half a dozen times and was continually interrupted by the secretary.

Mike and I thought we'd wasted our time. Was he just humouring us?

While we laced up the projector for reel two, Bob floored us with a question. 'How much do you want for it?'

We looked at each other, dumbfounded, trying to read each other's mind.

Bob Raymond smiled and, before we could respond, added, 'Okay, start the second reel and think about it.'

With the second reel's soundtrack loud enough to drown out our whispered conversation, my brother and I came up with a price.

Eventually we reached the end of the film.

'Well?' Bob asked.

'Fifteen hundred pounds,' we said, hoping to sound confident. In reality we had no idea what to ask, but that was about the total cost of the enterprise. So, if we got our money back, we thought, that would be great.

'Good,' Bob responded, without giving any hint of what he thought. 'I'll let you know how this goes down with the powers-that-be.'

We drove back to Newcastle with mixed feelings. He obviously liked it. Was the price too steep? Had we blown it? *Project 64* was, after all, the only game left in town. We waited.

When the call came, we had to go back to Sydney and repeat the whole exercise at TCN Channel Nine's board-room in Artarmon. Present were a number of executives, including Bob Raymond. At the end of the screening Mike and I were told they would consider the price and get back to us. What an ordeal!

Several days later, while I was at work, Bob phoned. 'I've been asked to ask you if you'll take £1200.'

'No. Fifteen hundred is the price!' we firmly replied.

'Very well. Fifteen hundred it is,' he said. Then added softly, 'I *did* have to ask, you understand?'

He knew it was cheap enough and had given a hint of that in the way he'd phrased the offer. I reckon if you offered a television network a programme for 20 cents, they'd automatically ask you to take ten.

Shortly after the deal had been struck, we were off to Sydney once more. We sat in a sound-recording studio with Bob prompting us to talk about the trip. It seemed like a conversation as he skilfully guided us through it. In the finished product, he used a mixture of our own voices and that of Channel Nine's professional voice-over man. The special projects division, with Bob at the helm, did the final edit and reduced the film to a one-hour episode.

Titled 'Down the Darling', it went to air on a Sunday night in 1964 as an episode in the *Project 64* series. It was an instant success with viewers. We too watched it for the first time when it went to air. Our family watched it in our parents' lounge room. It was an emotional night like no other. The professional editing and choice of bush music together with Raymond's skilfully crafted script gave the show a professionalism we could never have achieved with our limited experience.

The network was overwhelmed with praise and requests to see the episode again, so it was repeated within two weeks and pulled an even bigger audience. We were overjoyed.

The day after the show aired, we received a phone call from Melbourne. Lloyd O'Neil, the publisher and owner of Lansdowne Press, wanted to discuss the idea of us writing a book. He wondered if we thought we could do it.

'Yes, of course we can!' we told him somewhat audaciously, and arranged to meet him in Sydney the following week.

This was how Mike and I came to co-author our first book, *Great Ugly River: A Modern Adventure in Australia's Outback*. I was nineteen years old.

•

One day we received a request from our bank manager to come and see him. He offered the following advice: 'Get rid of the dead wood in your partnership.'

'Dead wood! What dead wood?' I exclaimed.

'Keith is a nice enough bloke, but you two are the heart of your success. He can't contribute anything that you can't do between you. Partnerships tend to fail. It'll be tough enough to make it work with just you. Better to split it up now than wait too long.'

I didn't agree: Keith had been in this from the start, and each of us had put our money in equally. He kept all the notes, did the majority of the research and had a greater understanding of natural history than us. He had been involved with the selling process and he was a full one-third partner.

Without much hesitation, Mike said, 'All right, but Keith has a one-third interest in everything. We'd need to pay him out and compensate him properly.'

The bank manager was willing to lend us any additional funds we might need for a fair compensation. Mike agreed on the spot without any consultation with me.

The whole thing came out of the blue to me. To me it felt like a huge betrayal of the trust we three had in each other, but Mike was undeterred. I felt like I'd been ambushed. I wondered whether the whole thing had been agreed to in advance and, as Mike knew I had a strong loyalty to Keith, set up the situation behind my back. I didn't want to believe it and reluctantly went along with it.

To Keith's great credit, he accepted the decision without a fuss. He remained a good friend and landed a job at NBN as a film cameraman shooting the news.

•

The next three years working at NBN were invaluable. Mike and I expanded our skills and fine-tuned our filmmaking techniques. We also developed a life outside television work.

Mike bought a new Land Rover and with Keith we joined the newly formed Land Rover Owner's Club. The three of us spent almost every weekend trekking off with half a dozen other vehicles into the surrounding Hunter Valley. Through the club we made many new friends, and Ted Hayes was one of them. An apprenticed motor mechanic, Ted became a very close mate, and before long the four of us were off enjoying the experience of discovering the outdoors.

We four blokes also joined the Newcastle Speleological Society, a group of enthusiastic cave explorers. This was an exciting prospect, but I had a problem, my claustrophobia. Most people think it is a fear of enclosed spaces, but in fact it's a fear of being encased. Trapped. The only exit blocked. I had managed to overcome my fear when I was in that suction head of the dredge in Newcastle harbour. Then I was running on adrenaline. This would be different.

Knowing that claustrophobia would be a problem for me when caving, I wondered if I could bring myself to crawl through tiny spaces. I was determined to overcome my irrational fear and just knew that the challenge of photographing myriads of beautiful limestone formations was something I had to try.

Ted had been caving many times, and one long weekend the whole club was off to Timor Caves in the Hunter Valley. Most club members arrived on Friday night and camped in a big open paddock near the cave entrance. When everyone had slipped into their sleeping bags after spending hours talking around the campfire, Ted and I gathered up our equipment and set off together.

There were commonsense rules imposed in the club: never go alone; carry two sources of light between you; let someone know where you're going; and never tackle something you aren't confident doing. Ted and I followed all the rules that night, except for letting anyone know we were going underground, and for the fact that only Ted was confident!

It was around midnight when we reached the entrance and crawled into the first opening, which was about the size of a car garage. We sat for some time adjusting to the enclosed feeling. So far, so good. Then, slowly, Ted led me into some of the tighter tunnels and narrow 'squeezes', as cavers call them.

That night I spent four hours underground. Thanks to Ted's seemingly infinite patience, I gradually learnt to control my apprehension. I was crawling through narrow tunnels, climbing over rocks and scrambling up sloping piles of rubble. I was okay if Ted was in front and I followed behind. I found I couldn't handle caving if someone was behind me. My irrational fear took over then; I felt trapped.

After this initiation, I became a fully active member of the club. Everyone knew about my problem and I was always tail-end-Charlie. Last in. First out.

My biggest test came several months after my night excursion, when the club president announced that he and a friend had uncovered the entrance to a hidden chamber that had never been explored before.

The dark black mud on the floor of limestone caves is often bat guano, dried-out bat excrement. One large cavern had more than a metre and a half of the stuff. To find out why it all flowed to one corner, the club president had dug down and discovered a narrow, tube-like sinkhole. He'd blocked it up immediately, and the next weekend the club went to explore it properly.

On the big day we formed a work party to excavate this hole. We were rewarded with an opening barely large enough to squeeze through. Worse, it had a 90-degree turn within the first half a metre, then sloped off to the right between two massive slabs of vertical rock. Exploring such a passage is dangerous: we had no idea if the air was stale, or even deadly.

The smallest club member went first, pushing a set of chemical air-testing equipment in front. We held his legs, ready to pull him out instantly if necessary. Slow and constant feedback was maintained as he gradually snaked his way along the thin passage and into the hidden chamber.

The air turned out to be safe and, remarkably, I was the third person to inch my way along that incredibly tight squeeze and enter the chamber. This was tighter than anything I'd tackled before, but by concentrating on the technicalities of the photographs I was taking, I was able to overcome my anxiety. I surprised myself.

What a feeling! Before my eyes was a jewelled chamber that had been sealed up for millions of years. Its walls were bedecked with millions of shining, pristine crystal-like formations, and there were stalactites and stalagmites in a forest of glistening limestone. (If you're wondering which are stalagmites and which are stalactites, it's easy—as all cavers know, *when the mites go up, the tights go down!*)

In the chamber I was elated and felt so privileged to know that no one had seen this before. A real sense of something special. I carefully moved my camera about, lining up the best angles I could and using my flashgun multiple times.

The results were stunning. I wrote a story about the experience and sent my pictures off to a national magazine. They loved it and ran a four-page spread: the payment I received was a nice little supplement to my income.

While caving was a fun new activity to master, we spent far more time exploring the fire trails of the forests and any other four-wheel-drive tracks we could get onto. All this time we were learning how to control and drive in 4WD. We learnt to judge the ground, to engage the correct gear for the terrain and to tackle loose sand on the beaches. Driving with the club was a great way to do this because, with several vehicles available, there was always someone on hand to pull you out if you ended up bogged. The more we mastered the skills of four-wheel-drive cross-country driving, the more we realised just how lucky we had been in South Australia when we came so close to becoming another statistic of misadventure.

In my second year at NBN I bought my own Land Rover, a long wheelbase version. I enjoyed bushwalking more than driving, which was merely a means to an end. I was acquiring an even deeper appreciation of the bush: a love of the wildlife and of the solitude. When we reached remote mountaintops I would trek off with my camera, recording everything I saw.

Mike and I were now preparing ourselves for another expedition. This time in four-wheel drives.

•

Most Friday nights, a large group of staff from NBN went to the nearby Delaney Hotel for a drink before heading home. I was frequently sharing Mike's car and we would end up there. Unlike my brother I didn't drink beer, or any alcohol for that matter. It's not that I hadn't tried beer; it was just a taste I didn't like.

One day the production manager bought a round of beer for everyone. I'd told him that I didn't drink, but he still placed a big glass in front of me.

'I told you I didn't want this,' I said. 'You must have forgotten.'

'No, I didn't. Now drink up and be a man.'

'No, I won't. Sorry.'

'Think you're too good for us, eh? Now drink it up. I paid good money for that!'

'Too bad,' I shot back angrily. 'You like it, you have it!'

I pushed the glass over to him, went to the bar, and bought a round for the whole group and a lemon squash for me.

The film editor came over and advised me to apologise or I wouldn't have a job on Monday. I didn't apologise, and on Monday nothing was said. Business as usual.

When Saturday nights became party nights at an NBN staff member's house, I'd go along with Mike to some of them. I would watch the blokes getting drunk and the girls getting ignored, then spend most of my time chatting to the girls while the blokes made fools of themselves.

I had no problem with socialising, but I couldn't understand why it needed to revolve around alcohol. My father was a heavy drinker and a chain smoker. I hated the idea I might turn out like him, so I consciously became a non-drinker. It takes a lot more courage and willpower to do that than to fall in with the majority. I didn't really conform to the crowd. The more they tried to get me to indulge, the more I resisted. Just think of the money I saved.

During this time Mike became involved with Pat Teare. She was the TV station's videotape operator. Soon she joined Mike on our weekend 4WD outings, became an active member of the caving club and within about one year, married him. I was not only Mike's best man, but also the photographer.

The dynamics of our small group changed, but we all shared the same interests and dreamt of doing something special together.

•

One time at work I had to photograph a newly released Mercedes Benz. I spent a lot of time in the studio setting up a complex effect of the car floating on water. The shot was used by the local car dealer, but Mercedes thought it was so good they put it on 24-sheet billboards all over the country.

I was called into the station manager's office. He demanded to know why I'd taken so long over a single photo. I explained that I was bored with taking shots in the local parkland and thought this might look better. He then advised me that the client had complained about the five hours of studio time.

'I see,' I said. 'But they must've been happy with the result—they're using it all over the place.'

'That may be,' he responded sternly, 'but in future, no more than one hour on a simple thing like that.'

I couldn't see what harm was done. The studio had been sitting empty. Besides, I'd thought I was applying myself. Doing something creative.

'You need to learn a lesson from this, Malcolm,' the station manager said. 'We don't want creativity. It's mediocrity that makes money. Understood?'

I left his office deflated. I knew I'd done a good job, but now I was supposed to go away like some robot and produce mediocrity. Although I liked my work, I was becoming disillusioned with my workplace. I raised this issue with the manager.

'If you don't like it, you can always leave,' he told me bluntly.

It *was* very tempting to leave then, but I already had plans. They involved a major expedition with Mike and I as partners, and Keith, Ted and Mike's new wife Pat making up the rest of the team. I chose to wait for the right time to hand in my notice, because all of us except Ted worked at NBN. My thirst for adventure was beckoning.

6

Big Plans and a Fortuitous Accident

What we'd achieved so far with 'Down the Darling' was just a rehearsal for the main event. Mike and I had tasted an amazing sense of achievement, but we ached to do something even better. Something that people would notice and, hopefully, that would set us up for a future in filmmaking.

While working at NBN, we used our spare time to plan a crossing of Australia by vehicle in as straight a line as possible: an 'Across Australia Expedition'.

We would start at Steep Point, the most westerly part of the mainland, and end at Cape Byron, the most easterly. Distance: 6500 kilometres. Estimated time: four to five months. Problem: the Simpson Desert was in the middle and it had no track across it. At around 180,000 square kilometres, it is the largest sand-ridge desert in the world.

In 1936 it was crossed by Ted Colson using camels. He took sixteen days to reach Birdsville. In 1939 it was again crossed by a camel expedition, led by Dr Cecil Madigan. According to our research, it had never been crossed by land vehicle.

All our planning revolved around this single major objective. We were in no doubt we could tackle anything else on the planned route, but for our expedition to be a success we had to cross the Simpson Desert. What a challenge!

We didn't have nearly enough money, but we reckoned that didn't matter: we'd overcome it somehow. We never even considered failure.

Most of our weekends were either spent planning or off somewhere four-wheel driving. When the Newcastle Speleological Society organised a two-week exploration of the Colong Caves in the Blue Mountains, we went along to film it. We shot in black-and-white and spent a lot of time capturing the exploration team as they investigated all the nooks and crannies of this extensive cave system.

Each scene took hours of setting up and dismantling the gear. It was painstakingly slow, but effective. We filmed an entire half-hour documentary underground.

For me it was a personal triumph. The prospect of being trapped underground still terrified me, but by forcing myself to concentrate on the job at hand, I managed to suppress my fears.

Mike and I edited the film at home and it came out as a half-hour television programme. We added a soundtrack of music and narration, titled it 'Expedition Underground', and then sent it off for assessment to the ABC, as they were the only broadcaster using half-hour shows. Based on our experience with 'Down the Darling', we expected a long wait before hearing back from them.

•

Preparations for our big expedition were well underway. We repainted both my Land Rover and Mike's red. Mine was overhauled mechanically from top to bottom: it was a 1958 model and we had to be sure it was sound. Ted Hayes and I worked on this tirelessly at night in my parents' backyard.

Over the Anzac Day long weekend, the speleological society was off to Kempsey to explore some limestone caves. Most club members left early on the Friday evening, but Ted and I laboured away until 11 p.m. to make some last-minute adjustments to my car.

When we finished up, I proposed that we should head off right then. 'The others are only five hours ahead. We should catch them up by morning.'

Ted agreed and suggested that we phone Keith, so we could go in convoy with him. The three of us set off for a night run north along the Pacific Highway. It was a cold night and we kept the car windows closed, with the heater on full blast.

Ted, exhausted from having worked every night for two weeks on my car, fell asleep on the front seat. The motor was humming reassuringly and kilometres sped by. I was becoming drowsy.

Then the forest echoed with the sound of tearing metal. My Land Rover crashed through three solid roadside posts and hurtled through the air like a missile. After landing on its nose, it twisted clockwise and came to rest as a mangled wreck.

I was suddenly awake. *Oh shit! Where's Ted?*

Both doors were missing. Amazingly the remains of the contorted vehicle were upright, but my passenger was nowhere to be seen.

The engine was roaring: the throttle had jammed on full. I fumbled for the ignition key, but it wasn't there. It had been spat out by the impact. The motor would surely explode if I couldn't stop it.

I didn't need to. Keith, bounding through the pitch black, reached the car and ripped the leads from the ignition coil.

An eerie silence descended on the curve in the highway just south of Kew, near Laurieton. It was 2.30 a.m. on Anzac Day, the 25th of April 1965.

Blood was pouring from a gash in my head. Had I killed my friend?

It was some time before Keith found Ted. He had flown through the air a considerable distance, taking out several saplings. He was unconscious.

It was half an hour before the police and ambulance arrived.

'Who was driving?' asked the sergeant.

'No one,' I replied flippantly, trying to add some levity to the situation.

The copper, obviously in no mood for nonsense, gave me a look that could kill.

'Technically, I was,' I hastened to add. 'Although I was asleep.'

He was not amused. I was, quite rightly, charged with negligent driving.

•

At the Port Macquarie hospital, a doctor declared Ted severely concussed: he was battered, but he had no broken bones. After tending to Ted's injuries, the doctor started sewing up the large gash in my head. We introduced ourselves and he told me his name was Malcolm Hay.

'You're not the same Dr Malcolm Hay who went to Heard Island in the Antarctic on a yacht called the *Patanela*, are you?' I asked.

'Yes,' he replied curiously. 'Did you hear about it?'

'Oh yes. My brother and I applied to join the expedition to take the film and still photographs, but we weren't accepted because some doctor got the job. Was that you?'

'Yes indeed!' replied my new acquaintance.

In the next hour or so we rattled on about expeditions and filmmaking. I told Dr Hay about the Darling River Expedition and our new venture, while also pointing out that all our planning was now down the drain. I'd wrecked my car and it would probably take a couple of years to save up enough to replace it.

The next day, Dr Hay kindly put us up at his home for a few days while we monitored Ted's condition. During this time I explained the full details of our Across Australia Expedition and Dr Hay listened intently. I told him about how the sand ridges in the Simpson Desert ran parallel north to south, and how we'd decided to tackle them from the western side where they had a gentler slope.

'How did you intend to fund all of this?' he asked.

I said that I didn't really know. We just reckoned we'd find a way.

'Perhaps I know someone who can help you,' he said.

George Sample had given considerable financial assistance to the Heard Island Expedition, and Dr Hay promised to drop him a line and tell him what sort of ideas we had. This sounded too good to be true. I accepted the note with Mr Sample's number and shoved it into my camera case, not expecting anything to come of it.

•

Several weeks later, I was surprised to receive a phone call from George Sample while at work at NBN.

'I've received a letter from Dr Malcolm Hay,' he said, 'explaining your expedition ideas to me. I was expecting you to call. So do you want to get together or not?'

I apologised that I hadn't got in touch, but I'd lost his number. He asked Mike and me to get to Sydney the following Sunday.

That day the two of us dressed up in our best suits and drove to Vaucluse. Mr Sample's impressive two-storey house lay at the end of a sweeping driveway, adorned by two gleaming Jaguars. The door was answered by his wife, Joan, who escorted us up the stairs and left us with her husband on the balcony. We were shocked to see him sitting in his underpants on a long deckchair, sunning himself.

'Get those jackets and ties off, boys. Relax,' he instructed. We eagerly complied.

Over the next few hours we outlined our expedition plans, showed a 16mm version of 'Down the Darling', and watched a lot of the footage from the Heard Island Expedition and Mr Sample's personal safaris in Africa. He then asked how much our Across Australia Expedition was expected to cost: we estimated $8000.

'What about cameras?' he asked. 'Are the ones you have good enough?'

We said yes, they were. We'd already used them on the Darling River.

'In my experience, you must have the best of equipment,' he advised. 'If you could have any camera in the world for a project like this, what would it be?'

Straight away we told him it would be either a German-made Arriflex or a French-made Eclair.

'Pick which one you'd have if you could.'

'The Eclair,' Mike decided. 'Although I've never used one.'

Mr Sample pulled out a small book and started writing this down. 'How do you spell that?' he asked. Then he asked who sold them. He wrote that down too, then signed the bottom of the sheet. He tore the page out and handed it to us. 'This,' he said with a broad smile, 'is an order for one of those Eclairs. Now go and place it.'

'But it will cost $6000,' I responded, my mouth open.

'That amount will become part of the loan I'm extending to you to get this show on the road.'

Loan? This was the first time we'd heard that word.

'Here's the deal,' Mr Sample said. 'I provide all the expedition expenses. You two organise everything and do the trip. You make the film and if it makes a profit, you can repay me. If it doesn't, I lose. It's my risk. But I'm a businessman, so there are conditions.'

Aha! I'd thought it sounded too good to be true. 'What conditions?' I asked.

'I will be a silent, one-third partner in this and all your ventures for the next five years. If you fail to make a profit, I suffer the loss. You get paid a basic wage throughout the term, hopefully from profitable income. This way you have an incentive to succeed. Profits will be shared one-third to me, two-thirds to you.'

Here was a man who didn't need the money.

'Why are you doing this?' I asked him.

He said he admired what we'd done so far with very little money. He had great faith in us and wanted to give us a chance to prove ourselves. 'There is no hidden agenda here. This is an opportunity. You decide if you want to take it up.'

We couldn't believe our luck. A few weeks earlier our whole expedition had been little more than a shattered dream. Now it was a reality. Philanthropists really do exist.

In the next month Mike and I revised our costs, and eventually our loan blew out to $15,000, including the Eclair. This was an amazing amount of money at the time. In the mid–1960s, a nicely appointed three-bedroom house in a good suburb of Newcastle would have cost about $6000, the price of the camera! The fifteen grand loan more than covered my replacement second-hand Land Rover. It was the same year model as my old one, but a station wagon configuration with five doors.

Of all the people who helped us with our careers, George Sample was the one who took the greatest risk and had the most confidence in our ability to succeed. We couldn't contemplate failure! We'd be letting down more than ourselves. Our expedition was at last ready to roll out of Newcastle and head west.

7

Wheels Across a Wilderness

In the darkness of 4 a.m. on a chilly April morning in 1966 I pulled away from home. I was in my Land Rover and had to pick up Ted and Keith along the way, and then join up with Mike and Pat in their Land Rover.

My vehicle was crammed full of filming equipment, fuel cans, water drums, dehydrated food and camping gear. I was also towing a heavily laden four-wheel trailer. It contained more fuel and water, as well as most of the expedition's emergency and recovery paraphernalia, including a shortwave radio transceiver. The trailer also carried a motorcycle to be used as a reconnaissance vehicle to scout for the best cross-country route over the desert regions ahead.

A feeling of overwhelming excitement surged through my veins. It felt exhilarating and daunting at the same time. A heavy cold mist hung over Wallsend. Nothing seemed to be on the road except me.

Years later, my mother told me she watched me pull away in the dark. She then moved off to the back verandah, listening to the burble of the Land Rover's exhaust. She told me how she feared that she wouldn't see her sons again: she pictured us perishing in the desert. She stayed listening until she could no longer hear my motor, then returned to bed and cried.

·

On the 3rd of May 1966, our two vehicles stood on the craggy limestone outcrop of Steep Point, the most westerly tip of the Australian mainland. The five of us had just made history: no vehicle had ever reached the Point before.

To get to our expedition's starting point we'd crossed the Nullarbor Plain from the east and driven north along the West Australian coastline. Our objective, the Point, had no track to provide access, so the final 42 kilometres had taken us two days, during which we'd bush-bashed through almost impenetrable scrub. An achievement in itself. The scrub was a metre and a half tall, and we needed to keep cleaning fine pulverised leaves out of the radiators.

We'd found an ornate wine bottle on the sandy beach south of the Point. It looked the right shape to suggest that a genie might appear if you rubbed it.

Now, standing on the outcrop, we dangled a billycan on a rope over the 20-metre cliff into the boiling surf of the Indian Ocean, then slowly hauled it up. This water was ceremoniously poured into the wine bottle and corked tight. We aimed to carry it across the continent and pour it into the Pacific at Cape Byron. The distance we'd need to cover was the same as that from London to Moscow: 5000 kilometres. Our journey, however, would be across red sand and wilderness.

We left a cairn of rocks at the point. It contained an oil drum declaring this as the start of the West–East Crossing Expedition and listing the expedition members: Mike Leyland, Mal Leyland, Pat Leyland, Keith Davey, Ted Hayes.

It took us a full day of rough four-wheel driving to return to our base camp, where the trailer and most of our equipment had been left.

Our intention was to follow as closely as possible the 26th parallel of latitude. For the best part of the trip we intended to use roads and tracks, but, when there were none, we would drive cross-country on a compass course. Of course, the greatest enigma of the entire effort was the Simpson Desert.

In Western Australia we used a track that cut through the desert, known as the Gunbarrel Highway. It was certainly no highway. In many places it had been washed away by cyclonic storms, and at times it was overgrown and blocked by fallen scrub. Ted rode the motorcycle to scout ahead, while we passed through seemingly endless kilometres of wilderness.

Along the way, the differential in my Land Rover smashed to pieces. Without it we couldn't drive the rear wheels, so we removed the drive shaft and continued on, just using the front wheels.

Breakdowns plagued the trip, but the highlights made up for it! We climbed to the top of some of the mesas that dot the landscape in the Gibson Desert, visited a small pond of water in the desert known as Lake Gruska and filmed the abundant wildlife that frequented it.

It took a month for us to reach Giles Weather Station, close to the Western Australia and Northern Territory border, and possibly the most remote such station in Australia. Here we had a chance to make some repairs to the trailer and carry out regular maintenance.

We continued east to the Northern Territory, monitoring the Royal Flying Doctor radio network to report our position and to send and receive telegrams. We were camped west of the Olgas when a message came through advising us that ABC TV wanted to buy 'Expedition Underground'. We responded with a price and this was agreed to. Negotiations took place over the radio network for all to hear. Possibly the strangest film transaction ever made!

By far the most sensational natural event on the trip occurred when we arrived at Ayers Rock on the 28th June. The sun was blazing and the Rock looked great: a massive monolith protruding from the almost–flat desert plain. I photographed it from all angles while Mike filmed it.

That night a howling wind blew in, accompanied by driving rain. The tent flapped violently and leaked profusely. Drops of chilly water woke me early. I quickly dressed and splashed my way to the door. It was a dull, wet morning. The grey outline of Ayers Rock was barely visible. Half a dozen frothy trails of water were running down the Rock's steep face. The beginnings of waterfalls.

The top of the Rock was shrouded by a thick foggy cloud that began to swirl and then headed skyward. As if a giant veil was lifting, the mist rose to reveal an enormous silver-grey mountain of glistening rock. The red surface was coated in a film of water that reflected the dull overcast sky.

More rain fell; it poured down. The waterfalls began to grow. At the top, a few hundred metres up, silver trails of froth scattered in all directions, eventually locating the time-worn channels that run to the edges of the world's largest monolith. A gathering of the waters took place until thousands of tons plummeted over the edges, creating countless powerful waterfalls.

It was a magnificent spectacle. Something like this only comes along once in a lifetime. How privileged we were to witness it, and to film and photograph everything. I found it, personally, very moving. I was saturated and cold from the blustering wind, but I couldn't contain the emotional sense that I was experiencing something very special.

This amazing storm lasted five hours, and then the clouds lifted and it was all over. We soon found out that we'd experienced the breaking of an eight-year drought. Never had so much rain been recorded at Ayers Rock in June.

This was also the first time such an event had been filmed and photographed. After we returned from the expedition, my pictures were sold all over the world and commanded a two-page colour spread in the *Australian Women's Weekly*.

Such luck not only gave us a unique photographic opportunity, but also soaked the Simpson Desert. This could only assist us in tackling the biggest challenge of the expedition. Desert vegetation would sprout, the sand would compact more with the added moisture and, with luck, our vehicles would have an easier time crossing those daunting sand dunes.

.

After a couple of days we took off, with Mike towing the monstrous trailer because of my broken differential. I wanted to stop and take a picture of our vehicles with the familiar silhouette of Ayers Rock in the background. At first Mike refused, arguing that we didn't need to.

I reminded him that my task was to record everything with stills. 'It's not all about the film, Mike!' I yelled. Ted and I unhitched the trailer beside the track.

Without a further word, Mike did a fast U-turn and drove off back towards Ayers Rock. Ted followed in my vehicle so I could take a shot of our whole convoy with the Rock in the background.

Within minutes the pictures were done, but Mike was still fuming. He left it to me to hook the trailer back onto the rear of his vehicle. Just as I got it attached, he roared off. He almost ran me down with the trailer. I dived out of the way as it swished past.

I jumped in my Land Rover and took off after him. My blood was up. My six-cylinder motor could outrun Mike's easily and I was gaining on him. I was getting closer. Soon I would pass alongside and force him off the road.

'Calm down,' Ted pleaded.

'No way!' I screamed back.

Suddenly my motor died. Just stopped. *What?!* I glanced at the ignition and the key was missing. Ted had removed it. 'You'll thank me later,' he said.

As Mike's vehicle vanished from view, I was ready to take my anger out on Ted, but I quickly remembered that he wasn't the one with whom I was upset. I regained my composure and Ted handed me back the key.

This is just one example of the many moments of frustration and anger that afflicted all of us on this long endurance journey. There were times when it might have been possible to cut the atmosphere with a knife. In most cases the perceived problems were disproportionate to the reality: Ted was lazy, or Keith was obstinate, or Mike was unreasonable in wanting to film every bloody thing, or I was just as stubborn with the still pictures. Of course, the seemingly unending series of mechanical breakdowns got to all of us.

Pat gave the impression of being miserable. She and Mike were having arguments whenever they thought we weren't in earshot. Afterwards she'd sink into a state of moody depression. If I wanted to take a photograph with her in it, she never looked happy. Mike was well aware of this, of course, and throughout the expedition he had a strained expression. He looked positively haggard at times.

When a small group of people spend so much time together, friendships are tested to the limit. Small, unimportant details are blown out of proportion. Considering the dynamics of our group, we managed quite well. Keith, Ted and I were only 21 years old. We all had a lot of maturing ahead of us.

•

The Finke is said to be the oldest river in the world. When we were there, it was flooded with creamy red water that flowed lazily under the railway bridge. Our camp was right next to this wide expanse.

When the sun set, the huge mud puddle turned to gold. Around the edges of the riverbank, the red soil was shrinking, creating a crazed pattern of cracks, a mosaic floor in the desert. Galahs screeched as they scrambled for suitable roosts for the night. As we watched the day fade out, our thoughts turned to the job ahead.

The town of Finke was around a kilometre away. Population: about a hundred, half of them white, half Aboriginal. This would be our last town until Birdsville, about 560 kilometres to the east. It was from near Finke, from Blood Creek Station, that Ted Colson had set out to make his first crossing of the Simpson.

We loaded up with additional food supplies, filled up with fuel and picked up the second-hand differential for my car that we'd ordered to be despatched to us here. Physically, we were ready, but mentally we each had our own demons to deal with.

We quickly covered the first few kilometres to Andado Station, where the owner, Mac Clarke, made us welcome. He advised us to give up our idea, or at least to travel south about 150 kilometres and try there. The sand ridges are lower near the border with South Australia.

We thanked him, but pressed on with our original plan. We filled our water tanks from his bore, and on the 74th day of the expedition, the 15th of July, we attacked the first sand ridge of the Simpson Desert. It was 30 metres high.

The top part of these ridges is dry and loose. It's known as 'live sand' because it is constantly being blown around by the relentless winds of the desert. Around the base of each ridge and in the inter-dune corridors are clumps of spinifex. These hard tufts are about a metre high; they have sharp, spiky, needle-like shafts. As wind whips around the tufts it creates hillocks, like thousands of anthills. Driving over this is extremely rough on the vehicle.

Inside the cabin, we hit our heads on the roof and whacked the side doors as if we were on a bucking bronco. To our amazement, both vehicles made it over the first ridge without much trouble, and mine had the heavy trailer in tow.

One down. One thousand, one hundred and four to go. Ahead was a sea of sand. We gave a hearty cheer and marked it off in the journal.

Our technique had been worked out well in advance. Ted on the bike would scout the easiest path. The rest of us would follow in the vehicles, with Mike's in front because it was the lightest. On top of each ridge I'd take compass bearings off our wheel marks to the west and we'd plot this on the map.

Soon the enormity of the task we had set ourselves sunk in. Every single ridge was a challenge. We would get bogged; we would winch our way out. We towed each other, joining the vehicles with a solid metal towbar: lashed together, we doubled the pulling power. An eight-wheel drive. Often it wasn't enough, and we'd have to disconnect everything and tackle a monstrous dune without the trailer. On reaching the live sand on the crest, we would turn my vehicle around, run a long winch rope down to the trailer and haul it up separately: an arduous procedure.

Metre by metre, dune by dune, hour by hour, we nibbled away at the desert. At the end of our first day we'd travelled a little over 6 kilometres. My mood was mixed. The vehicles were protesting. Creaks and groans and the sound of metal rasping against metal had accompanied us all day, along with the roar of tortured engines working hard in their lowest gear. I felt good that our techniques were moving us forward, but daunted by how much ground lay ahead.

On day two, another differential in my Land Rover shattered. When Ted pulled it apart, he found that the axle had broken too. We had a spare axle and, from the remains of the smashed diff, plus some surviving parts of the other broken diff, Ted managed to assemble a workable replacement. However, he warned me it would probably not last long.

The third day brought more of the same. The huge baggy folds of our tyres flexed and rolled over the spinifex clumps, making zipping sounds in the loose sand. But the ridge count began to build and, with it, our confidence.

Twenty kilometres in and having just crossed ridge number 54, we came across a track. It was a bulldozer cut running north–south between the sand ridges. We suspected that it had been cut in by one of the seismic teams working the northern part of the desert in search of subterranean oil deposits.

We made a decision to create a camp here. We'd unload my vehicle to basics, and Ted and I would drive north along the inter-dune corridor. From our position on the map I figured this should come out near a water bore marked as North Bore on the northern fringes of the desert: a distance of roughly 50 kilometres. We knew that a seismic crew had a camp there. From here, Ted and I could backtrack to Andado Station to seek help.

Ted threw in his toolkit and, apprehensively, we set off. The track was made up of very loose sand, and soon the repair to the differential gave up and was ground into bits. We carried on, using just the front wheels.

Our exit from the desert was a life-saving good move. At North Bore we were amazed to find that the seismic crew camp was well equipped with a workshop and transportable housing that had been dragged in by bulldozer. Ted, using the camp welder, made repairs to the cracked chassis. The chassis is the backbone of a truck. Without this skeletal frame the vehicle has no strength. I talked Artie Herne, a light-plane pilot based with the oil-search crew, into flying me over the desert at dawn to see what lay in front of us.

With the repairs completed, we drove along a bush track to Andado where we borrowed a differential from Mac. He kindly removed it from his brand-new Land Rover to help us out. I never fail to find such generosity overwhelming.

•

We'd been gone three days by the time we returned to Mike, Pat and Keith, using the same route via North Bore. I relayed what I'd seen from the plane at dawn. As the sun had begun peeping over the horizon, the long red fingers of light skimmed the crests of the sand ridges. Even though we'd crossed 54 of them and had studied our maps endlessly, I found the scene utterly awesome. Kilometres and kilometres of sand ridges, like a 500-kilometre-wide sheet of corrugated iron. A hopelessly impossible task, it seemed, to drive across it.

What I didn't relay is how I felt personally. The prospect of confronting this vast desert sent a shudder down my spine. Yet I also felt inexplicably drawn to it, as if wooed by a deadly damsel I could not refuse.

None of us expressed our true feelings. We stoically maintained an air of nonchalant optimism. Or was it denial?

We set off south along the dozer cut for a few kilometres before turning once more into the sand canyons to the east. The dunes were just as difficult as they had ever been. Birdsville was 400 kilometres to the east. The desert was just as formidable, just as unforgiving, just as terrifying and, above all, merciless. Would we succeed or fail?

The task became one of monotonous regularity. Our practised tactics were now fine-tuned. We knew we could pull this challenge off if breakdowns would leave us alone. And they did for a while.

Keith had been pleading with us for days to stop, so he could bottle, catalogue and record details of all his insect and animal specimens: he was gathering quite a collection. We agreed to a break.

His interest in natural history had been kindled on our Darling River expedition and he had spent a large part of the intervening three years honing his skills as an amateur naturalist. He had made good contacts with the Australian Museum in Sydney and wanted to make a collection from the Simpson Desert, as the last time such scientific specimens had been gathered was in 1939.

Pat took the opportunity to bake one of her magnificent loaves of bread in the camp oven. She made these treats a regular part of the expedition and we all looked forward to them. All the bread would go in one sitting. We may have been in the most isolated place in Australia, surrounded by the most fearsome desert in the world, but we still had, thanks to Pat, fresh bread.

On that particular break, Ted resumed his role as mechanic and carried out routine maintenance, including an oil change. Mike cleaned his camera gear and filmed anything that moved, including the capture of a few lizards, which Keith willingly carried out.

I decided to take a walk on my own. The heavy drift sand, fine and red, cascaded off my feet as I waded through it on the crest of a huge ridge, and ran like water down the steep eastern side of the dunes. I covered many kilometres in the two hours after I left our camp. In all directions I was surrounded by an ocean of red. The powdery sand had been blown into millions of ripples, each a miniature of the desert ridge of which they were part.

This seemed to be the most desolate of landscapes on the planet, other than the icy wastes of the Antarctic. I watched a small wave of dislodged sand slide away like a dusty avalanche, devouring the delicately formed ripples. Sitting on the crest of that massive dune, I watched the shifting sand reach the bottom.

This was true isolation. I couldn't see any sign of our camp. No sign of life. To stand where no one has ever stood before is humbling and hard to fathom. I could have been the lone survivor of some catastrophic event that had wiped humanity from the Earth. A sobering concept, and one that had a life-changing effect on me.

I knew we were in a difficult position, but I also knew we should be able to survive, because we'd taken every possible precaution. We had a transceiver, we had two vehicles and we had determination. But we had no guarantees. We could actually perish in this sea of sand.

As someone with no religious beliefs, this was as close to a spiritual moment for me as it could get. I felt an emotional attachment to the infernal desert. I'd entered the Simpson as an immature 21-year-old. On this day I experienced a sense of change: I became an adult. My development still had a fair way to go but I knew that even if I died in the desert, I'd arrived. Life was good and I did not fear death.

My moment of contemplation was broken by the chirping of a small flock of budgerigars. These lively green parrots, native to Australia, can only fly short distances from water: so somewhere in this wilderness, I thought, there must be some surface water. Where, I would never know.

The time had come for me to return to the camp and rejoin the team. Time to pull together. To get on with the long hard grind.

•

As we worked our way eastwards, the ridges became smaller but closer together. The red was not so intense. Slowly we were conquering the desert. Each night I plotted our progress on the map and filled my diary with entries that were as alike as the days they dealt with.

I used a bubble sextant to take altitude readings at solar noon; after a page and a half of calculations, I would pinpoint our position.

Six hundred ridges . . . 700 ridges . . . 800 ridges. Each day a new score. Each day, a growing confidence. We ripped a few tyres off the rims because we had their pressures too low, but we carried spares, so all we lost was time.

Now my calculations put us somewhere near the Queensland border. We could almost taste success. We mounted one big ridge and, off to the south, we spotted a lake: a flat open claypan covered with a crust of salt. We were on course. This tiny lake was on the map! A proper landmark. We knew where we were and I felt elated that my navigation had proved correct.

From here the ridges got bigger again, and we returned to lashing the vehicles together. Then, with an ear-splitting crack, my rear diff shattered. The fifth one to collapse! Ted rebuilt a workable diff from the remains of several others.

Cautiously we eased onward, winching up every slightly difficult hill. We'd almost accomplished our task; this was no time to get careless.

On the 4th of August we reached a track and camped for the night. It rained. How ironic, after so much dust and sand! Next day we reached Birdsville, which was awash: it resembled a quagmire. We'd crossed 1105 ridges since leaving Andado 22 days earlier, and clocked up 700 kilometres in low-range gear.

From Birdsville, after waiting for the rains to ease, we continued east.

On the 20th of August we arrived at Cape Byron. The crossing was complete. Both vehicles were in a bad way, but we were elated. As a group the experience had tested our loyalties and strength. Although we had each experienced our moments of discontent, all the differences and wounds subsided into an appropriate place. Those moments became insignificant in the full perspective of what we had achieved. Our successes smothered the problems and we all felt overwhelmed by emotion. Happiness replaced hardship and pride dared to emerge. All of our fears of failure or even survival were gone and not just for the expedition members. Our families too rejoiced at the news.

The final task was to pour the flask of Indian Ocean water into the Pacific. Mission accomplished.

8

The Movie Business
(How Hard Can It Be?)

'Not everybody in the film business is a bastard, but all the bastards are in the film business,' Tony advised us with a quirky smile.

Tony and his brothers owned a chain of independent cinemas in Adelaide. My brother and I were in the street outside one of them, leaning against Mike's Land Rover. Afternoon traffic streamed past and, amid the exhaust fumes and noise, we were negotiating with Tony to screen our film, *Wheels Across a Wilderness*, in Adelaide. This was the 100-minute production of our West–East Crossing Expedition. It had already established itself as a box office success in New South Wales and Victoria.

We were roadshowing our film around the country. In each town or city we'd hire a cinema or town hall, place advertising in the local papers, organise as much publicity as possible with radio and TV stations, and run the film ourselves on our own projector.

We hadn't started our screening tour in Adelaide. Five months earlier, on the 10th of May 1967, we had staged the world premiere in our home town, Newcastle, with the help of the local Apex Club. They promoted it and sold tickets, with all monies going to charity.

That was an emotional night. The theatre was sold out. More than a thousand seats. A brass band played in the street outside and we were dressed in dinner suits. All kinds of dignitaries arrived, including the Lord Mayor and Lady Mayoress.

After the screening, we went to the Newcastle City Hall, where a chicken supper was served with champagne. The Apex Club organised it all. After most of the guests were seated, we expedition members made a grand entrance. The hall was packed. It was overwhelming. About 900 people applauded while the band played.

Our parents were there, of course. After the initial applause died down, Mum turned to me with a tear of joy running down her cheek and said, 'To think all of this is for my two boys.'

The film was a huge success. Everyone told us so that night as we were ushered around and introduced to one and all.

Subsequently, after a fortnight of screenings in Newcastle, we had recovered and repaid all of Mr Sample's $15,000.

In New South Wales a film could only be shown in a licensed cinema and most were controlled by Hoyts or

Greater Union. None of them wanted our 'amateur' effort. If we could find an independent cinema owner willing to put it on, as we had in Newcastle, we could screen the show; but they were thin on the ground. So we went to Melbourne, where the situation wasn't so restrictive.

We began our roadshow in the Hawthorn Town Hall. We could only screen on Mondays to Thursdays, as dances were booked on Friday and Saturday nights.

By now we'd developed some newspaper ads and spent about $5000 inserting them in local papers. The results were sensational. We had to turn away a couple of hundred people every night. When the show ended, we were always rewarded with huge applause. After two weeks of packed houses, we extended the season for a fortnight. We couldn't extend further as other events were booked in.

Our last night was no different. People were spilling all over the streets wanting to get in, so we instructed the cashier to sell standing room. She did. The town hall staff were horrified, maintaining that we were exceeding the safe capacity of the hall, but it was too late. They were in.

Eventually, after a month in Melbourne, we moved on. In that time we'd taken $28,000! An incredible amount of money.

•

At Geelong we hired the Plaza Theatre. This was owned by the local amateur theatrical society and used for live shows. We booked four nights, concluding with Saturday.

We had tickets printed and placed them with the local booking agent, and waited for the sales.

They didn't happen. Only about fifteen were sold.

On the Wednesday afternoon, when we picked up the unsold tickets, we spoke to the theatre managers, then cancelled the ushers and the ticket seller. I would sell the tickets and Mike would run the projector.

The caretaker pressed her sons and husband into service. 'I told you Geelong was different,' she said sadly. 'Nothing works too well here.' She offered the help of her family free of charge, so we would limit our losses.

The show was due to start at 8 p.m. I took up my position in the ticket office, a small cubicle with windows on three sides.

My mental maths had always been poor, so I made up a chart. The number of adults was down the left side; the number of children was across the top. If a patron asked for two adults and three children, I could check the second row down, under the column for three children, so I knew the right amount to charge.

I was very nervous, but figured it should be all right. After all, we weren't expecting much of a crowd.

It was a freezing night; fog swirled outside in the streets. We had about fifteen minutes till showtime. A handful of patrons filed in, mostly to pre-booked seats. Ten minutes to go. A small crowd began to assemble in the front foyer. I was handling the cashiering well enough.

Then it happened. As if a huge floodgate had opened, hundreds of people descended on the Plaza. Inside the ticket box, I panicked.

Most people were tolerant and understanding as I fumbled away, desperately trying to work out the change. They shouted their orders to me: 'Three adults and four children' or 'One adult, one pensioner and two children.' I was out of my depth.

Soon we had just five minutes to start time and people were getting agitated—they didn't want to miss out. I had no communication from the ticket box to the projection booth, which was on top of the building. Mike was intending to start the projector at eight, as advertised, but the crowd had grown enormously.

Fortunately Mike, from his elevated position, heard the crowd. He descended a ladder on the outside of the building to ground level, then forced his way through the crushing crowd and got to me. 'They're all the way down the street,' he yelled.

'Delay the start!' I called back.

He nodded and pushed off, to climb the ladder and return to his post.

The cash drawer was a thin wooden thing with several compartments. It simply couldn't hold much money. I was trying to stuff in note after note, but it was no use. The drawer was overflowing terribly. I started screwing up the notes as they were handed to me and just throwing them to the ground. The floor was wooden and the cracks in it were wide. If I hadn't screwed the notes into balls, they could easily have slipped through and gone under the old building.

I kept at it; I could see that at last I was getting there. The anxious crowd was now being pacified by one of the managers, who was busy telling them that we would delay the start until everyone was seated.

The nightmare continued for about half an hour beyond our advertised starting time. By then my cubicle's floor was littered with banknotes, which were creeping up around where I stood. Past my shoes. Past my ankles. The tide of money kept climbing.

Now people were gazing through the glass at the overwhelmed and distraught cashier standing in piles of money: like a sick version of Uncle Scrooge in the *Donald Duck* comics. 'Look at all the money!' someone called out. So then even more people began to peer through the glass at the hapless idiot. The idiot with more cash than he'd seen in his life.

Finally the last one was in and the lights were dimmed. An enormous cheer roared from within the auditorium. Some customers had been seated for up to 50 minutes. It was a full house.

I gathered up the takings and shoved them into several calico money bags. Then I climbed the long steel ladder to the projection box and breathed a sigh of relief.

'Tomorrow night we pay for a proper cashier,' I gasped over the noise of the projector. Mike roared with laughter.

As the night went on, an extremely heavy fog descended on Geelong. It seeped in through the high ventilators and began slowly to fill the theatre from the top down. It became so thick that the projector beam was being diffused. Our helpers rushed to the upstairs seats and waved large sheets of cardboard to disperse the fog. The patrons laughed and ducked around one another so as to see the screen. What a fiasco! A real-life slapstick comedy.

Mike and I returned to our motel room after midnight. We should have been tired, but we were too restless. We made cups of tea and coffee, then started the task of counting the money. On the floor we flattened the balled notes out and made neat piles of each denomination, like we were still children playing with toys.

Eventually we counted the takings—$1200. Holy cow! That was serious money for one night.

Mike then horrified me by suggesting that we not bank it all. If we kept back about a third, he urged, and banked the remainder, no one would know.

While we'd repaid our loan to Mr Sample, under our agreement he was due for his share of profits over the next five years. Mike's suggestion wasn't something I was comfortable with. We debated the issue for some time, with Mike accusing me of being too honest. For me, honesty has never come in degrees.

When I finally laid my head on my pillow, I found sleep difficult. I was troubled by Mike's willingness to cheat, and the adrenaline released by our argument was still circulating through my veins. We would never have made the trip at all without George Sample's help; his belief in us and his trust in us had given us the chance of a lifetime. We made a deal and as long as I was breathing we would stick to it.

This was the first time I'd doubted my brother's honesty; but I put his attitude down to the heady excitement of the moment. An unfortunate lapse of judgement.

•

The rest of our season in Geelong was a sell-out every night. We left elated and we never again spoke of our differences that night.

In Victoria we'd been approached by various cinema owners willing to screen our film. We offered them all the same deal: after advertising expenses and staffing costs, we would split the takings 50/50.

Most independent owners jumped at this. Because we were in Victoria, if they didn't like our deal, we could hire any public hall and run our own show in their town. They'd get nothing and probably have an empty theatre on the days we screened. Cinemas weren't doing such good business at this time, as television was beginning to make big inroads.

In Melbourne we went to some well-known printers who specialised in roll tickets for theatres. These rolls had 'Admit One' printed on them with a number, and the numbers were sequential.

'How do you want them?' asked the printer. 'Ten per cent or 20 or what?'

'How do you mean?' we asked.

'Ten per cent has every tenth number repeated. Twenty per cent, every fifth.'

Suddenly the penny dropped.

'Can you print straight ones?' I asked. 'You know— with each one sequential. No repeats?'

'Yes, but it's been a long time since we did that,' he said with a mischievous grin. 'Cash business, you see, boys. Got to make it where you can.'

We were flabbergasted. From then on, Mike and I would insist that we use our own tickets. By now we were beginning to learn the tricks of cinema operators.

Most cinemas had auditors come around to check on takings. They represented the interests of the filmmakers, and they would stand in the foyer and watch the cashier all night. At the end of the night, the cashier would remove the starting float of change and the auditor would count the money. By subtracting the start number off the roll of tickets from the last number sold, he thought he knew how many had entered the theatre, but of course the duplicated numbers underestimated the size of the house. The cinema owner knew how much of the takings had to be siphoned off to make the scam work. The money always balanced, even though the auditor knew that somehow he was being diddled.

There are many other ways to fiddle the sales right under the nose of the most diligent auditor. For example, tickets were usually torn in half—but every now and then, the doorman would retain a ticket. When he had a few, he'd wander over to the ticket box, say a cheerful hello to the cashier and slip the untorn tickets back for her to resell. At the end of the night they divided the extra money between them.

We heard many such variations from the cinema operators. They would always try to get a little extra because the film distributors always tried to screw them: for instance, if a really good movie was released, the distributors would increase the percentage they received.

The cinema owners were struggling to survive in the economy of the day, but I don't believe they ever tried to diddle Mike and me. They respected us and our honest approach. Yes, not everybody in the film business is a bastard.

We moved on around the country screening our film, but still we wanted to show it in Sydney. We ended up striking a deal with Hoyts, a wholly owned subsidiary of 20th Century Fox. They had the cinemas; we had the film. Take out the costs and split the takings 50/50. Simple, right? This time however we were in the hands of really professional bastards.

Our film opened at the Palace Theatre, Pitt Street, Sydney. Hoyts hired a 16mm projector with a much more powerful light than ours and ran three sessions a day. The Christmas school holidays were on and it rained almost every day for six weeks. The show was huge: almost every session was packed. We were delighted, and for once we didn't have to run it ourselves.

Then, when the cheque arrived, we were under-whelmed. This couldn't be right! We demanded to see the details.

Under our contract, Hoyts had the right to recoup the costs of advertising, staff, et cetera—all running costs, in fact. We were staggered to find the front-of-house banner listed at $3000. Mike, as a sign-writer, pointed out that he could do the job for about $200. Hoyts showed us proper invoices. We asked why the cleaning bill was so high. They showed us proper invoices. We asked why the posters in the front of the theatres were so expensive. They showed us proper invoices from a ticket-writing company.

We left with copies of the invoices and had a search done on the suppliers. All were subsidiaries of Hoyts! The same applied to many other details of the over-inflated costs. So we received our 50 per cent of what was left. We had been done like a dinner. Yes, all the bastards *are* in the film business.

Of course, all in all we had a very successful film. We certainly didn't get our fair share of the profits, but we did well enough.

It might be difficult to understand, but we got tired of screening it all the time. Although the money was pouring in, we were bored. Bored with racking in money? Stupid, eh?

We had the 16mm film enlarged to a full 35mm and made nine copies. They went into general distribution with 20th Century Fox and were shown all over the country, including at drive-ins. More than a million people saw the film.

Mike was itching to get out of the screening business, and move on to making more films and having more adventures.

9

Gullible Americans

While we were running *Wheels Across a Wilderness* in Melbourne, we spent a lot of time planning our next venture. We had decided to take a 5-metre boat from Darwin to Sydney. Distance: 5000 nautical miles. Estimated time: six months. Objective: to retrace the voyage of the famous English navigator, Lieutenant Matthew Flinders, who made the trip in 1802 with his ship, *Investigator*.

We would name our vessel *Little Investigator* and, if successful, would complete the longest open boat voyage ever recorded.

This time we didn't need a loan to equip ourselves with the best of everything. Although *Wheels* had made us a small fortune, we hadn't been frugal: much of it was used up meeting the cost of our new expedition. We were

Our family on holidays in England 1948. Mum (Frankie) and Dad (Ivan) in the back row. Me on the left with Michael in the front row.

I started work as a cadet press photographer at the age of 17, working for the *Newcastle Sun*. I had landed my dream job but soon realised I had a lot to learn.

Poster for the Orient Ship *Otranto* that transported us to Australia in 1950. It is depicted passing through the Suez Canal.

Crossing the flooded Condamine River in Queensland on our first outback trip in 1961. Keith Davey and I sat on the front trying to keep the strong current from washing the lightweight vehicle away while Mike drove.

Travelling down the Darling River in 1963 proved to be a test of endurance and inventiveness. When the water ran out we had to push the boat through sloppy mud. Keith took the picture of me (left) and Mike almost at the point of exhaustion.

Manoeuvring the boat over the weir at Bourke during our Darling River Expedition. (Note the cine camera set up to record whatever was about to happen next.)

I was in my element on the Darling River in 1963. I took thousands of pictures, mostly black and white, but used the large plate camera for colour shots. The colour film was so expensive I was limited to 20 images for the entire expedition.

I sent despatches back from some remote places during our early expeditions. Here, I'm in the Gulf of Carpentaria, in 1968.

I was the navigator in our West–East Crossing Expedition in 1966. I used a prism compass for sighting across the seemingly endless sand ridges of the Simpson Desert to take bearings from our wheel marks in the sand. Mike, on the left, consults with me as I check and re-check our position.

Even though we were in the bush I managed to use a small camping tent as a darkroom to develop and print pictures to accompany the stories I had written. The enlarger was converted to run off a 12 volt car battery (1968-9).

Crossing 1,105 ridges of red sand in the Simpson Desert was the biggest challenge we had faced up to 1966. No one had completed this before and we had an enormous trailer of fuel, water and supplies to drag with us.

Ted Hayes, our mechanic, worked tirelessly to keep the old landy running. In total we smashed 5 differentials on our vehicle during our across-Australia expedition in 1966.

Drought-breaking rain fell on Ayers Rock/ Uluru and we happened to be there to capture it on both movie and still film. This is one of my most memorable shots as waterfalls cascade off the huge monolith (28th June 1966).

My first despatch from the West–East Crossing Expedition made the front page of the *Newcastle Sun*. It was syndicated to affiliated newspapers in Sydney and Melbourne.

Exhausted and having just survived a near-drowning, I was in no mood for Mike to film me. (Image lifted from a 16mm movie frame of film.)

During our voyage from Darwin to Sydney in 1968–9, the *Little Investigator*, was our 18-foot home for six and half months. Our daily endurance on the little boat became a relentless battle with the sea. Novices at first, we soon found our sea legs and slowly underwent a metamorphosis from land-lubbers to seafarers.

When we returned to Newcastle Mike and I spent months editing 'Open Boat To Adventure'. I used our editing machine to add sound effects to every single second of the two and quarter-hour film. It was a marathon task.

Crossing the Jardine River near the tip of Cape York Peninsular in1971.

When Laraine and I married in December, 1969, it was the start of a passionate love affair and a wonderful marriage, one that has never ended. Without her by my side I would not have made it through all the trials life has dealt us.

Camped on Fraser Island, Queensland, during the filming of *Ask the Leyland Brothers*. Carmen was introduced to camping early in life.

Laraine examines our Land Rover after it rolled on a rough bush track in the Kimberley. We were filming an episode of our *Off the Beaten Track* TV series. There was no serious damage, except to our egos.

so convinced that our ocean expedition would be just as successful that we overspent irresponsibly.

When we were in the final stages of organisation, I took a phone call out of the blue from Bill Cartwright, an American scout for the National Geographic Society (NGS). He'd been visiting Australia in order to investigate whether there was sufficient material here to make a one-hour television special. His recommendation had been not to bother but, while waiting at the airport for his flight back to the United States, he'd spotted an advertisement for *Wheels*. He cancelled his flight, took a taxi back to the city and watched our film in a Pitt Street cinema. He wanted to meet with us.

Bill was so impressed with our film that he would now recommend that the NGS buy the rights to it, cut it down to a one-hour show and use it. We were ecstatic. We loaded him up with a spare print and sent him back to the States.

Within a few weeks Dennis Kane, the executive producer for NGS television, phoned us. All was going well. There would be lots of editing to do to create good soundtracks. He would be getting in touch soon. We had cracked the big time. Their shows pulled an audience of 40 million. They had a budget of about $400,000 for each show! Serious money.

Agonising weeks went by. No word. Eventually, after two months, NGS made contact. They would not buy our film; instead, they wanted us to undertake another expedition across the country and they'd bring their own film crew to shoot it.

We were reluctant, because we needed to leave Darwin on our boat trip in a few months. We couldn't delay: we had to time our departure to fit in with the dry season. They offered us US$10,000 for six weeks. The money was excellent; but, on top of that, we figured this would place us in a good position to establish our names in the States and hopefully that would lead to more opportunities. So we agreed.

•

'The Leylands meet a bloke skiing behind a pickup truck as it drives through bulldust a foot thick.'

I was reading these lines from a manuscript of about 140 pages, and I couldn't keep a straight face. I burst out laughing as I tore the page out and threw it onto the rapidly expanding heap on the floor of the Sydney hotel room. Mike, Pat and Ted joined in the hilarity, all of us cackling somewhat insultingly at the naivety of the script we were reading. This was intended to be our pre-trip briefing!

The American team that had flown 'Down Under' to film their special included a director, a cameraman, his assistant and another advisor. They all looked horrified at our amused disbelief, but their script showed just how ill-informed they were about Australia: we were to ski along bulldust tracks, wrestle crocodiles and carry out a litany of other equally ridiculous activities that could only have come from the mind of a Hollywood writer who'd never stepped outside an air-conditioned five-star hotel.

The director, Bob, took our undignified contempt in good humour. 'Don't worry about it,' he reassured us. 'We just needed something to show the sponsors. They've signed up for some big bucks, so we had to demonstrate that we could make a worthwhile programme on Australia.'

It was on that day that I realised just how ignorant Americans were about the rest of the world. They had so little experience outside their own culture that they appeared to imagine Australia as some wild, untamed frontier.

We kept tearing out more pages until, in the early hours of the morning, the original script consisted of only a handful of ideas. Their team finally agreed to take our advice: we'd set off on the 12,000-kilometre trip and see what turned up.

•

The six-week odyssey turned into ten while the crew shot an unbelievable amount of film. By the time we reached Broken Hill, Bob had sent one of the team home. He simply couldn't handle the bush flies, and the travelling was too rough for him.

'Things get much rougher when we reach the Northern Territory,' we warned.

The cameraman, a dyed-in-the-wool Mexican, retorted with, 'You don't know what rough is. You should see *my* country. Then you'll see rough.'

This ultimately became a bit of a joke between us. He had a great sense of humour and was an excellent cameraman.

As we worked our way west, we'd often stop for tea beside the track. When the billy boiled, we'd throw in a handful of leaves, let it draw for a moment or two, then begin to pour. We each had a mug and they'd all be lined up in a row in the red soil.

One time, when we were in South Australia, I started pouring. I worked my way along the row of eight mugs and ended with Judy, the assistant.

'I've noticed that about you Aussies,' she exploded, 'You always serve the ladies last. Well, I'm a lady and I want to be treated like a fucking lady!'

I was shocked. Never before had I heard that kind of language from a woman: I certainly didn't expect it from a 'lady'. I couldn't help myself—I started laughing. I actually turned it on a bit thick and rolled around on the ground, roaring with forced laughter. Mike, Pat and Ted all carried on too.

'What?' Judy screamed. We kept laughing. 'What?' she demanded again. 'What's so funny?'

We couldn't control ourselves. The more agitated she became, the funnier it seemed. She had no idea of the incongruity of the statement she'd just made. Judy had a foul mouth on her and this was the first of many such outbursts; she used this kind of language in everyday conversation, as if it were perfectly normal. In 1968, swearing was unacceptable in mixed company. Standards have certainly changed, or should I say degenerated, since then.

Judy was also a trained nurse; she carried with her an enormous first-aid kit and she was fanatical about hygiene. Every mealtime she'd collect the utensils, plates and mugs that she had used and immerse them in boiling water over the fire for ten minutes. She would then air-dry them by waving them around, before inserting them into large plastic bags with zip seals. We'd never seen zip seals before; we'd never seen anyone do this before either!

Judy explained that she wasn't prepared to take the risk of cross-contamination by washing up in the same water as us. She also said our plastic mugs would harbour germs, which was why she'd chosen enamel. She obviously felt that she was in an unbelievably contaminated part of the world, where bacterial infections roamed in epidemic proportions. I couldn't help but feel sorry for her. She was outside America and therefore outside her comfort zone.

•

In South Australia we dropped in on a dingo trapper, arriving at his remote camp right at dusk. To preserve his anonymity, I'll call him Jack.

Jack was lean, tall and had a face tanned like leather. He had a scruffy beard and walked slowly and deliberately. He sashayed over and eyed off the strangers to his isolated part of the world.

'Can I help you?' he asked cautiously.

'Possibly,' I responded, and then asked him about the track and whether or not the rain would affect our journey west.

Jack began to respond, but was obviously very wary.

The conversation went on for some time. I hadn't yet broached the subject of us filming him at work, when Bob, the American director cut in. 'Let's not muck around!' he said. 'We're from the National Geographic and we want to film you trapping these wild dingoes.'

Jack stood and stared blankly at him.

'Come on!' Bob insisted, as he pulled his wallet from his jacket. He lifted out a handful of notes and waved them about. 'How much? Fifty? A hundred?'

Jack stared back at him. No sign of a response.

'Here. Five hundred!' Bob yelled. 'Should be fine—okay?'

Jack said nothing; he just turned his back and wandered off into the darkness.

'I told you to leave it to me,' I said to Bob. I explained that Jack lived out here on his own and didn't trust us yet. 'You're throwing money around like confetti.'

The American simply did not get it. So far as he was concerned, Jack obviously had nothing and he should have jumped at more money than he'd see in a long time.

'You don't know that,' I said. 'You know nothing about him.'

Bob asked what I suggested now. I said he'd probably blown it with Jack, and we should leave the trapper alone and move on in the morning. Bob looked so crestfallen that I agreed to try and find Jack, and see what I could do.

I searched for some time, but Jack was not to be seen. Then, just as we were getting ready to retire to our sleeping bags, he emerged from the dark and joined us round the campfire.

I spoke to him quietly, explaining that Dennis and his friends were Americans and couldn't really help themselves. They assumed it was always a matter of money. Luckily Jack had seen 'Down the Darling' and liked it, so he agreed to let us film him with his traps in the morning.

At sun-up we headed off, following Jack as he checked the traps from the night before and set new ones. He was marvellous and went out of his way to co-operate with the filming. He even began to open up and talk. We asked him about himself and why he lived out in the bush on his own.

It turned out that Jack was a multimillionaire. He'd been a structural engineer specialising in bridge building and was responsible for some of the biggest industrial constructions in Victoria. His problem was alcohol: he'd become a heavy drinker, and eventually a hopeless alcoholic. He told us how his addiction had ruined his marriage and broken up his family. The only way he could cope with life was to get away from the grog. Out in the bush he had none.

He lived in an iron-clad shack and received about a dollar a scalp for the foxes and dingoes he trapped. He didn't need the money; he needed the isolation. He told us that, if he returned to the city, he would get on the grog again so, for now at least, he'd just stay where he was. He enjoyed the quiet and solitude. We promised to move on at first light and wished him luck with his self-imposed exile.

In the morning I reminded Bob that he was paying us to co-ordinate this exercise, so he should let us do the talking from now on. He readily agreed.

●

The outback tracks in South Australia aren't so good in the rain. So, when it started to pour, we found ourselves driving through slush and mud, occasionally getting bogged. In camp I rigged up the Royal Flying Doctor Service radio we had on us and listened to the rainfall reports to see how widely the wet conditions extended.

Bob approached me to send a telegram to the NGS headquarters in the United States using the radio. When I saw the text of his message, I asked him whether he was sure he wanted to send it over the radio.

'Why not?' he asked.

I explained that everyone could hear one another's messages. There was no privacy. He told me to send it nonetheless.

I dictated the telegram:

WIRE TEN THOUSAND DOLLARS U.S. TO ALICE SPRINGS POST OFFICE IMMEDIATELY. B. RILEY.

The operator asked me to repeat the amount to make sure it was correct.

'Now everyone in the Northern Territory knows how much money you'll have on you,' I informed him, but he didn't see it as an issue. I pointed out that all our vehicles had National Geographic signage on the doors. With that much cash, we could be inviting trouble.

He didn't believe me but, when we turned up in Alice Springs about a week later, the bloke behind the counter asked Bob to follow him into a private room.

A few minutes later, a policeman arrived.

The clerk had called him to say that the Yanks had come to collect the money. The copper pointed out that almost everyone was aware that some Americans would be roaming about with huge amounts of cash. He advised extreme caution.

We broke the money down into several bundles and distributed them among the crew. If anyone was robbed, we'd only lose a portion. Fortunately all went well.

•

Heading north from Alice, we were all getting a little tired of camping, but there was simply nowhere to stay. We'd been keeping up our running joke with the camera-man. He maintained that nothing was rougher than Mexico, and we kept saying that things were rougher in the Northern Territory, which he'd laugh off.

One afternoon we drifted into a remote roadside pub and, to our amazement, saw that it had four transport-able fibreglass cabins as accommodation. 'I thought you reckoned we'd have to camp all the way to Darwin,' the Mexican declared.

We booked all the cabins and were grateful for a hot shower before moving over to the pub to seek out some tucker. The pub was a typical outback affair: corrugated iron walls, concrete floor, a small pool table, a dart board. A single bar and the owner behind it. I shall not name the pub.

A couple of Aboriginal blokes were buying flagons of wine. They looked pretty unsteady on their feet but, once served, they went outside to drink it.

We asked if the kitchen was open for business and, if so, what was on the menu.

'There's the cook,' said the barman, pointing to a middle-aged woman sitting alone and drinking beer. 'Ask her.'

We did. She eyed us up and down. Eight hungry city slickers waiting anxiously to hear what culinary delights she had to offer. She staggered to her feet, using the table to steady herself, and downed the rest of her schooner before she spoke with a mumbled drunken slur.

'It's bacon and eggs.' She swayed her considerable bulk about on unsteady legs. 'And you'll eat it or you'll bloody well wear it.' We watched her wobble across the concrete to the door of the eatery. She turned as she steadied herself against the doorframe. 'How many?'

'Eight,' we responded.

About 20 minutes later, we seated ourselves at the milk-bar-like laminated tables while she staggered from the kitchen, somehow managing to balance four plates of greasy bacon and eggs. She slowly returned with the other four. The eggs, floating in a pond of grease, were three to a plate with a generous heap of bacon. We ate in silence—in no doubt that, if it wasn't all consumed, we would indeed be bloody well wearing it.

Our hunger satisfied, we turned to the pool table and started playing about with the balls and cues.

Suddenly there was a loud crash from behind the bar. The only other customer got up from his stool, peered over the bar at the floor, and then promptly sat back down to finish his drink.

When a few of us wandered over to take a look, we saw the owner lying on the floor. Out cold. He didn't look so good.

'Is he okay?' Bob asked the customer.

'Yeah. No problem. He does that about this time every night.'

I was standing next to Bob. The bloke on the floor was very pale. He started going grey around the eyes and mouth. Judy was quickly summoned.

She took one look, checked his pulse, then rushed outside and returned with her enormous first-aid kit. Using her nursing skills, she checked his vital signs.

The cook came in and stood in disbelief as Judy knelt over what seemed to be a dead body. We all watched. Judy tried valiantly to revive him. She tried mouth-to-mouth resuscitation. She tried thumping his chest to restart his heart. Nothing.

The patron left the pub.

We eventually got the Alice Springs hospital on the phone and spoke to the duty doctor. He called out instructions, which Judy followed, but the pub owner was dead. Judy had done her best; he was probably dead before he hit the floor.

Without warning, the Aboriginal men came marching through the door. They had plenty of mates with them.

They strolled into the bar, stepped over the dead body, ripped open the massive refrigerator and started handing out the grog. Flagons. Boxes of beer. Cans. Bottles. Everything and anything.

'Free grog!' one of them yelled out, and soon a steady stream of beverages was being whisked outside, where the men were consuming it in the car park.

After the raiders had left, a couple of us bolted the door. We counted the money in the till and put it aside, then covered the corpse with a bed sheet provided by the cook, who was inconsolable.

I rang the police at their outpost further north. The copper advised that he'd be there as soon as possible, but there would be a bit of a delay. Could we continue to take charge of the situation and wait inside until he arrived? We agreed.

It was about two and a half hours later, around one in the morning, when he turned up. In the meantime the Aboriginal drinkers had run out of grog and were banging on the door, demanding we open up. The copper blew the horn of his truck and, shortly after, rapped on the door. We opened up.

He was a big man—at least 6-foot-4 and 14 stone. He asked where the body was and strolled over to the bar. He was followed by about five drunken Aboriginal men. When he realised this, he turned around; without hesitation, he decked the first man with such a quick blow that he hit the floor hard. When another man stepped up, the big copper decked him too. Then another, and another. After that, the rest of them stopped at the pub doorway.

'Give us a hand to put the rubbish out,' the copper instructed us, as he grabbed the feet of number four and dragged his inert form across the concrete, out the door and down the steps to the gravel car park. We complied, although it took two of us to manage one of the fallen men.

Then we introduced ourselves. For the next hour he took statements from all of us and we signed them. He thanked us for our efforts in keeping some kind of order, and then asked for help to carry the body out to his ute.

As we approached the vehicle, our noses wrinkled. There was a putrid stench.

'Sorry about the smell,' the copper explained. 'I had to pick up another body this afternoon. Been out in the bush for weeks. Full of maggots. I was unloading it when I got your call. I hosed the ute out, but it'll stink for weeks.'

We held our collective breath and loaded our bloke on top of the slimy ooze in the back of the copper's ute.

'Thanks for the help. Better get some sleep now,' were his parting words.

We wandered over to the fibreglass cabins. *Shit!* Could we sleep after all that? The night air was chilling. The stars glistened in the darkness and our tragic black comedy was almost over.

The Mexican turned to me with a mischievous look on his face. 'You were right, Mal,' he said, grinning impishly. 'Things really are a bit rough in the Territory. It's like the Wild West.'

'You should be here on a Saturday. Gets *really* rough then,' I kidded him.

We all had a laugh. What else could we do?

10

Three Men in a Boat

A full-blown gale is battering our small boat. The 5 metres of aluminium skin feels like a cork in a massive washing machine. It seems like it could be ripped apart by the angry sea at any time. I'm gripping the gunwales of the fragile little vessel with every fibre of my being. My life depends upon it.

The sky is inky black. I'm about 40 miles out to sea in the dead of night, in one of the worst gales to hit the Queensland coast in years. The *Little Investigator* is being battered by thousands of monstrous waves, some as high as two-storey buildings. I am alone and desperately trying to keep my balance while our stricken vessel is dragged through the water by a thick towrope attached to a 15-metre fishing trawler. I can't actually see this boat even though it's ploughing through the sea only 90 metres away. Each wave of raging terror rises from the black depths like a living monster. A multitude of unstoppable liquid mountains.

I've been enduring this ordeal for about four hours. Occasional flashes of lightning illuminate the scene like giant flashbulbs, showing me frozen images of the mountains of water. Otherwise, the darkness is absolute, except for the light of the small waterproof torch around my neck. I can see nothing other than the defunct motor sitting lifeless. It's a useless block of metal.

I'm weak and in excruciating pain from constantly working the manual bilge pump. First came the blisters. They were bad enough, but then they grew huge and felt like liquid-filled plastic bags on my palms and fingers. Eventually they burst; the skin on both my hands is reduced to bloody tatters, but I can't stop. The pain is excruciating.

I have to keep pumping even though my hands are bleeding. My body wants me to stop, but my mind is overriding the message: *Keep pumping. Keep the water down. Mustn't stop. Can't stop.* Mind-numbing willpower overrules all logic. *Stop and I die. Can't die. Everything we've achieved in the last few months would be for nothing. I must not fail.* The water is sloshing around my feet.

I can tell when the trawler is climbing a huge wave up ahead: the *Little Investigator* stops moving for about ten seconds, as though cut adrift from the towrope. The forward movement stops. Then suddenly it lurches forward and accelerates, while the trawler careens down the wave, and my boat is whisked along and up.

The tops of the giants are breaking and tumbling down upon me. Wild foamy crests engulf the vessel and the floorboards are awash once more. *Keep pumping! Must get the water down.* The howling 75-kilometre-per-hour wind is tearing at the boat, its deafening roar mingling with the sound from tons of tumultuous water.

The waves have been coming in sets of four. The first three are not too bad—about 7 metres each—but then the big bastards follow—12 metres at least.

The towrope goes slack. I know it'll be big.

Hang on with both hands. Wait for it.

Then I zoom forward as though on a speedboat, and within a few seconds hit the angry wild water on the crest. It jolts the towrope, twanging a shudder through the vessel. Engulfed by foam, I feel my body being grabbed by the water.

Then it stops. I emerge from the breaking crest and surf down the other side. Into the darkness. The most terrifying ride in the world.

On all sides, the ocean glows a luminescent green-blue wherever there is turbulence. This effect, known as phosphorescence, is caused by huge blooms of microscopic phytoplankton. Anyone who's been at sea at night under the right conditions has seen it. It's eerie, as if the ocean is a living thing and the luminous glow within it, a ghostly apparition without form.

Keep pumping!

I feel the rope go slack yet again. *Hang on.* As the trawler rushes down the other side of the massive wave, I'm being whisked towards the top at enormous speed. Before I can reach the crest, the bow of the *Little Investigator* is pulled through the water. Instantly I'm in a washing machine.

About half a ton of water dumps into the boat. I try to hang on, but the water's crushing power is too much. I lose my grip and, in a split second, I'm washed out the back. I catch a fleeting glimpse of the receding transom. My only light is the radiance from the phosphorescence that envelopes my body, and the dull glow of my torch tied around my neck.

My energy is all but gone. Fear grips my mind. Our boat, our home for the past six months, is disappearing into the storm. Mike and our mate Trevor are on the trawler with its captain. They will never know exactly how it happened.

Then, with a sharp jolt, the 3-metre-long safety rope tied around my chest snaps taut. It feels as though it will rip my body in half. I am being pulled through the water like a piece of meat. The trawler continues forward unrelentingly, dragging the *Little Investigator* and me in its wake. I will surely drown. My energy is at rock bottom. I can't haul myself towards my boat. *Too weak.* Perhaps a shark will rip me apart. I know I am doomed.

My brain is racing. I am spluttering and coughing. I try not to swallow water. The water pressure on my head is enormous; I'm gasping for air to fill my lungs.

The ocean is unforgiving. When things go wrong out at sea, there's no escape. The ocean is the master. It can easily consume huge ships, so my body is nothing.

I expect to die tonight, probably in the next few minutes. This grim prospect slows my brain down. I feel so weak that I relax; somehow it feels peaceful. The water rushing past becomes a whisper as I withdraw into a silent place. I am resigned to my fate. *Just let it happen. It's so easy. Just give in and let the ocean consume me.*

The sea is dark and silent. *Am I drowning yet?* Reality ceases to exist. Overlapping memories return like a slow-motion replay, and my mind drifts back to the beginning of this mad adventure.

•

Six months earlier, in Darwin, the harbour master told us we'd surely come to grief in such a small boat. We had crossed the Simpson Desert when everyone said we would die in the attempt. This should be no problem! What a cocky, arrogant pair of smartarses Mike and I were. We had a lot to learn.

On the 17th July 1968 we gathered on the shore at Darwin's Doctors Gully. Pat waved a teary farewell to Mike; if all the sceptics were to be believed, we were doomed to perish, and husband and wife would never see each other again. Trevor Teare, Pat's younger brother, was our third crew member. He too displayed deep emotions, as he was leaving behind his bride of three months, Barbara, to tackle the unknown. Being single, I had no one to see me off.

Adventure was calling. It was time to go.

As soon as we rounded the first point, our 5-metre craft was smashing into a sharp south-easterly chop. *Slap, slap, slap!*

It quickly became obvious that a small open vessel, barely bigger than a dinghy, was not a great choice for the marathon ahead. We had no accommodation and no protection from the elements. The bow thumped into each wave, sending needles of icy water into our faces. Our T-shirts stuck to our saturated bodies in drooping folds. Welcome to the next six months.

On board we had 340 litres of fuel, 225 litres of drinking water, dehydrated food, two rifles, our cameras and plenty of film. We towed a small aluminium dinghy: this was to be our lifeboat if the worst came to the worst. In the event of a capsize, it would flood with water but remain afloat. The dinghy was stocked with more drinking water and food rations, as well as emergency flares, basic camping utensils and a small fold-away motorcycle for explorations ashore.

I was the designated navigator again. As we intended to stay in sight of land, it couldn't be too tricky, I thought. Keep the land on the right and sea on the left, and we should reach Sydney eventually.

In spite of the uncomfortable conditions, initially our spirits were high. It was already clear that because of the two-month delay with the NGS, we were going to cop the constant south-easterly winds that we'd hoped to avoid. Would we regret working with the Americans?

•

At the end of day one we'd covered a tiny fraction of the 5000 miles. We camped on a sandy beach near a spot named, somewhat ominously, Fright Point. The mozzies ate us alive while we scrambled under our insect nets and crawled into our sleeping bags.

Our boat was excruciatingly slow. Six knots. The head-winds sent endless showers of spray into it. We rigged up a tent-like canvas cover across the boom and tied it securely around the gunwales. This sent most of the water over the sides, but left our rear exposed. The helmsman had to perch on the back and steer via a tiller handle, wearing his spray jacket to keep from freezing. The water and wind made for chilling conditions, even though it was blazing sunshine.

On our third night we anchored in a few metres of water. Using the dinghy, we set off to camp ashore. Soon the water was too shallow, so Mike leapt over the side to wade ashore, carrying his backpack of camping gear.

In a few seconds, he was encircled by sharks. One was quite large, its menacing dorsal fin slicing effortlessly through the water. My brother hadn't seen them.

'Sharks!' Trevor and I yelled as loudly as we could.

Mike turned, spotted the danger and beat a hasty retreat towards us. Grabbing our .22 rifle, I pumped shots into the dorsal fin. When Mike reached our dinghy, he tumbled in headfirst; his feet and calves were caked in slimy grey mud. Undeterred, the biggest shark circled us as we headed back to the *Little Investigator*.

We decided to stay on the vessel for the night. With our .303 heavy-duty rifle, we blasted away at the big shark's head as it continued its menacing patrol. Then the ugly brute shimmied off into the inky void of the ocean amid death throws, and we settled in for our first night of sleeping on board.

Soon we heard a gurgling sound. In the north of Australia, the tidal rise and fall is huge. About 10 metres. We swung our hurricane lamp over the side of the boat and watched the last of the tidal waters rushing seaward. In minutes our craft was sitting on rippled grey mud.

'You can walk ashore now,' I suggested to Mike in jest.

He smiled and leapt into the custard-like slush. He was instantly up to his waist. The more he moved, the deeper he sunk.

I slipped over to help. Big mistake. I too began a descent into the creamy ooze. The two of us flustered about; we looked like drunken idiots with feet of glue. We began to laugh at ourselves. The more we laughed, the more Trevor, high and dry on board, laughed too. He must have thought us quite mad.

These days I tell people to pack everything they think they're going to need when planning an outback tour, but not to worry if they leave something behind, so long as they bring their sense of humour. Never leave home without it, for it's sure to be needed before the trip is over. We needed ours right then.

Finally, after much struggling, Trevor hauled us free. The Leyland brothers stood naked on the bow of the *Little Investigator*, caked in slimy, smelly, foul, grey mangrove mud.

The funny side faded rapidly when we realised we had no water with which to wash it off: our drinking water was too valuable. We sat solemnly until the stuff dried, then picked it off in chunks, wincing as it took clumps of hair with it. Trevor quietly giggled to himself.

We then had a miserable night lying awake until three-thirty when the boat floated free from the clinging sludge with the return of the tide. We moved out into deeper water and dropped anchor for a few hours' sleep before sunrise.

•

The coastline of northern Australia is fringed with a barrier of mangroves, so thick they're almost impenetrable on foot. Perhaps the most uninviting coast anywhere.

Van Diemen Gulf lies to the north-east of Darwin. It's a huge area that could be crossed quickly enough in a ship, but we had to skirt our small craft around its perimeter, hugging the shore and keeping the mangrove jungle always in sight. It took us two weeks.

In that time we had a number of mishaps. First, we ran into a reef and badly damaged the propeller. Worse was to come.

We had a following sea that sent large swells rushing into our slow-moving vessel. These filled the dinghy, causing it to capsize. In the three-hour ordeal that followed, we lost the motorbike in 30 metres of water, plus about $500 worth of camping and survival gear. Owing to the delay, we ran out of daylight and chose to camp on board in a protected alcove.

Next morning we rounded the notorious Cape Don to reach its lighthouse. The lighthouse keeper advised us that the morning tide was the only safe time to tackle the rough seas around the cape. In the afternoon, the tidal currents that surge from the gulf mingle with those of the Arafura Sea: a highly dangerous combination that produces rip currents of 18 knots and waves that would surely have sunk us. Our little boat could manage 6 knots at best.

The dinghy capsize had delayed our progress but saved us from the catastrophe that would have awaited us. Pure chance. Nothing to do with good planning.

•

At the lighthouse we met Dave Lindner, the ranger for the Cobourg Peninsula, a huge wildlife reserve. We learnt that we were about to pass through his patrol territory. He invited us to drop in at his camp about 35 kilometres around the coast. Then he sped off in his boat with its 45-horsepower outboard, while we chugged along at our steady 6 knots.

I was receiving a drenching on the tiller as our little boat slammed incessantly into the unrelenting headwind and the accompanying steep-sided chop. This continued for the next three hours. The coastline was too rugged to call it quits and head for shelter. Anyway, there was no shelter we could see. No inlets. No beach.

The boat was still taking a pounding when I felt an excruciating shock. The water washing across the floor had shorted out the starter motor, causing it to throw into gear. Because this had happened with the motor running, the starter had turned into a generator, sending a huge electrical current along my arm and directly through my saturated bum to short out via the aluminium hull.

Trevor pulled the stop control, turning everything off.

My whole body was shaking uncontrollably: it seemed as though all my nerve ends were on fire. Most of the charge had passed through my testicles. I can't hope to convey how much agony this produced! Much worse than a kick in the balls! I thought I might have fried my family jewels beyond use and, what's worse, I hadn't even used them yet. Bugger!

I had burn marks on parts of my anatomy that don't normally see the sun, but the prospect of my possible impotency was something to worry about on another occasion. Right then the starter motor was cooked and, with no hand crank, we had no way of restarting the engine. We drifted for two hours.

Fortunately Dave turned back, found us and took us in tow. He knew a small sandy beach and managed to get us to it. Then he returned to his ranger quarters.

Next morning Trevor worked tirelessly to fix the starter motor. He soldered every single strand of copper wire back into place. It didn't work. We weren't going anywhere. All we could do was wait until Dave decided we were overdue.

The ranger's boat turned up at 10 p.m. He offered to tow our stricken vessel the 16 kilometres to his camp right then and there, advising that the seas usually died down a bit at night. We completed the exercise in two and a half hours, filled up on hot drinks and collapsed on the floor of his house for a well-earned rest.

In the morning we used the radio to order a new starter motor, then settled in for a wait of one week, when the next supply ship was due.

Dave's ranger quarters were located within a natural harbour, Port Essington, and we used our enforced break to explore the area. With Dave as our barefoot guide we visited most of its extensive coves and bays. It's roughly the size of Sydney Harbour and, at one time in history, high hopes were held that it would become the centre of enterprise for the north.

Named in honour of Queen Victoria, this small settlement was expected to grow into a great city but it was fraught with problems. Totally dependent on supply ships from Sydney, it was a hopeless failure. They came with everything needed to create civilization in the wilds of the north. They had cattle, sheep, goats, pigs, building supplies and, most importantly, they came with pioneering families and high hopes for a new exciting future. A garrison of soldiers were based here and for some time the future looked assured. They constructed family homes using local stone and timber, and a real village streetscape styled after an English hamlet was hewn from the wilderness.

The tropical monsoons, isolation, biting insects and unrelenting heat wore down the resolve of those hardy pioneers. The settlement was abandoned in 1849. Now, 119 years later, it had almost been obliterated by nature. Their homes and graves are now abandoned relics barely discernable among the tropical forest vines and decaying vegetation. I left feeling moved by the courage of those pioneers but saddened by the futility of the enterprise and misplaced optimism for those whose names are lost to history.

•

When our starter motor arrived we resumed our voyage with renewed enthusiasm, nibbling away at the seemingly endless coastline. The south-easterly winds were just as persistent and our days at sea were usually copies of one another.

Fortunately the coastline offered some fascinating diversions. This is traditional Aboriginal country, and in 1968 was still referred to as an Aboriginal Reserve. We dropped in at many of their camps and settlements, where we were given a privileged look at their way of life. We were always made welcome; on our arrival on the beach or mudflats, we'd be greeted by a sea of smiling children's faces.

On one occasion we went out all day in our dinghy to film two men hunting a sea turtle from a dugout canoe. The old man in the back patiently made silent strokes with his single paddle, while his younger companion stood in the bow, poised with a long pole: a sharpened nail in the end served as a harpoon.

After six hours without a break in the blistering sun, they spotted telltale movements near the water's muddy surface. A few deft strokes of the paddle and the canoe swung into position.

The harpooner lunged forward, putting his entire weight into the long shaft as he entered the water with a huge splash. The nail penetrated right through the shell of the turtle, which suddenly took off while the harpooner scrambled back on board. A long rope was attached to the harpoon head and it effortlessly pulled the heavy wooden dugout after the turtle. After some time the turtle weakened, and with considerable effort the men hauled their 140-kilogram catch into the canoe.

With just a few centimetres of freeboard, they returned to their camp with the turtle still alive and flapping on its back. It was slaughtered on the beach.

Life in these parts hadn't changed much in 40,000 years: it felt as if we'd been transported through time.

•

During the next few weeks we were battered as we headed into the cursed south-easterly winds. A bucketload of salty water would cascade over us with every choppy wave.

However, we were encouraged by the knowledge that we were achieving what no one had done before. We doggedly stuck to our plan: camping ashore when we could, stopping at mission stations for fuel and food, transmitting our position every day, and enduring the mind-numbing repetition with stoic determination. At least we had no trouble catching fish, often cooking them whole in the coals of an open fire.

We depended on the mission stations to buy our fuel, but unfortunately some of them were extremely low themselves, so we set off into the Gulf of Carpentaria with a half-full tank.

After studying the map for some time, I suggested we leave the coast and head on a compass course to Maria Island, before continuing on to the mouth of the McArthur River. Borroloola, our first town since Darwin, was located about 70 miles upstream from there. There was no way our fuel was going to last, but this course would cut about 50 miles off the voyage.

It was the first time we'd travelled out of sight of land. Our compass bearing proved accurate and, to our great relief, we reached Maria Island just on dusk. We anchored the *Little Investigator* and went ashore with the dinghy.

In the morning I felt refreshed and pretty good about my first true navigational test. We boarded the dinghy and set off to reach our boat.

A strong current, which tore around the island, created turbulent rapids that swamped the small petrol outboard. As hard as we tried, it would not restart.

The current was rapidly drawing us away from the anchored *Little Investigator*. Mike and I rowed furiously, but we couldn't make headway. For half an hour we kept up a superhuman effort. No good. We were weakening and our mother vessel was vanishing from view. The current was pulling us to the north, into the vastness of the Arafura Sea. The next landfall would be Papua New Guinea!

Trevor was valiantly trying to get the motor going. We had hardly any food or water, and *no radio*. How utterly stupid! We were about to become a statistic. I could easily imagine the headlines:

THREE FOOLHARDY ADVENTURERS
LOST AT SEA

The mystery of their abandoned vessel is puzzling as everything on board the Little Investigator *seems to be in working order.*

Whatever happened to the Leyland brothers and their companion?

Without warning, Trevor leapt overboard and started swimming against the tidal current. Mike and I continued to paddle with ever-weakening strokes, but by now the tide had won. We were on the point of physical collapse. Trevor however, to my amazement, was slowly making headway in his seemingly impossible task.

The *Little Investigator* was a small silhouette on the horizon. Trevor ploughed on. Mike and I were gasping for breath. Trevor was a good surfer and a strong swimmer, but this was the ultimate test. Could he do it? Our lives were in his hands.

Although his pace slowed, he kept gaining ground against the tidal rip. Soon my brother and I could barely make out what was happening.

We stopped paddling as soon as we saw a puff of black smoke from the exhaust. Trevor had the motor running! The little vessel came to pick us up! I'd never been so pleased to see it. Well done, Trevor! What a great choice for our crew. Without him we would have certainly perished that day.

•

We undertook the next leg of our voyage with a new appreciation of our cramped but trusty boat. We were once more out of the sight of land almost all day, until we reached the McArthur River mouth. Our fuel was desperately low, so we sat in the rear of the boat to raise the bow, allowing the last drops to run to the back and be drawn into the motor by the fuel pump.

Twenty miles short of Borroloola, as we were going up the river, the inevitable happened: the motor conked out. We pressed on using the small petrol outboard motor. Somehow Trevor had got it going after drying it out, but it was painstakingly slow.

Having been away for two months, we'd covered 1000 miles of our 5000-mile journey and learnt a few valuable lessons. No one dared suggest we give up, but I'm pretty sure we all thought it. I know I did.

11

Untamed Coast

Borroloola turned out to be little more than a trading post and a pub, but it did qualify as a town and boasted a post office. I sat in our small two-man tent, processed some pictures and wrote a despatch to send back to the *Newcastle Sun,* where they ran it front page.

Loaded to the gunwales with supplies, we motored down the McArthur River and returned to the Gulf. The monotony of a low, almost indiscernible line of mangroves slid by.

An opportunity to break this repetition occurred when we altered course and headed north to reach Mornington Island. Here we were invited by the Aboriginal locals to go out hunting in a dugout canoe. Burid, one of the tribal leaders, wanted to show us the traditional way to harpoon a huge dugong.

These amazing creatures are mammals. They graze on seaweed with a pig-like snout and have narrow slits for eyes. It's believed they gave rise to the ancient mariner's myth of mermaids, perhaps because the females lie floating on their backs to suckle their young, revealing full breasts, not unlike human breasts. Their grossly ugly faces, however, would only appeal to the most desperate of sailors.

To kill the dugong, the Aboriginal hunters simply thrust their harpoon into its thick skin and let the poor creature haul around the heavy canoe until it is exhausted; they then hold its tail out of the water and try to drown it. However, this dugong wasn't giving in without a fight, and snatched gasps of air while struggling violently.

Finally Burid jumped overboard, wrapped his legs around the mammal's head and held it underwater. The powerful dugong kept up a valiant fight. I knew this was a traditional way of obtaining what the islanders prized as a delicacy, but it still seemed terribly cruel. The struggle for life was going on for far too long.

We'd been filming the hunt from our dinghy, as we wanted to show how these people lived. Although we'd agreed not to interfere, in the end I produced our .303 rifle and offered to put the animal out of its misery.

Burid dragged himself from the water and tumbled back into the dugout. 'Why didn't you *say* you had a gun?' he called to me between gasps of breath.

'We wanted to see the traditional way of life!' I yelled back.

'Bugger tradition!' Burid smiled. 'Shoot him in the head, Mal.'

I did, and instantly the dugong was dead.

The hunters towed the body to a sandbank and dissected it, leaving the offal and unwanted bits at the water's edge. Within minutes, hundreds of small sharks rushed in and devoured these remains.

We returned to Mornington Island for a huge feast of dugong meat. It tasted like lightly salted pork. Quite a welcome change to our repetitious diet of fish. The turtle meat we had sampled earlier was quite good too, although the fatty bits were a greenish colour that I found a bit off-putting.

•

After several days, we waved goodbye to our friends on Mornington and resumed our voyage. The monsoonal wet season was fast approaching and we had to make better time. I suggested we travel at night, taking three-hour shifts on the tiller. Dave the ranger had told us the seas are calmer at night when the winds ease. We could use the stars to keep a compass course.

Mike and Trevor were hesitant, but I argued that we could chalk up eighteen hours of travel a day, and that this was essential for us to complete our voyage. We all agreed to give it a go and it worked out well. We were making real progress: on some days we managed 100 nautical miles.

On the 107th day since leaving Darwin, we reached the Torres Strait. It was blowing a 45-kilometre-per-hour wind with 2-metre waves, but we braved the open waters to head north to Thursday Island, with its cosmopolitan population of islanders, Aboriginal mainlanders, Chinese, Malays and whites.

As we wandered up the street to the town, women of all shapes and sizes hung out their windows and called for us to come in 'for a good time'. Some were quite pretty. Some were elderly! They all made it quite plain what they wanted.

Thursday Island had a reputation for its free-living girls and their easy-going approach to sex. The men from the island mostly went to the mainland for work and, as a result, females outnumbered males by about eight to one, so the girls were lonely and frustrated. We waved back and smiled as we walked on into town.

We soon heard about a big ceremony taking place on the island of Badu, about halfway to New Guinea: a tombstone opening. These festive occasions are carried out several years after someone of importance has died and been buried, when enough money has been accumulated to buy a fitting tombstone. The stone is wrapped in brightly coloured cloth, then unwrapped before a crowd of wailing and singing relatives and friends. This is followed by a big feast and dancing.

The tombstone opening on Badu was being held to honour the life of an important chieftain of the region, who had been responsible for bringing peace to the islands in the old days. This ceremony was to be the largest in 25 years.

Our time on Badu was like being transported to another world. On the first day, pearling luggers, crammed with thousands of islanders, sailed into the bay. Our *Little Investigator* was anchored among them.

We woke the next morning to the loud tolling of a bell, which signalled the start of a procession. The population of the island and most visitors marched slowly, six abreast, down a roadway lined with red and white flags, chanting and wailing. The procession included a priest and altar boys swinging incense burners: it was a unique mix of Christianity and island customs.

At the grave, the tombstone was revealed amid much weeping, chanting and more wailing. This was one of the oddest events I've ever seen, but we also felt privileged to witness it. Only three other white men were allowed to be there.

As dusk descended on the island, the dancing commenced and it carried on all night. The feast was amazing: pork, turtle and dugong were cooked underground with stones heated in open fires. All the vegetables and yams, plus some other items I couldn't identify, were cooked the same way, and then served with a sauce made from pig's blood. It was delicious!

The beating of the drums, the chanting and the dancing went on without a break. A mesmerising experience. We returned to our small craft in the early hours of the morning and collapsed on our bunks. The sound of the drums continued to drift across the cool night air to the bay with its flotilla of luggers.

•

In the morning we needed to head south. We were now roughly halfway through our 5000-mile voyage. The entire east coast to Sydney was still ahead of us.

To our amazement, the north of Australia offered us some of the calmest weather of our trip. We made good time across Torres Strait to reach the mainland and Cape York. From there the run south was monotonous but beautiful. We camped ashore whenever we could on countless unnamed, pristine beaches. Most were fringed with coconut palms, and soon we developed a taste for the fresh milk within each nut.

As carefree and Robinson Crusoe-like as this sounds, it was fraught with one overriding menace. The wet season was fast approaching, though the days were calm and still. The calm before the storm? Absolutely. We knew it and made the best time we could.

Our boat, reliable as it was, became the curse of the expedition. We hated its painfully slow progress, and the thump of its diesel engine almost drove us insane. We just wanted to get a move on and finish.

We passed Cooktown, Cairns, Townsville, Mackay and Rockhampton, clocking up fifteen to eighteen hours of travel each day. Plugging along the east coast had one great advantage: the towns are about 100 kilometres apart from each other, perfect for a full day's travel. We had the luxury of sleeping on board in the relative calm of small harbours and safe anchorages.

Sydney was getting closer. We could almost taste success. The longest open boat voyage was nearly ours. Surely nothing could stop us now!

The water was crystal clear, reflecting a deep turquoise blue. The Pacific Ocean swept gently from the east in long, slow swells. On a day without wind, the ocean rose and fell like the breathing of a dormant monster.

Our little boat chugged along reliably and we had great faith in its ability to get us through to the end, but we also had respect for the fearsome reputation of the east coast with its gales, cyclones and wild storms. Could we reach Sydney without having to find out just how fearsome it could be?

•

Fraser Island is the largest sand island in the world, and it runs parallel to the east coast south of Bundaberg. When we reached its northernmost tip, we had to decide whether to travel on its eastern side, open to the Pacific swell, or take the shallow but protected channel on its western side. We chose the channel.

Apart from running aground twice, we found the channel uneventful until we reached the southern fishing port of Tin Can Bay. We were topping up our fuel tanks and making ready to cross the sandbar, when local trawler fishermen told us not to attempt this. They had been 'bar-bound' for two days, waiting for the sea to calm down.

We were impatient to get moving, and so we set off to take a look. The sandbar was a seething, foaming mass of white water. It sent a chill down my spine. We'd never needed to cross one before.

Trevor, who was on the tiller, eased us near the edge of the turbulent water. Then we all noticed a flat spot, where no waves were breaking.

'What do you reckon?' Trevor asked.

'Hell, let's go!' we urged, and he opened up the throttle.

I was with Mike under the canvas cover, which stretched tightly across the boom. I glanced back to see a horrified look on Trevor's face, then I gazed through the murky plastic windscreen just in time to see a series of massive waves rushing straight at our little boat. Nothing for it but to hold on and hope for the best.

A leaden thump, followed by an avalanche of foaming water, accompanied each of the monsters. Some waves were deep green, and one was so big that it ripped the canvas cover from its lashings. I thought we must surely sink.

Instead we were airborne. The motor revved up into a scream and I expected it to explode, but we crashed back into the water and it made an awful jolting sound. Water sloshed across the floorboards as the stern sank deeper into the cauldron of foam. I grabbed my knife, ready to cut my way free from the canvas and ropes.

Then, surprisingly, the *Little Investigator* came upright and we were through the worst of it. Our marvellous boat burst from the foaming mass and proceeded seaward. We'd crossed the bar! We motored out into deep blue water and relaxed, looking forward to a nice calm day's run.

Two hours later I was on the tiller when sounds like gunshots emanated from the engine. I slowed the motor, but they became louder until, with an ear-piercing metallic thud, the engine stopped dead. We'd snapped a crankshaft; a direct result, no doubt, of the strain of crossing the bar.

We were just off Double Island Point and drifting perilously close to the rugged rocks, where waves were being dashed to spray. Our small outboard motor and the sail got us out of trouble, and we just managed to sneak around the protruding finger of the point so we could enter the comparative calm of the bay.

To our delight a prawning trawler, the *Yulgibar*, was anchored there. We introduced ourselves to the skipper, Joe Flaherty. He was an ex-navy man and knew the dangers of the Tin Can Bay bar very well. He thought we were extremely lucky to have made it out.

Joe was doing night-time prawning while using the bay as a daytime anchorage. He kindly offered to tow the *Little Investigator* back to his home port, Mooloolaba, and we gratefully accepted. He advised that a gale warning was out, so we should set off immediately. However, by the time we rigged up a 90-metre towrope and a harness around our boat, the daylight was almost gone.

Mike and Trevor went on board the *Yulgibar* with Joe, while I volunteered to stay on the *Little Investigator* to keep it safe and afloat. The logic behind my thinking went that since I was unmarried, I was more expendable!

The night was black as pitch. Lightning slashed the sky. Wind and rain roared at about 30 kilometres per hour. I had radio communication with the trawler, but the sea was a savage violent mass of turbulence: hell-bent, it seemed, on destroying our small craft and its only occupant. I hung on for the most frightening experience of my life. If I was to survive this night's ordeal, I would be changed forever.

•

So, dear reader, you know now how I came to be dangling with a rope around my waist, gasping for air and resigned to the fact that I would soon drown.

The pain from my blood-tattered hands had gone: replaced by numbness, as though they were anaesthetised. Phosphorescence enveloped me in a cocoon of eerie blue. My energy had left me.

I wasn't much more than dead meat when the trawler started to climb another monster wave and the *Little Investigator*, just a dim white glow in the black void, stopped moving. I suddenly snapped out of my mesmerised state: *Haul yourself forward! Reach the boat! Save yourself NOW!*

With a last shot of adrenaline, my body leapt into action: hand over hand, I pulled myself along the rope. Pain returned with a vengeance. My palms were bleeding. Inch by inch, faster, faster . . . until my bloody right hand slapped down on the metal gunwale of the transom.

With one last burst of energy, I crashed into the back of the boat, landing in a heap on the floor next to the defunct motor. I was alive! Just.

I lay resting for a few minutes, and then crawled to the radio and called Joe.

'It's no use,' I screamed into the microphone, 'I'm exhausted! Can't keep the pump going any longer. The boat is sinking!'

'Hold on!' came the reply. 'We'll winch the boat close up to the trawler and try to get you off. I'll cut your boat loose.'

Had it really come to this? Had all our efforts been in vain?

I resumed pumping for about ten minutes while the winch drew the two craft together. I staggered to the bow in the pitching sea and clung to the mast. Spots of water felt like small stones. The trawler's floodlights, normally used for sorting the catch, illuminated the black sea as if it were daylight.

One minute I was looking down on the stern of the trawler deck at Mike, Trevor and Joe, and the next I was in a trough staring up at the underside of the trawler while its propellers turned uselessly in the air. Our attempted rescue was at risk of turning into tragedy. The vessels were only a metre or so apart, and slicing up and down with the passing of each wave.

As he'd done during our near-disaster at Maria Island, Trevor suddenly dived into the water and swam back to the *Little Investigator*. Joe let fly with curses at his recklessness, but Trevor was fine and scrambled on board.

'New man for the pump!' he screamed to me over the roaring gale.

We both hurried to the rear of our mighty little craft, and Trevor immediately started work on the hand pump. I was grateful for the fresh energy he brought to the task, but also for the company, someone with whom to share the fear.

'Watch out for sudden waves,' I warned him, as I gripped the radio under the canvas in the front of the boat. 'They come right after a slowing down. You should tie your safety line around your waist now.'

'I'll get the water down first,' he replied, but no sooner had he said this than a wave hit the boat. By the dull glow of the torch around my neck, I could see a wall of foamy white water fill the stern.

When it cleared, Trevor had gone . . .

Well, almost. His fingers were clinging to the stern. There was a row of white knuckles, with Trevor dragging behind. I rushed up and helped him back on board.

'Are those the waves to watch for?' he asked flippantly, with a trace of fear in his voice. Only his swift reflexes had saved his life.

Trevor quickly attached his safety rope, and silently we resumed our night of hell. Here, in this tiny metal shell, bouncing endlessly as the forces of nature tried to rip us apart, I began to reflect upon this trip and my life. Up to that night, I'd been living for the adventure. I loved the photography and the challenge.

Alone in the dark and dragged along by the rope, I'd come so close to drowning that I underwent a transformation. Looking death in the face had been a sobering experience. I wasn't ready to die. Partly because I was still a virgin; I don't think anyone should die a virgin. I promised myself that I'd make a conscious effort to meet some girls. Hopefully, the Right Girl. I had a lot of living yet to do. Lost time to make up.

First things first, however. We needed to get through the rest of this mess: we were still at the mercy of the untamed coast. It took eleven hours of alternating shifts on the bilge pump before Trevor and I came to the end of our ordeal and slipped into the tranquil waters of the Mooloolah River.

Our progress had been monitored over the radio by the fishing fleet anchored in the river. As we passed them, the skippers blew their whistles. It seemed as though all the fishermen had come out to watch the survivors with their bedraggled and battered little boat. The men wanted to wave to the three insane boys who thought they could sail from Darwin to Sydney in a 5-metre tub.

Joe Flaherty had saved our lives. He was the hero of the day.

I found it difficult to stand when we finally stepped from the boat onto terra firma. I was weak in the legs and my hands were raw, but Christmas Day was two days off and we already had our present. We were alive!

After a phone call to Perkins Motors in Sydney and a long discussion with a disbelieving executive, during which he maintained that Perkins don't break crankshafts, a cheerful mechanic arrived with a complete replacement engine in his service ute.

It was Christmas Eve. He and Trevor worked tirelessly to install the new motor.

Job done, he shook our hands, wished us luck and, just as he was about to leave, paused beside his car and said, 'By the way, I have a message from the boss in Sydney: "Perkins Marine Engines don't break crankshafts."'

We watched him drive off; we hadn't signed any papers or paid any costs. They obviously had a reputation to protect. Great service for Christmas Eve!

•

The rest of our amazing adventure was relatively easy. We hopped between towns and anchorages. Each small harbour was within a calm day's cruising. Our routine started in the dark about 4 a.m. and we spent every day of fine weather clocking up the kilometres until dusk. The Pacific swell rolled in unrelentingly, but never again were we put to the test with storms or rough seas.

The towns slid by and the great urge to finish drove us on, day after day until triumphantly, on the 174th day since leaving Darwin, we entered Sydney Heads. The Bridge had never looked so good! The three of us went through a bout of backslapping, handshaking and hugging.

We ended our odyssey at Farm Cove under the glare of TV news cameras, in a scrum of reporters and photographers. Pat and Barbara, along with our parents, greeted us like long-lost souls back from the dead.

We had completed the longest open boat voyage in the world: 5000 nautical miles. Time to settle down and put the bloody film together!

12

Off to see the World and
Falling in Love

We were on the 22nd floor of a skyscraper in New York City. Mike and I sat facing a huge mahogany desk. I stared between the soles of two large leather shoes, resting on the desk, at a proportionately large, jowly man. He sucked on a massive cigar, puffing billows of tobacco smoke into the ever-increasing cloud that threatened to fill the oversized office. I'm sure its size was meant to impress us.

We were in the office of 20th Century Fox studios, trying to sell *Wheels Across a Wilderness*. Hollywood is where they make the films: this is where the money is.

'I've taken a look at your little movie,' the man finally said, 'and you should be proud of yourselves.'

I breathed a sigh of relief. *He likes it.*

'However,' he continued, almost without pause,

'although it certainly performed well in Australia, we can't see it working with an American audience.'

'Why not?' I asked.

'Americans like to see other Americans doing things, and your film is about a group of young people crossing a desert they never heard of, in a country most of them have only heard about vaguely. If you two guys were Americans, we'd run the film as is. But in its present form . . .' He paused, puffing away, then asked, 'Have you still got those vehicles?'

We nodded.

'Take them back to the desert and refilm the finish. What we need—' by now he was waving his arms around in exaggerated gestures, meant to encompass the whole world '—is a *sensational* ending. Have one of the trucks catch on fire. You guys barely survive, and crawl out of the desert on your hands and knees.'

Angry by now, Mike and I reminded him that *Wheels* was a documentary record of a real event: the first time that vehicles had crossed the Simpson Desert. We couldn't rewrite history.

'It's only a movie, boys.' He made a dismissive gesture. '*We* know how movies are made. Everything is staged for the camera. It's only entertainment.'

'None of it was staged,' I protested. 'It was filmed exactly as it happened. Surely it's worthy of a test as it is.'

The big man moved slowly in his chair and dragged his hefty feet off the desk. We at last got a proper look at him.

'If we release this movie,' he said, 'we'll be making at least 200 copies of it. We'll have an east coast release followed by one on the west coast. Now *that's* a big investment. But . . . we have a committee who viewed your film here in New York, and we all agreed it needs spicing up at the end.'

'Two hundred prints!' Mike repeated. 'That seems a hell of a lot.'

'Sure is! And with the publicity and advertising we're looking at, *millions* of dollars. We just don't reckon it's worth the risk—in its present form, that is.'

'What kind of money do you reckon it could take in an altered form?' I asked.

'We're thinking of a return of ten to twenty times our investment,' he said flatly, as though discussing the cost of an ice-cream.

Mike and I looked at each other, flabbergasted. Twenty million dollars made the money our film had taken in Australia seem like chicken feed.

A huge knowing grin emerged from the big man's face as he rocked back on his chair. 'It's my job to know what works and what doesn't,' he said smugly.

'Can we talk again tomorrow and give you our decision?' we asked.

'Sure, talk it over, but I know what you'll say. Make a time with my secretary on the way out,' he added, like a school headmaster dismissing us from his office.

We wandered back to our dingy hotel room on 57th Street to contemplate our next move.

Our trip to the United States had come about because the National Geographic Society was screening their TV special featuring us on NBC to an audience of 40 million.

We reckoned it would help open doors for an American release of *Wheels*.

Next morning, while perched on bar stools eating pancakes and maple syrup at a drugstore counter, Mike and I discussed the pros and cons of doing a deal with 20th Century Fox.

Later we kept our second appointment with the big man.

'Do we have a deal?' he asked, while chewing on an even bigger cigar.

'Not exactly,' I informed him, then went on to explain.

We conceded that he no doubt knew his country well. He could pick any town he fancied and we would go there, help promote the film and see how it went. We'd use one of our 35mm prints. If the film worked well in the town, Fox could run off their 200 copies and let it go out into general distribution. If the trial failed, Mike and I would go home with our tails between our legs and a lesson learnt.

The big man considered this proposal without giving us any hint of his thoughts. Just more belches of cigar smoke.

Finally he spoke. 'We don't do things that way here. We know what works and it will if you reshoot that ending,' he stated bluntly, before adding, 'I can't believe you didn't jump at the prospect of all that dough.'

'If that's your final decision, I guess we'd better be getting along.'

I rose to leave. Mike followed.

'Good luck, fellas,' the big man said, shaking our hands

as we said our goodbyes. 'If you change your minds, you know where to find me.'

•

Mike and I spent fourteen days amid New York's seething mass of human energy. We then took a shuttle flight to Washington DC for an appointment with the head pictorial editor of *National Geographic* magazine. I had hopes of selling a story to what I regarded as the ultimate pictorial magazine in the world.

The editor was a delightful man who greeted us warmly and invited us to join him in the huge picture editing room. Rows and rows of white laminated benches ran the entire length of the building. Dozens of people sat on bar stool-like seats that rolled along chromed rails. They could stop and peer at 35mm slides through powerful magnifying viewers. Thousands of images were in the process of being selected down to the few they would use. It was all spotlessly clean.

I immediately recognised my slides, which I'd sent ahead several days earlier. This was encouraging. They were on the light bench, hopefully making the cut for the final selection.

This proved to be false hope. My pictures were laid out simply so that our helpful guide could explain what had caused them to be rejected. The West–East Crossing Expedition photos were considered very good, but the story too old for use. The shots from our boat trip were also considered worthy of publication, but the voyage hadn't been an NGS-sponsored undertaking.

As we rode the lift to the ground floor, Mike made the cruellest comment he'd ever come out with.

'Congratulations,' he said with a smug, I-told-you-so smirk, 'you've failed!'

What a bastard. Did he imagine that the runaway success of *Wheels* was all due to his efforts, and that my photography was just some leisure pursuit of his little brother? This was my first insight into how Mike viewed our relative contributions to our enterprise: clearly he considered me to be less able and less important.

'You know how to kick a bloke when he's down don't you? You bastard,' I responded with real venom.

From my reaction to his comment, Mike quickly realised he'd offended me and tried to laugh it off with an 'Only kidding!' I wasn't convinced.

•

We flew out the next day for London, where we were met by our uncle Ron, Mum's younger brother. He drove us back to Hitchin, our old home town. I was surprised to discover that I remembered the route I'd once walked to school as a four-year-old. Of course, everything seemed smaller than in my memory.

Mike and I then caught the train back to London, in an effort to sell some of my most recent pictures and stories to magazines or newspapers. Fleet Street was the place to go, so that's where we went.

I was pleased to get an appointment with the pictorial editor of the *London Times*, the newspaper I considered the most prestigious in the world. As I showed the editor black-and-white prints from our boat trip, including those of the Aboriginal people of Arnhem Land, he expressed appreciation of my work.

A flap broke out in the reporters' room and the newspaper's editor burst in, looking for a photographer. None were available: they were all out on assignments.

Then the pictorial editor looked at me and asked, 'Do you have all your gear in that camera bag?', pointing at the black leather case on my shoulder.

'Yes. Two Nikons and a full set of lenses.'

On the spot I was offered not only the assignment but also a permanent job with the *Times*.

I honestly didn't know what to do. Here I was, having been ridiculed by Mike a few days earlier, trying to decide whether to take up a job on the *Times* or to return to Australia and help complete the film we'd just shot. To have abandoned Mike would have been a betrayal, and I could never do that.

My decision was perhaps the most difficult I'd ever made. I hesitated for a bit, knowing that this was a dream job, and then gracefully declined. Mike chose to remain silent. I have often wondered how it would have panned out if I had chosen to stay.

Mike and I left the building. As we walked the streets of London, stopping off at coffee shops and taking pictures of landmarks, I felt like I was really at home. It was an even bigger city than New York, but it felt more inviting. It seemed right for me. Comfortable. The weather was foul, but then it was mid-winter.

This was the swinging sixties, all the girls looked fabulous. Everywhere I looked I saw beautiful women, happy and carefree. Many seemed about my age and they all wore miniskirts. Yes, I thought, I could live here and get to know some of these scrumptious girls!

However, my decision had been made. We returned to our editing rooms 'Down Under' to cut that enormous pile of film into a movie.

•

Our rooms were in a disused old shop in an inner suburb of Newcastle. For months we worked at the film every day, gradually putting it together. At 40 hours it was way too long and so the cutting needed to be severe, and the task of synchronising the film with the appropriate soundtracks was massive. This was my job, along with writing the script and researching background information.

During this time I was living back at my parents' house. One night Mum was hosting a jewellery party: a dozen or so friends came around while a salesgirl demonstrated various bits of jewellery and took orders that would be delivered in a few weeks' time. Like a Tupperware Party, except with jewels instead of plastic containers.

There was no way I wanted to be around for *that*, so I'd arranged with Mike for the two of us to go off and work on the film. This suited him as he was dropping Pat at Mum's to make up the numbers.

I was relaxing in the lounge room in a scruffy pair of old jeans and a somewhat battered jumper when the doorbell rang. Probably Mike and Pat arriving early, I thought, but no, Mum greeted someone at the door. I heard the voice of a young woman, and then she walked into the lounge.

I turned in my chair. There stood the most beautiful and immaculately groomed girl I'd ever seen, adorned in a rich blue dress. Realising how grubby I looked, I felt blood surge through my face, blushing uncontrollably while Mum introduced us.

'Malcolm,' she said, 'this is Laraine, Betty Dempsey's daughter.' Betty was one of Mum's lawn bowls friends. 'Laraine's brought the jewellery tonight.'

My head was spinning. The lovely Laraine had shiny dark-brown hair and the deepest brown eyes I'd ever seen. They glinted in the light like mysterious pools of ebony. She had the most wonderful smile and a bright, sunny disposition. I felt like a lovesick teenager.

I volunteered to help set up the tables and lay out Laraine's samples before the guests arrived, even though I felt embarrassed standing alongside her in my dingy work clothes. I helped with as many chores as possible, and Mum made a strategic exit and left us alone.

Eventually the guests arrived. When Mike turned up, I gave Laraine one last look, soaking up the impeccable vision before me, and then took off in my brother's Land Rover to go and do a night's work.

'Did you notice the girl who brought the jewellery?' I asked him as we motored through the chilly April night.

'Not really,' he replied. 'Which one was she?'

'The gorgeous one, with the dark hair and the blue dress.'

'Oh! Can't say I did,' he mumbled.

The editing wasn't going well that night. I couldn't quite get that girl out of my mind. Besides, it was cold in the old timber building. Our small electric radiator put out a pitiful amount of heat.

'How about we go home now?' I suggested. 'The party should be over and Pat will be waiting to go.'

Mike agreed, and in about fifteen minutes we pulled up outside Mum and Dad's house. To my delight, Laraine's red VW Beetle was still parked out the front. I rushed in to find Mum, Pat, Betty and Laraine chatting, with the jewellery still on display.

Pat and Mike left immediately, then Mum made herself scarce. I volunteered to help pack things up for Laraine and carry them out to her Beetle.

The more I saw of this girl, the more I liked what I saw. I know it sounds kind of clichéd, but there is such a thing as 'love at first sight'—it happened to me that night in the lounge room when Laraine walked through the door and into my life.

I had a problem. I was very shy with girls and didn't know how to handle things from there.

The atmosphere between us seemed to have a kind of electricity in it, but this didn't help me with my inexperience in such matters. In the end, Laraine smiled sweetly, said goodnight and left to go home. I stood in the cold night out the front of the house and watched her red Beetle vanish into the darkness.

•

Three weeks later I was in the darkroom that we'd constructed in the far end of Dad's garage when there was a knock on the door. I was developing a print under the red safelight, so I called out, 'Is that you, Mum?'

'Yes. Will you be long?'

'About twenty seconds.'

I opened the door to find Mum standing there with Laraine. She'd dropped by to deliver all the jewellery that had been ordered at the party, and she looked just as beautiful as I recalled.

'You remember Laraine, Malcolm?' Mum asked.

Remember? I'd thought about her every day. I'd been unable to forget her.

'Yes, of course,' I replied.

'I told her you were in the darkroom and suggested she might like to see how you make photographs.'

My mum, the matchmaker, wasn't very subtle, but I certainly approved of her actions. I invited Laraine to join me in the very tiny room, closing the door on Mum and letting her know not to disturb us for a while, as I had to keep the door closed and the light out.

I was dressed in daggy clothes covered in chemical stains, and I warned Laraine not to get anything on her lovely dress. I turned off the white light and we were soon enveloped by the safelight's warm red glow.

This was a great opportunity for me to impress Laraine, but I was just as stupefied as before. I spent the next twenty minutes demonstrating the art of making a good photographic print and processing it.

I must have come across as a bumbling idiot; I hardly stopped talking in my effort to cover up my nervousness.

I don't think she was really all that interested, but she smiled her sweet disarming smile, listened intently and generally kept very close in the tight confines of the darkroom. I could feel her breath on my neck as I leant over the processing dishes. Occasionally she brushed up against my back, and I could smell her perfume and feel her warmth. In the red light, she looked perfect.

She could have stayed all night as far as I was concerned, but I realised prints must be of limited interest, so I switched the white light on, opened the door and once more escorted her to her red Beetle. My head was spinning. I was smitten.

•

The Friday following our darkroom encounter, Laraine telephoned me and asked if I would like to accompany her to a friend's 21st birthday party. I said yes.

On the night, she looked gorgeous. I was terrified of mucking things up. The party took place in a hired public hall and I knew no one, so I sat next to Laraine and quietly munched on peanuts. What a bloody dill she must have thought me!

When I took her home at the end of the night, I plucked up the courage to ask her to come out with me the next day for a picnic in the bush. I needed to record some bird calls for our film and suggested we go to the Mount Sugarloaf Reserve, just west of Newcastle.

Everything went well. I cooked steak on an open fire and made billy tea. She took a keen interest in the complex sound–recording equipment and naturally I produced my camera. I started taking pictures of her, but she was camera shy.

I felt so buoyed just being with Laraine that I asked her out the next night to go to the movies. I didn't care what was playing, for I was in love and I was going to give this courtship thing the best shot I could. Believe me, I found it more difficult than battling tropical gales or crossing more than a thousand sand ridges.

We went to drive-ins, cinemas, restaurants and midnight coffee lounges, and talked in the car. About three weeks after our first picnic date, we were at the drive-in and it was here that I held her hand for the first time. I know this sounds odd for a 24-year-old bloke, but I didn't want to rush things. I didn't want her to think I was only trying to get in her pants, although the thought never left my mind.

Soon our courtship blossomed and, feeling more comfortable and confident, we kissed for the first time. I can still recall the heady experience. It was as if nothing else in the world existed. Just the two of us locked in each other's arms with the blood surging through our veins. I'm not exaggerating one bit when I say that I was light-headed—I nearly fainted. We devoured each other with as much passion as we could muster.

It was only a kiss, but what a kiss! My hormones were running riot. I'd never experienced anything like it and never wanted it to end.

We started going out every night unless Laraine had some other commitment. I realised I wanted to spend the rest of my life with this girl.

Three months after we first met, I asked Laraine to marry me. She said yes!

The next day I bought an engagement ring and she booked the church: St Luke's in Wallsend. Our marriage would take place on the 13th December 1969. No one else wanted that date because it was considered bad luck, but we just wanted to marry before the film was ready to roadshow. There was no way I wanted to go away screening it all over the country and not see Laraine for twelve months. Mike was best man and Keith the official photographer. After the wedding we had a small gathering of family and friends at her parents' place before setting off in our Land Rover for our honeymoon. We had just two weeks, and planned to drive to Melbourne and back.

On our wedding night we reached our pre-booked motel and checked in as Mr and Mrs Leyland. It sounded odd.

The awkward part of the evening was fast approaching.

I had the first shower and waited on the bed until Laraine emerged, wearing a silky, full-length nightie. I was shaking with anticipation. She glided over to the bed and lay beside me.

'Do you come with an instruction book?' I asked.

'Instruction book? For what?' she responded with a whimsical expression.

'You know.' I was grinning from ear to ear.

She smiled beautifully and then said, 'I expected *you* to have all the answers.'

We cuddled up, laughed at our naivety and, in spite of several clumsy attempts to consummate our marriage, we couldn't get it all figured out and fell asleep in each other's arms.

When we awoke in the middle of the night, nature took its course. It was wonderful and, I'm convinced, all the more beautiful because we lost our virginity to each other in one shared, breathtaking moment. Old-fashioned thinking perhaps, but not to be underrated.

·

Laraine's upbeat enthusiasm for everything was infectious. My life was revitalised. I often reflect on how glad I am that I didn't stay behind in England and take up that job at the *Times*. We would never have met.

During our courtship I managed to convince Laraine that she is photogenic, and I've taken thousands of great portraits of her since. My wife has worked as a successful model, run her own modelling agency and appeared in hundreds of TV commercials. I like to think I had a hand in that transformation, and I still cherish those first portraits we took so long ago.

Laraine is the love of my life. We've been married for 45 years and I hope for many more to come. She's stood by me through thick and thin, and played an important part in our filmmaking career. I'm convinced that I couldn't have done it without her. The best question I ever asked was, 'Will you marry me?'

13

'Roadshowing' and a Return to TV

The film was now complete. Over a period of nine months we'd reduced 20 hours of film to 135 minutes. We called it *Open Boat to Adventure*.

Mike and I delivered the narration, 50 per cent each. We lashed out $15,000 to have a theme written. The music was scored just like that of an acted feature film. It was performed by a fourteen-piece orchestra and recorded in Sydney.

I argued with Mike over the length of the film: I thought far too many sequences went on too long. I argued with Mike over the cost of the music: I reckoned that mood music would have done just as well. I argued with Mike over how long it had taken to edit. He insisted that it was our best film so far, but I was sceptical.

Mike's ego and my concern for the bottom line were at loggerheads. In the end I lost the battle and the total cost came to $28,000. Enough to buy four good homes at the time. Would we recover the money?

On the 5th of January 1970 we staged the world premiere of the film at a gala event in Newcastle. Laraine and I had been married less than four weeks. She took it in her stride, even though she told me she was shaking like a leaf.

We drove home about midnight and sat in the car outside.

'The film is a flop,' I declared. 'It may be made to a higher standard, but it's not as good as *Wheels*. It's far too long and it didn't work with the audience.'

Laraine was stunned, but it was true. Most of the time the audience had just sat impassively, unmoved. Uninvolved. With *Wheels* they'd been with us all the way and the atmosphere was electric.

Laraine couldn't believe what I was saying. 'Everyone seemed to like it,' she said gently, trying to raise my spirits.

'Oh yes, they all said so, but it was a charity night. They were just being polite.'

•

As a prophet of doom, I proved to be accurate. In the next few weeks, playing two sessions a day, we took about half as much as we had with *Wheels*. The film was struggling to show any reasonable profit.

Our roadshowing tour of the country was already planned. We were to play Sydney and then Melbourne, before taking the film west to Adelaide and Perth.

We set off with our vehicles packed to the gills. We spent a fortune on advertising and also had a lot of free publicity, with reviews and write-ups in many newspapers but, no matter how many posters we placed all over the city or how many radio interviews we conducted, mostly the film only achieved half-filled cinemas. At least the audience that did come said they loved it.

In Melbourne we used the Hawthorn Town Hall once more, but we could never duplicate our previous success. In order to save money on theatre staff, Laraine did the cashiering. She was a trained cashier when we met and, unlike me, she loved it. She quickly became a vital and much appreciated member of the team.

To make up for the poor attendances at our evening screenings, we directly contacted schools and offered special matinee sessions in their halls. The children would take home a promotional flyer and then bring 60 cents to school to see our film. Ten per cent of the takings went to the school P&C Association, to be used in whatever way they saw fit.

This method doubled our takings, especially in larger towns like Ballarat with many schools. Soon we realised that the cost of running the film in a town could be reduced to next to nothing by concentrating on schools only and avoiding cinemas. We ran the film in many school halls, turning it from a total fizzer into a reasonable earner. We were still a long way from paying it off, however.

A welcome windfall came while we were in Victoria. We received word that *Wheels* had been bought by Nippon TV for US$6000: the first time an Australian production had been sold to Japan.

I had to fly back to Newcastle for a week to do the complex task of making copies of the film's music and sound effects. Nippon needed a copy of the script too, so they could produce a Japanese translation and add their own narrator.

Laraine and I had only been married about four months at that stage. I reluctantly left my beloved bride to help run the show with Mike and Pat.

I returned to her in the middle of the night, on a small commuter plane that touched down in Bendigo. We rushed towards each other as if in a Hollywood movie and embraced on tarmac shrouded in a light fog. It was freezing cold, and Laraine wore a light black overcoat over her miniskirt.

It never felt so good to hold her close. I hate being separated from her and have always tried hard to avoid it.

•

We were in the middle of our screening run in Adelaide when we received a phone call from an old friend we'd worked with at NBN. He now ran a large advertising agency in Sydney, and he had a proposition for us. He represented AMP, one of the biggest life assurance companies in the country. Did we have any plans for a TV show and, if so, what was it and how much would it cost to make?

'Of course we do!' I informed him. In truth, we had no plans.

'Good,' he said. 'Come to Sydney and present your story. I'll arrange a meeting with the client.'

Oh shit! What to do now?

Mike and I put our heads together and came up with the idea of filming a half-hour series featuring expeditions into wild places around Australia. We tentatively titled it *Off the Beaten Track*. We'd travel by four-wheel drive and include as much wildlife and adventure as possible. It would involve our wives and, in Mike's case, his first-born baby daughter, Kerry.

A few weeks later we were in Sydney, sitting in an opulent boardroom talking to the man in charge of public relations and promotions at AMP.

We presented our concept for thirteen episodes and, when asked for a budget, I suggested $12,000 each: a cost of $156,000 over a three-year period of production. He didn't flinch at the price, and asked if we'd be willing to put a sign on each of our vehicles promoting AMP. Yes, we thought that would be okay; but we would need to clear it with our buyer, which we nominated as the Nine Network.

'Do you have a contract with them?' the man asked.

'Not as yet,' I responded cheerfully, 'but I've spoken with them and they're keen on the idea.'

'Great! Get the details sorted out and see if we can do business.'

The fact was that by then I'd spoken with Len Mauger, the network executive at Channel Nine and the Packer family's right-hand man there. He'd liked the sound of the series and asked for a full presentation. With AMP's backing seemingly secured, I put together the proposal and asked Nine for $12,000 per episode.

'But that's the same price you quoted AMP for their contribution,' Mike later pointed out.

'Yes, I know,' I explained, 'but it should be enough, just on its own, to make the series and to show a profit too. If AMP pulls out, we still have a viable series. If they stay in, we get paid twice.'

As it turned out, AMP did pull out, but by then Nine were keen for us to get on with making our new series. They wanted one-hour, not half-hour shows, and our biggest dilemma was that we had no money.

Some of the best ideas end up as just that. Ideas. They often never see the light of day because of lack of funding. Television shows are no different.

Luck was on our side. In 1970, coinciding perfectly with our embryonic idea for *Off the Beaten Track*, Prime Minister John Gorton set up the Australian Film Development Corporation, a government department charged with the task of fostering Aussie productions. The corporation had several million dollars at its disposal and, according to the story I read in the paper, was asking producers with ideas to make written submissions for grants.

The man in charge was Tom Stacey. Now it happened that Tom was a business acquaintance of ours, through his previous job as head of one of the biggest film-processing labs in Sydney. He'd been involved in blowing up *Wheels* to the 35mm version used by 20th Century Fox.

We arranged to meet Tom in his Sydney office, where we explained our programme idea. The first thing he asked us for was a cash flow spreadsheet.

A what? We'd never carried out such an exercise before. I explained that we knew how to make films but nothing about cash flow, whatever that was!

Tom looked at us sympathetically and, realising that we tended to fly by the seat of our pants, offered to work up a written application for us. Ours was the first accepted by the fund. We were offered the choice between a grant, with the corporation owning a share of our programme, or a loan of $45,000. We chose the loan, even though the interest rate of 12 per cent seemed steep. (At that time, 6 per cent for a mortgage was at the high end of the scale.) Our repayments were to be made from the licence fees when we received them from the broadcaster.

Off the Beaten Track was about to become a reality. Our first task was to equip ourselves for three years on the road. We took out a further loan and bought two new Land Rovers, and organised sponsorship support that provided us with two new caravans, especially modified for editing. Bit by bit we accumulated everything we needed, including generators, lighting gear and a 4-metre dinghy. The vehicles were overloaded, but somehow we crammed everything in.

•

For the first episode we chose something close to home. We'd navigate 115 kilometres down the Colo River, from the old abandoned shale-oil mining town of Glen Davis to where it joins the Hawkesbury River. We decided to use inflatable rubber rafts and paddle them by hand. Laraine and

I would take a small yellow one, bought from a camping store, and Mike and Pat would use a bigger Zodiac.

Several months of planning went into the trip. We limited our personal gear to 20 kilos each. No tents (saving weight; we'd use small groundsheets if it rained), no fresh water drums (the river was drinkable), no radio (who would we call? and too heavy anyway), dehydrated food (rationed out to last fourteen days), plus lots of optimism. The main bulk of our load consisted of cameras, film, a tape recorder and a hefty wooden tripod. In all it came to a staggering 115 kilos.

Sixteen millimetre film is very heavy stuff so, prior to setting off down the river, we took our vehicles into the rugged mountain country through which the water carves a canyon-like course. Our intention was to walk in to a point about halfway along our planned journey, find a cave somewhere in the sandstone cliffs and hide a cache of film. We'd camp overnight and retrace our footsteps the next day.

Brian, one of Pat's younger brothers, was a keen bush-walker and reckoned he could guide us into the Colo Gorge. We left our vehicles and set off through the rugged terrain. Brian led the way. There was no track and the country is extremely rugged.

Laraine had never been camping before, other than on Christmas holidays as a child, and that was in a 4- by 4-metre family tent, complete with stretchers and portable kitchen equipment. This would be a real test for her. She was now part of our team but, as a woman more at home in high heels and fashionable clothes attending

Saturday-night dances, she was being thrown in at the deep end to see if she could swim. She had the best new camping gear, though: bushwalking boots, a backpack and a highly efficient sleeping bag.

All was going well, it seemed, as Brian charged through the bush, employing his supposed knowledge of the area. As the afternoon progressed, rain began to drizzle down and the light was fading fast. Eventually Brian admitted that we must be in the wrong place, and it was only then that he produced his compass. He confessed he was lost. It was a hopeless situation, but it was now dark. We were on a sloping piece of ground and it was raining.

We opted to camp for the night. We'd be able to see more in the morning and, hopefully, find the deep gorge we were looking for.

In the drizzling rain we rigged up a couple of small army disposal groundsheets as fly covers and slipped into our sleeping bags. We lay directly on the ground, but the water invaded our space with rivulets of mud. To make matters worse, Laraine and I kept sliding down the hill. We were continually trying to get comfortable and drag ourselves back up. The shelter proved barely able to cover us.

In the morning, dishevelled, tired, saturated and fed up with our guide, we opted to abandon the plan. We found our way to the vehicles and drove back to Newcastle.

What an introduction to Laraine's new life in the great outdoors! If she could put up with that fiasco, she would do me. She must have thought us a bunch of hopeless idiots. To her great credit, she didn't complain at all.

A week later, when we finally set off on the snake-like river, as it wends its way downstream through canyons of fallen boulders, laughter echoed around the high bluffs. We were making a terrible job of paddling the inflatables. Without a keel or rudder, we were bumping into logs, grassy banks and rocks the size of cars. One minute the river would be shallow with a sandy bottom; the next it would be deeper and flowing reasonably fast through rock chokes.

Our progress turned from hilarity to hard grind. Rock bar after rock bar backed the water up into small deep pools, which then cascaded over rapids and dropped a few metres. We dragged our boats over these rocks while standing in the water, our legs scratched by sticks and submerged stones. At least the water was crystal clear, and the heat was made bearable by our continual dunking.

The rafts weren't handling the rough treatment too well. We were ripping holes in their floors almost every day, and using plastic strips and contact cement to repair them. When we came to the larger rapids, we had to unload every item and portage the gear around to the next pool with sufficient water to float the boats. Of course we had to film everything as we went, and that made it doubly difficult.

The serpentine course of the Colo River was slowly being conquered. Day by day we ate away at the challenge we had set ourselves. On our best days we tallied up 30 rock bars and rapids.

Laraine was holding up well; she and I made a good team. Our raft was lighter, but we also seemed to have a more co-ordinated paddling technique. As the days clocked up, we often found ourselves getting ahead of Mike and Pat, and we'd wait on sandbanks for them to catch up.

Much of the river was beautiful. Delicate maidenhair ferns fringed the banks, moss-covered rocks glistened with dew in the morning sun, and the delightful sound of tinkling bellbirds echoed through the low forests, while wallabies slaked their thirst in quiet, sheltered spots between the massive boulders. In all, it was a kind of paradise, and few had seen this canyon of red sandstone.

So far the weather had been sunny. As we progressed, there were fewer rock chokes and more long, still ponds. The filmmaking was going well.

Our diet of dehydrated food and rice, with dried fruit and soup made from foil sachets, was monotonous, but then Pat managed to catch a couple of bass using a handline and lure. They were a welcome change, appreciated by all of us.

Mike, though, had gradually become short-tempered and frustrated. I think he was worried there wasn't enough interesting stuff for the film. He also appeared to resent the fact that Laraine and I would paddle off effortlessly.

Then the magnificent sunny days turned to menacing grey. On a day towards the end of the journey, rain threatened. Laraine and I were quite a distance ahead of Mike and Pat. As we hadn't seen them for some time, I suggested we stop at the first suitable spot and make camp before the storm broke.

We found some large overhanging trees. Perfect. Here

we gathered up wood for the evening campfire and laid it in a pit of sand, as was our custom. We emptied out our raft, propped it up with the paddles and strung a ground-sheet from it as a kind of tent.

From the start I'd argued that we should all carry matches in waterproof containers, just in case we were separated. Mike had refused, insisting that he and Pat would carry them all: she was a smoker, so he was trying to make sure she didn't run out. Even matches had been rationed to keep the weight down.

The rain began to fall, but there was still no sign of Mike and Pat. Laraine and I were saturated to the skin by the time they pulled into the camp. Mike stepped off the raft and started up the bank.

Laraine, fed up with being cold and wet, yelled at him, 'Why can't we have some matches? We could have had a roaring fire by now.'

Mike looked dumbfounded, but he didn't reply. He acted like she hadn't spoken. Laraine, now furious, stepped forward and repeated her question, pushing him by his shoulders.

Mike, still holding his camera, stepped back. 'What's the problem with you?'

Laraine turned her back on him and walked off.

I explained that we'd set up the camp; all we'd needed were some matches, so he and Pat could have arrived to a lovely warm fire.

He was furious that Laraine should challenge him, and let fly with a mouthful of profanities. After so much hard manual labour, tempers were frayed.

Over time, of course, we cooled down and went about our camping chores. Then Laraine and I retreated to our makeshift tent, and Mike and Pat rigged up an identical set-up for themselves.

•

Fortunately the rest of the trip was pretty uneventful; well, Mike slipped on some rocks and cracked a rib, and I lost one of my Nikons in a deep pond.

This had been Laraine's baptism of fire. Or should that be water?

In spite of the hardships, bruises, cuts, scratches and frayed tempers, we all reckoned it had been a great experience. Laraine was now a fully initiated member of the team. For a city girl, she'd done well.

The film came together well too. We called it 'Ride the Wild River'.

As for every episode we made for Channel Nine, to get paid we had to present a rough-cut to an executive producer in Sydney in case further editing was needed. (A rough-cut is a black-and-white working copy with the completed soundtrack on a separate synchronised tape recording.)

Mike and I sat in his office in the 'hot seat' while he scrutinised every bit of our film. In the end he declared, to our great relief, that it was okay, and confirmed that we should proceed with the final colour print. We'd get paid when this print was checked and passed fit for transmission by the technicians.

However, he didn't think the film had lived up to the expectations we'd created with my persuasively written sales pitch. He felt it was 'a bit lame, but usable'.

The network put it on hold and waited until we could get the next episode shot and edited. It would need to be better, so we applied ourselves to come up with the most impressive adventure possible. We would challenge one of Australia's wildest places. One that could truly be described as off the beaten track.

14

Off the Beaten Track: a Successful Accident

Our second *Off the Beaten Track* episode took place on that wild triangle of land known as Cape York Peninsula, which stretches from Cooktown up to the Torres Strait at the northernmost point of the mainland. Back then the old telegraph maintenance track (4WD only and for the use of telephone linesmen) was the only way to the Cape, but recently it had been badly ravaged by the heaviest wet season rains in about ten years.

Our vehicles were set up with extra-wide flotation tyres. We left all unnecessary items behind, including the caravans, and headed off. We were eager to be the first to reach the Cape after the wet.

The journey turned out to be a 4WD thrash to the top over trenches and ruts big enough to swallow a car. The track was no more than a twisting, furrowed, liquid trail of mud. It was crisscrossed by washouts and flooded rivers.

We spent most days winching through obstacles and digging with our pitifully small trench shovels to rebuild washed out parts of the track. On occasions we had to bush-bash around impassable sections, and at one spot we built a log bridge to cross a huge gully. It was exceedingly tough on the vehicles, but even more so on all of us.

Laraine was amazed at where we took the 4WDs, but to my delight, she had a confidence in our ability to get through, based on her assumption that we knew what we were doing. Little did she know that this was the toughest and roughest off-road driving we'd ever taken on and there were 1120 kilometres of it.

In spite of the rough conditions, or perhaps because of them, we were getting a great yarn on film. We filmed plenty of wildlife, including freshwater crocodiles; we caught fish and yabbies in the creeks, and stopped at gold-mining ruins.

Eventually we reached the Jardine River, just 80 kilometres from the top. It was running about 2 metres deep and 150 metres wide. Not an easy obstacle! The bottom was sandy, and from soundings made in our dinghy, we determined that the deep section near the northern banks grew shallower after about three vehicle lengths. Waiting for the river to go down could take months.

Then we heard the approach of some other intrepid 4WD adventurers. We'd taken four and half weeks to reach the Jardine; taking advantage of our efforts to rebuild the road, they'd caught up with us just five days after leaving Cairns.

They were a great bunch of folks and one of them, Rod, was a qualified motor mechanic. So, how to cross the river?

We combined the winch ropes off all our vehicles to tow my Land Rover across. This towrope was stretched over the river and through a snatch block on the northern bank. Rod stripped my vehicle of its electrical instruments and then waterproofed the motor as best he could with dobs of grease. Another of our newly acquired friends attached the towrope from his vehicle to mine, then drove south from the riverbank, hauling my vehicle into the water.

Because we had several joins in the steel rope, it was necessary to pause every now and then to open the snatch blocks and pass the join through the wheel, before resuming the towing exercise. Luckily we had plenty of helpers.

Mike filmed from our boat with Laraine taking still pictures, while I stayed in my vehicle to try and steer it in the right direction.

In the shallow water all went well, but by the time I reached the deep section, an intensely strong current was pouring past. My vehicle dropped into the deep section and took off downstream, almost floating. The flat aluminium tray-top was acting like an aeroplane wing in the water.

'Drive faster!' was frantically yelled along a chain of onlookers to the driver of the tow vehicle, who sped up to about 25 kilometres per hour. My Land Rover took off and rapidly shot through the water.

In the cab I had about half a metre of air left. The dash-board was submerged, as was the motor. It was getting dangerous. Seeing the possibility of the vehicle being picked up and rolled over, I was ready to bail out.

With a mighty jolt, the car hit the steep northern bank and shot out like a leaping dolphin. About a ton of water poured out of the cabin as, heart-in-mouth and with blood pumping furiously through me, I tried to relax.

I was glad to hear that Mike had captured it all on film and Laraine had secured action stills!

Soon everyone involved, including our new friends, piled onto the back of my Land Rover to tackle the last 80 kilometres to the tip of Cape York.

Finally, we reached the rocky outcrop and stood gazing at the ocean. It was a triumphant moment for us all, and one we wouldn't have been able to achieve without the help of fellow adventurous travellers.

For Laraine it was particularly special. When she married me, she couldn't have imagined such a vastly different life. In spite of the hardships of roughing it in the bush, the biting insects and the heat, she often still refers to our Cape York journey as the best experience of her life.

•

It was obvious from our hard labour on the trek north that our small folding trench shovels weren't a good choice for excavating heavy trucks from bog holes. One of our newly acquired friends had a nice long-handled shovel with a pointed end slightly cut off. We borrowed it and found it perfect for the job.

When we asked him about it, he said it was called a 'number two rabbiter'. We all burst out laughing.

While in Cairns we dropped in at a big hardware store. This well-known trader sent supplies to cattle stations all throughout the north and the Pacific Islands. Among other things, they had a huge range of shovels and spades.

I walked up to the counter and approached the assistant. 'I'd like a number two rabbiter,' I said impassively, expecting to receive a blank response.

'Anything else?' he enquired, as he wheeled around and plucked one from the shelf, then slid it across the wide timber counter.

I was staggered. Apparently it was the proper name.

'Yes, please,' I managed to say without laughing, 'and I'd like another one.'

'Number two? Or a number one?' He held up a similar shovel with a narrower mouth.

'Number two, thanks.'

I suspected it was a Far North Queenslander expression.

The shovels proved to be great and travelled all over Australia with us over the next six years, digging us out of countless bogs.

Years later, when in Broken Hill, we'd left home without them. I wandered into a well-stocked hardware store and asked for a number two rabbiter. To my amazement, I was handed an identical replacement. It really is the proper name for these tools! Incidentally, we never used it for digging out rabbits.

•

When we presented our Cape York show to the Nine Network, we were greeted with unprecedented praise.

They chose it to be the first episode to go to air. We called it 'Trek to the Top', and the publicity department got right behind it.

Of all the 300 shows we made this one stuck in viewers' minds. When it first aired, it attracted a larger audience than anyone had anticipated. We had a rating of 43 over 60, meaning that 60 per cent of TV sets in the country were switched on and 43 per cent were watching our show. It was a massive result.

Buoyed by the success of the first few episodes, we returned to the road. We abandoned the caravans and spent the next three months travelling through the north, camping out in two-man tents. Our idea of filming all the inaccessible parts of our great country and bringing their stories to TV was a great challenge.

In the Kimberley we filmed the wild ways of life on remote cattle stations. This took a month. It was October and the Kimberley dry season was nearing its end. The humidity was around a hundred per cent and it was unbearably hot. Locals referred to this time as 'suicide month'.

Fortunately the property owners were very helpful and allowed us access to lots of places on their private land, so the episode was coming together well. We filmed the last sequence at a rodeo on Mount House Station: a rip-roaring affair with lots of folks from surrounding cattle stations gathering for three days. They used their own cattle for roping and riding, including some of their prize stud bulls.

Then we packed up our camp to get out before the wet season rains made this impossible. Electrical storms were lashing through the night skies every day, but so far the monsoon hadn't started in earnest.

Some property owners suggested we take a shortcut that had just been put in by bulldozer. It passed through rough country and had never had a vehicle over it, as it wasn't officially open, but it would eliminate a lot of backtracking. The owners pencilled a line onto our maps and we took off.

We soon discovered it was as rough as guts. The cut through the scrub was okay, but in the rocky, hilly country it was a track composed of loose boulders, some of which were more like steps.

I had a broken secondary leaf on the rear of my vehicle. This caused the left rear corner to sag badly every time we went over rough stuff. If the ground sloped to the left as well, the vehicle lent over further, with the front right-hand wheel lifting off the ground. It was a matter of gently easing the four-wheel drive over the rocks in the lowest gear possible. A hair-raising, heart-in-mouth experience!

We reached a particularly rough section of narrow track that cut across some diagonal strata: this was like driving up the steps of a building at 45 degrees. The right-hand wheel lifted off the ground for a few seconds while I backed off the throttle, and then continued to lift until the vehicle rolled onto its side.

Laraine was on the left. I came crashing down on top of her, along with loose items in the cabin, including our dog Gypsy and a small tomahawk. The axe missed Laraine's face by centimetres, slicing past her eyes and slamming into the steel bar on her sliding window. A slightly different angle and it could have been fatal.

We scrambled from the cabin. It was so hot that touching the vehicle was almost impossible. I ripped the bonnet open and removed the battery because acid was spilling all over the motor.

The heat was blistering. In the shade of a few small shrubs and still shaking from the accident, Laraine and I rested. We then unloaded our vehicle, which didn't appear badly damaged. Engine oil was running across the hot rocks, and the left-hand door and mudguard were dented, but otherwise all seemed intact.

Mike had been in the lead and in spite of our convoy travel rule of keeping an eye on the rear-view mirror, he'd driven on oblivious to our plight. When he and Pat turned up after almost half a day, Laraine and I were furious.

After a quick exchange of frayed tempers, we settled down to getting the vehicle back on its wheels. It was relatively easy, using a block and tackle plus a snatch block. We reloaded and took off slowly, with Mike vowing, and me insisting, that he would use his rear-view mirror more often.

How easy this would be today, with hand-held and CB radios. Dick Smith hadn't yet achieved his ambitions, and so such things were unavailable. Also, that track has now been fully developed into one of the main tourist roads of the Kimberley, known as the Gibb River Road.

'The Wild North West', as we titled this episode, became one of the best-loved of the series.

•

I don't have space to tell you about everything we filmed during the next three years, but there were some notable highlights.

In Tasmania we bushwalked the Overland Track, a hundred-kilometre trek over some of the world's most spectacular mountains. It wends through beech forests and rocky crags, beside sensational highland lakes and past some of the most picturesque waterfalls in Australia: a wilderness relatively untouched since it was first accessed by loggers years ago.

In that year, 1972, fur trappers' huts were scattered through the mountains. No longer in use by trappers, they were situated about one day's walk apart and made a welcome break from the long days of trudging with our heavy backpacks. We had to carry everything for the twelve-day trek including, once more, our cameras, film and sound-recording equipment.

This hike resulted in another of our most memorable episodes, but it was also a personal triumph for Laraine. She had a heart murmur from a valve damaged by child-hood rheumatic fever, which left her breathless whenever she exerted herself. Knowing of this disability, she always had to pace herself. To ready ourselves for the arduous trek, the two of us had engaged in a fitness programme months before leaving for Tasmania.

On the steep mountain country, some of which was akin to climbing, and on the long uphill slogs, Laraine had to stop and rest frequently. I stayed with her. It wasn't easy, but our magnificent surroundings made it worth the effort.

I took some of my best wilderness photographs on that trip and, to Laraine's credit, she managed to do something many people with 100 per cent fitness have not. It was a remarkable achievement by a woman who'd traded her high-heeled shoes for bushwalking boots.

•

We'd been intrigued by the Far North's wet season for years, so we decided to undertake an overland, and in part over-water, monsoonal journey. We would head through western Arnhem Land to Jim Jim Falls, which plummet a few hundred metres into a canyon. Millions of litres of water thunder over a cliff and then rise up in a fine mist when they crash on the rocks below.

Pat decided to stay behind with my young niece, Kerry, so for the first time our expedition consisted of just Mike, Laraine and me.

In those days the track was unsealed, so once more we found ourselves winching through sloppy goo and 4-metre-high spear grass. Getting bogged in custard-like mud and camping in sticky black muck was just as diffi-cult as we'd imagined, but we persevered.

Eventually we reached the South Alligator River and established a base camp. Here we launched our 4-metre boat, planning to reach the falls by travelling upstream against the strong flow of floodwater.

The heat was in the forties and the humidity a steady 100 per cent. The mosquitoes weren't as bad as in the dry season, but still made us uncomfortable. Laraine just about lived in her bikini, and the storms were so intense that Mike and I occasionally took showers by standing out in the rain with a bar of soap.

When we set off to reach the falls we had plenty of fuel on board, but against such a strong current it was consumed fast. We spent hours in vast flooded swamp country, trying to work out where the river course was: the trees that lined the banks were mostly submerged.

A lot of guesswork mixed with careful map and compass navigation brought us at last to the roaring rapids of Jim Jim Creek. These however were flowing too fast for us to proceed. Our fuel was too low. We tried to walk, but the distance was going to beat us. So we returned to our camp, disappointed and with hardly any fuel.

To complete the film we hired a helicopter from Darwin. The pilot flew Mike and me towards the base of the falls, but as we got closer, the massive downward thrust of water created a dangerous situation. My brother and I leapt out onto a sandbank and the pilot headed downstream. Much lighter, he was only just able to get airborne, almost skimming the treetops.

The plan was for us to walk the remaining several hundred metres to the base of the falls, get our filming done, and then climb to the top of the escarpment. The pilot would land there and wait.

The initial walk was tough enough, but once we reached the falls it was like being underwater. With the air so full of water vapour, it was difficult to breathe. To film or take still pictures, we each had to whip our camera out of a plastic bag, then grab a quick shot before wrapping it back up again. Cleaning water from the lenses was impossible; we did the best we could.

Hoping we had enough decent shots, we scrambled back over boulders the size of buildings, working our way downstream. The roar from the falls was so great our bodies were shaking. I could feel the soundwaves thumping against my chest.

After an hour, we reached the section of the canyon where we were to start our climb to the top. It was arduous and energy-sapping in the heat, but after about 40 minutes of climbing, we made it.

The flight back to Darwin was uneventful apart from having to skirt around a large electrical storm.

What made the trip so memorable was experiencing the wet season in the wilds of one of the most remote regions in the world. Today it's part of Kakadu National Park. I'd been able to share it with Laraine and, although it was uncomfortable, it was also unforgettable. Of course, having the love of my life running around in a skimpy bikini for about a month wasn't too hard to take either.

•

The cost of making the programme was creeping ever higher with each episode. A couple of the original story ideas were abandoned in favour of cheaper options, but most of the time we were able to keep the standard up.

For one exceptional episode we undertook a trip across the Simpson Desert, repeating our 1966 crossing but this time along a road using Honda motor tricycles: an eight-day jaunt from the western side of the desert at Oodnadatta to Birdsville in the east. Compared to the earlier trip, this was expected to be a breeze, although we did have to bring two Land Rovers to carry supplies and equipment.

By 1972 there was a road known as the French Line that followed roughly the border between the Northern Territory and South Australia. It had been cut through by French seismic crews searching for oil. In the early seventies hardly anyone knew about it, but today it's used as the only road across the desert, which has become a national park.

The trikes handled the dunes without any trouble. The problem came with the four-wheel drives. They were continually getting bogged in the live, moving sand on top of the dunes.

Pat drove Mike's vehicle, with young Kerry as a passenger. Laraine drove mine, which was capable of carrying all three of the trikes if needed, and also carried all the fuel. In the episode we didn't include my Land Rover at all: it appeared that Laraine only rode her bike. In reality, although she rode it a lot of the time and was often doubling back, only Mike and I rode all the way to Birdsville.

Our greatest drama began when my vehicle became bogged on the soft crest of a sand ridge while Laraine was driving. It looked like we'd have to winch it over the top using Mike's vehicle as an anchor.

My brother charged up the ridge on foot, demanding that Laraine get out of the driver's seat. He took over, revving the hell out of the engine. Then, slipping the clutch, he changed gears from forward to reverse in quick succession. This technique can work in mud, as long as it's not too deep, but with the chassis touching the sand, the wheels simply dug deeper trenches.

Eventually a horrible burning smell filled the air, along with lots of swearing from Mike. We had to winch the Land Rover off the dune.

After we let it cool down, I made an inspection. The clutch plate looked burnt to cinders. As the day wore on, I removed the gearbox to gain access to the clutch. Using a file, I cut grooves into the charred plate, then smeared it with contact cement and coated that with sand. It looked like the roughest sandpaper ever made but, if we could get it back together, I thought it would work a few times.

Although the vehicle took off a bit too rapidly, as if the clutch had been dropped suddenly, it did drive. Unfortunately, it didn't last long. A couple of dunes and we were in the same predicament.

Once more I stripped out the gearbox, then we used the radio to make a call to Pecky, the owner of Oodnadatta's general store and a bush pilot. Prior to the trip, we'd made arrangements for him to fly over our anticipated course if he didn't receive news that we'd reached Birdsville within ten days.

Our call went to the Flying Doctor base station in Alice Springs. I gave our latitude and longitude, and the nature of our spare-parts needs but, just as I was reaching the end of the call, the radio went on the blink because the output valve had overheated. We had no idea whether the message had been understood.

At least we had the second Land Rover. If nothing happened in a few days, we would abandon my vehicle and carry on to Birdsville with the other one and the bikes. Luckily it rained, so we caught some water running off the lean-to tent on Mike's vehicle.

Two days later, Pecky flew over our camp. He circled once and then dropped a parcel out his side door onto the soft sand on top of the nearest ridge. We grabbed it, tore it open and found a sparkling new clutch plate wrapped in frozen steaks.

We signalled 'thumbs-up' but, unsure if he knew our radio was defunct, I ran to the top of the dune and scribbled 'RADIO OUT' in large letters in the sand.

Pecky circled once more and then, to our amazement, took off east and not west back to Oodnadatta. Within ten minutes he was back over the camp and pointing frantically to the east.

Mike and I sped east on our bikes. After about 10 kilometres we reached a flat claypan, with Pecky's Cessna parked down one end. He had drums of fuel and water for us on board. After a quick discussion, he took to the skies while my brother and I returned to our camp. We had agreed that if we didn't reach Birdsville within a week, Pecky would fly back over our route.

I spent most of the night fitting the new clutch by the light of a hurricane lamp. The job would have been near impossible in daytime temperatures, which soared to the high 30s.

All went well after that, except for a ferocious dust storm that flattened our camp one night and half-buried the bikes.

Finally we arrived at Birdsville and sent a telegram to Pecky in Oodnadatta:

MISSION ACCOMPLISHED

The episode, 'Sea of Sand', was generally well received, although a couple of critics accused us of setting up the dust storm and the radio breakdown!

•

Off the Beaten Track was bleeding us dry financially. The costs were rising, so we asked Nine for a slight increase in the licence fee.

'No way!' I was told by the station manager in no uncertain terms. 'A deal is a deal, so manage with the money you agreed to.'

We were being paid $12,000 per episode: we asked for an additional $1500, or just $500 each for the final three. After all, costs had risen in three years, but our pleas made no difference.

We almost went broke making that first TV series, but we managed to pay back every cent we'd borrowed from the Australian government, including the interest, and came through it ready to tackle something new.

Our viewers loved the series, and now we were a family show. The inclusion of our wives and children became a hallmark of our programmes. We were, after all, an average family, but doing what most people only dreamed of.

15

Behind the Scenes and Another TV Series

One day in 1971 I called George Sample's Sydney office. I was told that he no longer worked at the company and that his son, John, had taken over. I was astonished but soon discovered that this had occurred due to some kind of forced takeover within the family company structure. I called George at home. He came across as a shattered man who could barely believe what had happened. We would need to deal with John from now on.

Our agreement with George had been a handshake: although the draft of a written agreement was typed up, it had never been signed. Now John was insisting that he owned everything, including our camera and production equipment.

It all came to a head when we received notice that a dispute was to be heard in the equity court in Sydney.

Sample Electronics, the company George had used to loan us the original $15,000, was claiming that Mike and I were simply employees. What a lot of rot!

A close friend, Wal Payne, who had been our business adviser and manager for several years, attempted to negotiate, but ran into a brick wall. We ended up briefing a solicitor in readiness for the day in court. I couldn't believe it had reached this point. We were advised to go to court and argue our case. What a ridiculous situation! The only people to make money out of that would be the legal fraternity.

I took matters into my own hands and tried to make contact with John Sample. According to our solicitor it was unethical for me to talk directly to him: because litigation was now in progress, only lawyers could talk to lawyers. Undeterred I persevered until I had John on the phone.

As soon as he found out it was me, he said, 'Sorry, I can't talk to you. This is in the hands of the legal people now. We'll have to sort it out in court.'

I wasn't going to be fobbed off that easily. I said that we were all intelligent, civilised people. Surely we could get together, talk things through and work something out. The lawyers were the only ones who were going to gain from this. Finally John relented and agreed to see us the following week.

We gathered in his boardroom. On one side of the long, highly polished mahogany table sat Mike, our advisers and me. On the other side were John's two lawyers, his accountant and John himself. We got down to business.

I reminded John that although the agreement between his company and us remained unsigned, it had been prepared by his father and its intent was obvious. We recognised that his company had a one-third interest in the equipment we had bought and the films we'd made during the five-year period of our association.

The next half-hour went slowly. John maintained that Mike and I worked for Sample Electronics and that the company owned all our equipment.

'So where are the tax records showing Mike and Mal as employees? Where are their group certificates?' Wal asked.

They all looked stunned. A quick huddle and a shrug of the shoulders.

John suddenly burst out with: 'Right, let's sort this out right now! How much are you suggesting is a fair amount to settle this thing once and for all?'

'Six thousand dollars,' we said, presenting him with a sheet outlining how we'd come to that figure.

'Good, then that's the end of it,' he responded.

'Only one problem,' I added. 'We don't have the money, so we'll need to organise a bank loan or something. How much time can we have?'

'Forget the loan. Just work out a payment scheme with my accountant over, say, five years. How does that sound?'

'At what interest rate?'

'No interest. Just 60 monthly payments. Okay?'

Okay? It was generous.

What a turnaround. 'See you in court' one minute; all sorted the next.

A big lesson here. I've never known a dispute that couldn't be worked out with sensible discussion and hard facts. Compromise is needed, of course, but, with goodwill on both sides, a settlement can always be reached. Perhaps the problems in the Middle East are an exception.

•

Mike and I added a second string to our bow, employing a bloke from Melbourne to screen *Open Boat to Adventure* in school halls. This worked so well that we hired more people, arming each of them with a projector, screens, blackout material and a film print. We called it Leyland's School Screening Service, and by the mid-seventies it was earning more than we were making from television.

Laraine and I moved out of the small flat we'd shared since our newlywed days, and bought our first home in Newcastle, a modest three-bedroom house.

I'd been taking lots of pictures of my wife and, believing she had what it takes to be a model, suggested she try a modelling course. She completed one in Newcastle and a second in Sydney at the famous June Dally-Watkins model school.

After that, she got work doing fashion parades and then, with the help of a few advertising agencies, some TV and newspaper jobs came her way. In no time she was earning more than I was getting out of my partnership with Mike. I encouraged her to pursue her career, and over the next couple of years it grew and grew.

She excelled at it. I would front up at parades, sometimes in large shopping centres, just to see her strut her stuff. She was good at photographic modelling, but she enjoyed the catwalk most of all. From shy and lacking in confidence, to swishing around in the latest fashions; a remarkable transformation.

Meanwhile, filmmaking needed to progress, but Mike and I were running out of wild places that could genuinely qualify as *Off the Beaten Track*. So we decided to make a new series with three episodes per year. We called it *Trekabout*.

We negotiated a better licence fee from the Nine Network, as well. The six episodes covered a variety of subjects, including two exceptional ones that focused on wildlife: one featured Australia's birds of prey and another was on the animals of Tasmania.

Then we received an unusual request. We were contacted by Stein Frich, a Norwegian glider pilot who'd seen *Wheels Across a Wilderness* and wanted to do the same thing in his glider: fly right across Australia from west to east. We agreed to pay all the costs, as long as we had the film rights for the expedition.

It was a huge logistical exercise, of course. The time for the trip was estimated to be six weeks. We planned to use a trailer to transport the glider to Western Australia, and to recover it if Stein needed to land unexpectedly. But we had a problem: there were two other pilots as well as Stein to share the flying. We only had two vehicles and really we needed three. By now we'd ditched the Land Rovers and were using Jeeps, which were smaller but more powerful and less prone to breakdowns.

Mike suggested we leave our wives behind. I protested strongly. I felt the family element of our shows was part of their appeal; besides, the girls were getting more fan mail than we were. He didn't think it mattered this time. In the end I gave in and was separated from Laraine for six weeks.

There's no denying the exercise was interesting. We would launch the glider from paddocks and bush tracks using a long nylon rope, then drive off until we reached 80 kilometres per hour with the rope coiled up on the ground. Like an elastic band, it whisked the glider into the air at an extreme angle. This is known as a reflex launch, and a good one can flick a glider up to 600 metres. The pilot circles around to find hot rising air, then circles in this air until he reaches about 2000 metres and glides off in the direction of travel. In our case, to the east.

We cheated, though. It was impossible to complete the undertaking in the time we'd allowed, so we used the trailer to cover hundreds of kilometres of boring country by road with the glider in tow.

An unforgettable part of the trip was when we dropped in at Maralinga, the ghost town in the middle of the South Australian desert where thirteen atomic bombs were exploded by the British military in the 1950s. At that time it was a military base, the land having been ceded to the United Kingdom for the tests.

In the seventies there was still a huge airstrip, but it was disused, with weeds protruding from cracks in the bitumen. The hangars were like a fully fitted-out workshop that had been abandoned overnight. Wind whipped down the streets of the town, blowing roly-poly tufts of grass.

When we got there, Maralinga had one resident: the caretaker. Every day he'd start up the huge diesel generators in the power shed to keep them in working order. He also took us on a tour of the place, including the test sites where the bombs had been exploded. The ground was barren. No vegetation at all!

Maralinga had the spooky atmosphere of how the world might look after a nuclear war has destroyed humankind. The empty chapel (with prayer books still on the pews), the huge mess hall (with tables and chairs in neat rows), the rust-filled swimming pool and the beautifully equipped cinema (with a strip of film dangling from the projector) all contributed to the *Day after Doomsday* feel. I was pleased to get away from the place.

When we landed the glider on the beach in Wollongong, the journey was over and so too was the charade that we'd glided all the way across the country. I was only too pleased to return to Newcastle and into the arms of my darling wife. The resulting film turned out to be very popular but the truth of how we had claimed it was the first continuous glider flight was never revealed; until now.

•

'Journey to an Inland Sea', a documentary in the *Trekabout* series, depicted a four-wheel-drive journey from Ayers Rock to Lake Eyre in South Australia. Laraine was heavily pregnant at the time.

At the beginning of the filming we had an upsetting experience when camped overnight at an abandoned goldmining town east of Alice Springs. We were the only people there and so we set up our two tents and the Jeeps in a circle, like a ring of wagons in the American west.

We were especially cautious because there had been an incident in Alice just a few weeks earlier. A group of drunken Aboriginal men had attacked a woman on a street at night and savagely raped her. This incident had the whole town so tense, it was like an explosion waiting to happen. We'd heard all this in gory detail while we'd been in Alice stocking up for our journey south to Lake Eyre.

In the middle of the night, we were awakened by a vehicle approaching. Who would be coming out to a dead-end track at 3 a.m.?

Soon the vehicle stopped right next to our tents. The air was filled with the sound of inebriated Aboriginal men swearing and yelling at the top of their lungs.

'It's a whitey camp!' one of them slurred. 'Let's wake 'em up and thump 'em.'

It sounded as though there were six to eight of them. I grabbed our number two rabbiter, which was just near the tent door. If they came near me or my wife, they would wish they hadn't!

We waited in silence, hoping they would leave. Then Sandy, Pat and Mike's youngest girl, who was about eighteen months old, woke up because of the noise and started crying. It was obvious we were awake, so Mike yelled out from his tent, 'Shut up, you lot. You've woken the baby.'

I yelled back, 'Yeah, keep it down or you'll wake up the other blokes.'

We started up a back-and-forth banter, trying to give the impression that there was a whole bunch of us. We disguised our voices to convince the intruders there were plenty of angry blokes about to come out and take them on. They then called out that they needed oil for their Land Rover.

'We haven't got any,' I yelled back. 'Now piss off and leave us be!'

One of their crew, obviously not as drunk as the others, said to his mates, 'Leave 'em alone. They've got kids.'

The engine started up and they drove off. Then Mike and I charged out of our tents and both of us stood listening to the sound of the vehicle as it bumped down the track. After a few minutes, we could hear it was bogged in sand and the motor was being thrashed.

Eventually it went quiet, but my brother and I stayed up until dawn, patrolling the camp with our number two rabbiters, like something out of *Dad's Army*.

The next day we set off early. We saw their passed-out bodies scattered all over the side of the track, next to the hopelessly bogged vehicle. Only one man managed to sit up and stagger to his feet as we drove by.

•

Six weeks later, in August 1975, back in Newcastle, Laraine gave birth to our daughter, Carmen. The arrival of our child was naturally a big event for us, but, because Laraine had the heart murmur, it was potentially dangerous for her.

About two weeks short of full term, Laraine was with her obstetrician for a routine check-up when she had a fainting spell due to a sudden blood-pressure fluctuation. The obstetrician, well aware of her heart condition, booked her into the hospital the next day, and he and two heart specialists commenced the induction process.

It ended up taking all day, with nurses and doctors popping into the delivery room every fifteen minutes or so. Apparently this was an extremely long time for such a delivery. Eventually the contractions started, but Laraine was so dosed up with gas she was off on another planet. The contractions became more frequent; I was by now recording the information for the nurses, but I was getting extremely hungry because I hadn't left the room in eleven hours.

The head nurse suggested I grab a bite to eat. The contractions were still well spaced out, she said, so nothing was likely to happen in my absence.

There was no canteen at the hospital, so I drove to Mum's house, about twelve minutes away, where she had a roast dinner waiting for me. I scoffed it down and wanted to go back, but she delayed me by asking lots of questions and plying me with cups of tea.

When I did arrive back at the hospital, the nurse on duty outside the delivery room said, 'Oh, Mr Leyland, I'm so sorry.'

The blood drained from my face and I nearly dropped to the floor.

'No! No!' she cried. 'Nothing's happened to your wife. She's had the baby. Sorry you missed the birth.'

The nurse tried to stop me, but I was too quick and pushed past her into the room. Another nurse was busy cleaning up the afterbirth, which she covered up like it was a dead body. I rushed over to Laraine and gave her a huge hug. She was indeed all right, but couldn't remember the birth. All I wanted was to hold her.

The nurses were looking amused, then one of them spoke. 'The baby is fine. It's a girl, by the way. Would you like to see her?'

'Oh yeah, I suppose so. Where is she?'

After a few minutes more with Laraine, I was taken to look at the baby. Carmen was, without doubt, the best-looking child in the nursery; and that's the unbiased opinion of the father, right?

Laraine was badly affected by the birth. For the next six months she couldn't even carry Carmen in her little bassinet, so I did this. In time, Laraine recovered her fitness, but doctors explained that another pregnancy would be increasing the already high risk to about a hundred times that for an average woman.

We decided we'd got it right the first time and considered ourselves lucky to have Carmen. I was also lucky to have Laraine: I would have been shattered if I'd lost my lovely wife and had to raise Carmen on my own. We reckoned we had a nice-sized family. No more children for us.

16

The Show
Nobody Wanted

'No one will bother to write you any letters. You'll have to fake them,' declared Len Mauger, the network programme buyer for the Nine Network.

Mike and I had just presented an idea for a new programme. We called it *Ask the Leyland Brothers*: it was an idea inspired by an American show, *You Asked for It*.

The concept was simple. Viewers would write in and ask us to film whatever subject they nominated, and we would travel anywhere in Australia to do so. This would result in a series of five-minute segments and make up a half-hour show.

The American series was hammed up with an obnoxious presenter, but the content was often interesting and the viewers were doing the research. Our approach would be more laidback: Mike and I would do the presenting, filming and editing, while our wives would act as camera operators and sound–recordists.

We'd run out of adventurous places to go to, and we were ready to gear up our production and churn out 26 programmes in one year, rather than our usual three. We needed to make some proper money. Our wages were low to average.

Len, however, didn't reckon it was much of an idea. 'Give us more shows like *Off the Beaten Track*,' he told us. 'Don't change what's worked well, boys. We just want more of the same.'

The idea for *Ask the Leyland Brothers* had come out of a discussion between Mike and me some five months earlier. I'd suggested we could make a programme like *Weekend Magazine*, a fifteen-minute show on ABC-TV that featured in–depth short subjects from all over the country. By copying the viewer involvement of requests from the American programme, we felt it would be like *Weekend Magazine* but by request. However, for it to work the show needed to air every week. It had to have continuity.

Mike argued that this was impossible. People would expect to see their letters read out the week after they sent them in. Besides, how the hell were we going to film so much stuff?

He had two good points there, although we ended up convincing ourselves that the first didn't matter. Filming so much material, however, was still an issue until I made a radical suggestion.

We'd been using tape recorders for sound and 16mm cameras for images. Some cameras, like the ones used for news, now recorded both sound and film. We could switch to this method and put the original film directly to air: cheaper, faster and more efficient. If we split into two teams we could double our output.

It isn't widely known that our partnership was under great strain at this time. Mike would come to work at our editing rooms and complain to me that he and Pat weren't talking. I'd noticed she would go into prolonged periods of sullen silence when we were travelling together, but I'd put this down to the fact that she didn't really want Laraine and me there at all. Until Mike started complaining to me that this was happening all the time at home, I hadn't realised there was more to it.

Mike would vent his frustration and I'd listen intently. A sounding board was all he needed, and I was it. He would say, 'I have to decide between my marriage and our business partnership.' He told me that Pat couldn't stand the fact that both our families were 'in each other's pockets'. Usually in a few days it would blow over and all would return to normal. I'd seen this happen many times.

Now I took the opportunity to point out that with this new show we'd be filming as two units with Mike and Pat alone together, just as she wanted. We'd organise our own travel arrangements, edit our own films and only get together to compile the programmes. We'd all contribute to every show, but the viewers need not know who was filming what.

Mike could see the merit in this: it seemed a practical solution to the amount of filming we'd need to get through, and it would keep some sense of harmony going.

It did, however, require a major investment in some very expensive cameras.

At this point, I made a suggestion I knew Mike would oppose.

•

For Christmas one year, I'd bought Laraine her own AGFA 8mm camera. She loved it and started shooting little home movies of our trips. I played around with it a lot myself, and we ended up with plenty of typical picnic and Christmas Day footage. I'd noticed how remarkably good the quality was.

Our TV programmes used a negative from the original 16mm film we were using at this time: a second-generation copy went to the TV station for broadcast. I reckoned the original 8mm film from our home movie camera was as good as the prints we were sending to the network. To prove it, I shot some scenes using both techniques and set up a demonstration in our own theatrette for Mike to view. He agreed, but couldn't see the point of the comparison.

I explained we could use 8mm film with cheap sound cameras and save heaps. Predictably, he was appalled. After seeing my demonstration, he couldn't claim it wouldn't be good enough for broadcast, but he was nonetheless concerned that Channel Nine wouldn't buy it.

'Don't tell them,' I urged him. 'We'll transfer the film to broadcast videotape and they needn't know how we shot it.'

'No way!' Mike shouted. 'I'm not running around with a toy camera like that. That's for amateurs.'

My plan was that we'd buy better ones, with sound-recording systems and good lenses. Our discussion ended with my suggestion that I buy a high-quality super 8mm camera with a professional lens.

Mike and I took this gear to Central Australia and filmed a test story at the Pichi Richi outdoor bird sanctuary, just south of Alice Springs. Mike was unfamiliar with the camera and many of the controls were automatic. He was all thumbs, reckoning the switches and buttons were too tiny. At one point, he almost refused to keep going. He even belted the camera with his fist, breaking the handle off it. The camera was a mess and he hated it, but the film was shot.

Back home the sound and picture quality were outstanding. Mike reluctantly agreed that it might be good enough.

We knew the show would need to be on air every week in a half-hour format. I worked out a budget for 26 episodes and it was this presentation we put to Len in Sydney. We now had a good idea and a practical method of filming it, but no buyer. What to do?

•

Our two earlier series had been sponsored by Caltex Oil, so we knew the PR man there, Mark Farmer. I phoned him and organised a meeting in his office in Sydney, where I explained how *Ask the Leyland Brothers* would work. He liked it.

'So what's the problem?' he asked.

I explained how Channel Nine didn't reckon anyone would write in, but that we already had plenty of unsolicited letters from viewers suggesting things to film. Surely if we asked them to write in, we'd have no trouble filling a show with interesting stuff. Our viewers would do the research for us. They'd get to hear us read their letter out and have their name on TV. It had to work!

'I agree. So how can I help?' he asked as he sucked on his pipe.

In preparing for this meeting, I'd made a lot of phone calls and obtained a copy of Nine's advertising rate card. I now presented a case to Mark for Caltex to sponsor the show. They'd get an opening and closing billboard, plus ads in every break, and have exclusive advertising rights to the show. I didn't know how much of a discount they'd get for buying such a large number of shows, while the cost to them would be in the millions. In effect, I was acting as a salesman for Nine without their authority or knowledge.

Mark Farmer considered my carefully presented written proposal in detail.

'This is a lot of money and it all goes to Nine. How will you boys make anything out of it?' he finally asked.

'They'll pay us for broadcast rights,' I replied. 'The same as usual.'

He was sceptical that we'd actually make this number of shows in one year, but I told him I was sure we could. In truth, I didn't really know.

We left our presentation with him. About a week later, he advised that he would be willing to sponsor half of it.

We'd need a second sponsor to share the cost. Find one and we had a show.

Who could be co-sponsor? We reckoned the ideal timeslot for the programme would be 5.30 p.m. on a Sunday, just before the six o'clock news. Who wants to reach that audience at that time of day? We came up with Cadbury Schweppes: they flogged chocolate in the winter and soft drinks in the summer. Ideal.

After much chasing and lots of phone calls, I reached the man in charge of their advertising department and put our case. He liked it and agreed to be half sponsor.

Now, armed with letters of intent from both sponsors, we fronted up to Channel Nine once more.

'This is the same programme idea we rejected before. I told you to come up with something else,' Len protested.

'I know it's the same, but *this* is different,' I replied, sliding the letters across the table.

He picked them up and read them carefully. He looked astonished. 'How did you manage this?'

'It wasn't easy, but, as you can see, it represents millions of dollars for your network, and your advertising department doesn't have to do a thing.'

Len was curious as to how we'd arrived at the rates. When I confessed that we'd used their rate card, he was not amused. 'You had no authority to represent our network like that,' he said sternly. 'We may have been in delicate negotiations with Caltex, and this could have upset things.'

He was also dubious that we could make 26 shows per year given our previous output. When we explained we'd be using new cameras and handing over ready-for-broadcast tape, he wondered whether we had costed it properly. I assured him we could make each show for $6000.

'That seems a bit low,' he said, surprised. 'Are you sure you haven't missed anything?'

'Well, perhaps another $500 per episode would help a bit.'

'Go home, boys, and double-check your costs. Then get back to me and I'll have our legal department draw up the contract.'

In the end we were paid $6500 per episode and the network had the right to play them three times each. Caltex came through, and when Cadbury Schweppes pulled out at the last minute, Nine had no trouble replacing them.

To produce the programme using 8mm film, we had lots of technical challenges to overcome. Convinced the savings were worth it, we worked our way through a series of tests in readiness to tackle our huge task.

Twenty-six episodes per year: the prospect was exciting and daunting at the same time. We had talked the talk. Now we had to walk the walk.

17

Interactive TV?
Ask the Leyland Brothers

To launch *Ask the Leyland Brothers* we made a pilot episode. This consisted of several short subjects. Nine agreed to air the pilot show in its anticipated timeslot. In it, we asked our viewers to write to us with any ideas for inclusion in the series. We also took out a full-page advertisement in *TV Week*, in which Mike and I made a request for ideas.

The pilot went to air and a week later we turned up at the post office to see if we had any mail. Nothing! The steel box was empty.

Almost. Lying on the bottom was a small handwritten note: 'Please go to the front counter of the post office.'

Mike and I discovered that, far from having no mail, we had masses of it! We were handed three huge canvas post bags brimming with thousands of letters.

'We couldn't fit them in the box, fellers,' the bloke behind the counter told us.

So much for Len's predictions of doom. In fact, *Ask the Leyland Brothers* became the most successful show we ever made. We produced 230 episodes, the last of which went to air sixteen years after we got the go-ahead.

The Provost Brothers sang the catchy theme song which I recorded in our studio facility in Newcastle. Then we contacted one of the world's best exponents of the harmonica, Horrie Dargie. He listened to the tune and wrote about an hour of musical snippets: all variations on the basic theme song, in different moods and with different tempos.

The music was recorded in Sydney using a bunch of professional studio musicians. Many of the moods were created by the different instruments: timpani for drama, strident brass for action, soft clarinet for rainforests, and of course harmonica for the deserts. It cost a lot of money but it was a cheaper option than paying royalties on pre-recorded music. We got the whole lot for less than half the cost of the score for *Open Boat to Adventure*, and we were still using it sixteen years later, so the amortised cost against each show was extremely small.

Mike and I had a big difference of opinion over the vehicles to use in the show. I felt that, since most folks didn't own expensive four-wheel drives, we should do our travelling in conventional cars. I reckoned our average viewer could relate more to a Ford or a Holden. In the end, we settled on VW Kombi vans. These had plenty of clearance, and room to sleep when needed for camping;

they were low on fuel consumption and could handle outback tracks no problem.

So I'd talked Mike into two ideas: two-wheel drives and 8mm film. When it came to the latter, in the first year of production alone we saved $36,000 in film costs, compared with using 16mm film. In 1976, that was a hell of a lot of money.

Not only did we pioneer a cheap way of making TV, we also broke new ground by producing interactive contact with our audience. Our ratings grew rapidly. The show almost always won its timeslot.

Today I meet people who tell me they grew up watching our show every Sunday night. It was simple, honest and a family programme. What could be better?

•

After the hard grind of getting the show up, we now had to perform. The first trip Laraine and I took was to Victoria. We had letters asking for something to be filmed at every place we visited: Ballarat, Bendigo and parts of the Great Ocean Road.

Our day would start before dawn. Get ourselves and baby Carmen fed and on the road. Arrive at our anticipated story locations and film the segment. Return to a motel or camp in the Kombi, clean the cameras and pack up the exposed film to send to the lab. Write up all our notes on the day's work, use the phone to arrange the next day's travel and collapse into bed. Seven days a week with no time off. It was exciting and exhausting too.

Laraine and I were together, alone with our baby, and it was one of the most enjoyable memories I have. We chalked up thousands of kilometres and met some wonderful people. We had a privileged look at how artists worked and at all kinds of folks doing all kinds of things. It was the best mind-broadening experience one could hope for. We were welcomed wherever we went and no one ever made us feel like we were intruding, even though we often did to get the film we needed.

After six months of both teams filming all over the country, Laraine and I would work on how to assemble the episodes. We rated them as human interest, wildlife, action, adventure, sports, craft and weird. They also got a rating for their interest value: 'A' was the strongest; 'C' the weakest. To mix and match these stories we had a big whiteboard on the wall of my editing room.

Laraine tackled the job of juggling the stories so as to create the best balance in the episodes. This was a tricky job for which she had a natural talent. We needed to estimate the length of each story, so that became another factor in the juggling act.

As you can probably imagine, Laraine and I had no life outside our work and child. We were either filming in the field or back home compiling programmes, and Laraine also kept working as a model. I had to edit the final cut of each story we'd filmed to the precise second; Mike carried out the same task for his stories.

There were about 800 stories in the series. Some were amusing, some were dangerous, some were exciting; but all were, at least to us, fascinating.

The Leyland gang ready for another filming trip for our *Ask The Leyland Brothers* TV series. Left to right: Carmen, Laraine, Mal, Mike, Pat, Kerry, Sandy and Dawn.

Our orange Kombi was a home on the road for our family and over the years became somewhat of a Leyland Brothers icon.

Laraine (recording sound) and Mike (on camera) filming one of our camps for an episode of *Off The Beaten Track*. The series of 13 shows was filmed from 1971 to 1973.

I'm filming a segment for *Ask the Leyland Brothers* on Franz Joseph Glacier in New Zealand. Later that same day I came perilously close to losing my life.

Mike was never happier than when he had a movie camera in his hands. The track to the tip of Cape York Peninsular was scarred by monsoonal rains in 1971. I'm carefully picking a path through the washed-out gullies while Mike films our slow progress.

Laraine carries baby Carmen around the Warrumbungle Mountains in NSW along the Grand High Tops walking track. The papoose carrier was great for outdoor work when filming with the family as the crew.

Laraine and I tackling the rapids of the Colo River in the Blue Mountains in NSW (1971). This was Laraine's first filming trip and although she was more at home in high heels and a skirt, she adapted quickly to the rigours of the outdoor life.

Our first attempt to cross the Jardine River, North Queensland, in 1971 was a failure. Laraine, new to our team, must have thought us mad. The vehicle was brand new.

Laraine modelling country clothes. Taken at the height of her modelling career when she was not only doing fashion shoots and catwalk work, but was also training about 70 new models each year at her modelling school.

It cost more than a million dollars to build our Ayers Rock-shaped building at *Leyland Brothers World*. The construction was delayed almost a year due to wet weather.

Above, our big Ayers Rock is pictured during construction and, at right, when completed.

Me (left) and Mike with our Bush Basher six-wheel-drive vehicle. The circuit ride took patrons on a bush track through deep water crossings and over rugged and steep hills. It was enormously popular.

Building a home in the bush at Mount Mitchell near Glen Innes NSW. I felled the trees to mill the timber and constructed our house between the two shipping containers. The day I put the last of 62 stumps in the ground was a milestone in a project that was to take seven years.

Our stand-alone solar power shed stored the energy in batteries and kept the house and outbuildings supplied with 240 volt AC and was not connected to the power grid.

The house was far from finished for several years but the snows came every winter and at last we had a roof over our heads.

Laraine and me with half an hour's yield from our garden. There is nothing to compare with fresh, organically grown chemical-free produce.

Laraine and I are proud of what we managed to create: a simple, practical and cosy house. It was rustic but it was also a home made with our own labour and love. We called our property *Lara's Valley*.

Laraine and me in the Keep River National Park. The light was fantastic, the scenery spectacular, but I was now expected to live for no more than 18 months. I threw my watch away and stopped counting the days.

A new TV series offers the chance to claw our way back from financial oblivion. Carmen and Robert (left), joined me and Laraine to film a 26-part series titled *Leyland's Australia*. We all travelled around the country together with two caravans. It took three years.

Laraine and I with our granddaughters, Samantha (left) and Jasmine (right) at Lara's Valley during the spring harvest season.

Camping in style about 60 kilometres west of Cameron's Corner in big sand ridge country while on our way down the Strzelecki track 2012.

By the second year of production, Mike's family had expanded with the arrival of Dawn, his third daughter. The Kombis had to go. Too small. We used Ford F100 4WD trucks. Mike's had a canopy on the back tray that was set up with seats for the children. Mine carried a slide-on camper: Laraine and I loved the idea of having a self-contained comfortable unit like the Kombi, but bigger. Almost a motor home.

During those heady days of production we received thousands of letters. It was obvious from the comments that viewers related well to our families. They wanted to see as much of them as the places and things we filmed.

I encouraged Laraine to be in the films more. She'd walk into the shot and look at whatever we were filming; occasionally she made on-camera comments. On several shows I even talked her into narrating some of the stories. Mike and I were still the hosts, but our wives began to have a real presence. Our viewers liked this and fan mail poured in.

We broke the request letters down into regions. Simply categorising them into the states and territories wasn't enough: we had ten regions, including New Zealand. Mike and I would work out where we were going next, and then set off with the entire file for that area.

The business end of our activities was getting bigger. We'd expanded the School Screening Service and now had eleven representatives showing our films all over the country. Life was hectic and, on top of everything else, I was lumped with the responsibility of running the business. I hated paperwork, but Mike hated it even more; he simply took no interest in it.

I needed help to get through all the work, so we decided to employ someone to create a third filming unit. We approached Phil Lloyd, a director working at NBN Channel 3. Laraine knew Phil pretty well through her work as a popular model in Newcastle. He accepted our offer to join the production team.

We gave him an identical set of filming equipment and a vehicle. He filmed the 'B' subjects that didn't involve our being there on camera, like how to make mead, produce wooden toys and turn banksia nuts into ornaments. He would film outside the location and show our vehicle pulling up.

The scene where Mike or I read the letter was filmed after Phil returned to Newcastle. He'd find a suitable background to match the wide shot of the vehicle and, in a medium shot, we would step from the car, read the introduction and walk out of the scene. The illusion that we were there was perfect because Phil was a perfectionist who matched backgrounds and lighting carefully.

Phil worked with his wife, Margo, as a husband-and-wife team, just like us. Their work relieved our load, while viewers were unaware of a third team: Mike and I presented Phil's stories as our own about 50 per cent each. It made a big difference to our lives.

•

Before the third season started, Laraine and I organised ten weeks off and took an around-the-world holiday with Carmen. My parents accompanied us as we planned to have six weeks in England: they hadn't been back since 1950, 27 years earlier.

We'd been trying for years to sell our shows in the United States and United Kingdom, but still with no success. I was determined to give it a good go.

We hired a car in Los Angeles and drove to several potential buyers. We'd sent a beautiful rich red leather-bound presentation book to each of them, and this was to be an in-person follow up.

My highest hopes for selling *Off the Beaten Track* were with Screen Gems, the TV division of Columbia Pictures in Hollywood. At the appointed time, Laraine and I found ourselves seated in their programme buyer's office. He had our presentation book in front of him.

'I've looked at this,' he said with a smile, 'and I've also viewed two of the six films you sent me.'

So far, so good. What now?

'I'm sorry to say this to you but . . . if only your films were as good as this beautiful book, we would buy them.'

'What's wrong with the films?' I asked incredulously.

'You must understand that no one in this country gives a damn about Australia. Most don't even know where it is.'

'If you had no intention of buying them, why did you agree to see us?' I asked, somewhat pissed off to be hearing the same crap we'd received five years earlier.

He explained that the book was an excellent presentation and he didn't want to shatter my ego too savagely. He felt a compliment would soften the blow. 'In all my years in this job,' he explained, 'I've never come across anyone quite as determined and persuasive as you have been on all those phone calls. I just had to meet this brash young guy from Down Under.'

Wonderful! So this interview had been nothing more than his chance to satisfy his curiosity. He went on to explain that he'd probably lose his job if he aired our shows, because they didn't feature Americans. Nothing had changed. Whether it was Hollywood or New York, self-centred Yanks hadn't yet matured enough to realise that there was a world outside their country.

We'd planned to fly to the Big Apple, then on to Toronto. However, disillusioned with the American attitude, and because there was the threat of a pilots' strike that would have left us stranded, we headed straight for Canada, where we could catch a flight to London on a 747.

The five of us arrived at the airport early as instructed, because at the time terrorists were hijacking planes and blowing them up on airfields. Security was high and extra time was needed to get through the check-in.

When we reached the counter, the female check-in agent on the other side accused us of having too much carry-on luggage.

'No,' Laraine said, 'we have just one for each passenger.'

The agent was indignant. 'You have too many!' she insisted, raising her voice.

One of the things I love about my wife is that I always know where I stand with her. She has a feisty personality and a short fuse to go with it. This was the last straw after an early start to our day.

'Can't you lot count?' Laraine screamed. 'Look!' She picked up our hand luggage and threw it onto the counter.

Dad and Mum were most embarrassed. We were holding up hundreds of passengers, and Laraine was in full voice. I knew she'd sort it out, and besides, she was right. We had just one piece each.

By now the raised voices were causing quite a stir. A large crowd of disgruntled passengers had moved in closer to hear more. The check-in agent was sticking to her guns, while Laraine was counting our bags. 'One. Two. Three. Four. Five! Now where's the problem?'

'Five is the problem,' responded the agent and pointed to Laraine, me, Mum and Dad. 'You only have four people and four tickets.'

'Open your bloody eyes. The first thing I gave you were the tickets. If you took the trouble to count them, you'd see there are *five*.'

The agent now realised her error and burst out crying. In between sobs she told us she'd thought that Carmen, being only two years old, was going to be nursed and didn't have a ticket. She was inconsolable.

A PR man, dressed in an immaculate suit, arrived while she disappeared. This smooth-talking fellow with a strong French accent couldn't apologise enough. He organised our seating and even personally escorted us to our seats.

To our amazement, we found ourselves smack bang in the middle of the centre aisle. Two rows in front and two behind were empty. We were occupying an island of isolation!

The plane took off. Then, as soon as it began to level a little, our smooth-talking Frenchman appeared like magic, poking his head between Laraine and me.

'Is everything satisfactory?' he asked politely.

'Crikey, mate, what are you doing here?' I asked him.

'Oh! I sometimes jump on board to make sure things are running smoothly for special passengers.'

Special passengers. Was he talking about us?

'I've brought a bottle of our finest French champagne for you, madam,' he said, with the biggest smile he could muster, as he looked at Laraine. 'Our airline prides itself on its good service. Perhaps this will help you forget, eh?'

Of course, I don't drink, but Laraine had a glass of champers with Mum and we had VIP treatment for the entire flight. We stretched out over our rows of seats to sleep most of the way. Laraine's feisty nature comes in real handy sometimes!

In England we went back to Hitchin, where I had a chance to show off my 'bonzer Aussie sheila' to the relatives. Laraine and I went to London to do some business with potential film buyers, but spent most of the time being tourists. We drove up to Scotland and visited many places familiar to us from TV shows.

•

Once we got back, our first trip was a six-week run west through Broken Hill and up through the Strzelecki Track to Innamincka and Cooper Creek. Phil Lloyd came with us, making a tight squeeze in the slide-on camper. It was a training exercise for him: he needed to become familiar with the 8mm equipment and learn how we kept our travelling budget down to rock bottom.

By now the licence fee from Channel Nine had crept up a bit. Since we'd switched to 8mm film and the simpler editing gear, we'd moved our film post-production to our homes. Mike had a set-up at his place on Lake Macquarie, and Laraine and I used a spare bedroom.

Life was great. I finally had time for hobbies and bought a 1944 ex-army Jeep. I fully restored it and loved charging off into the bush. It was an escape from the daily routine of editing and office paperwork.

Laraine started up her own business, training young models. She developed an extensive course and conducted it from home. We used the double garage as a studio for still photography, and we filmed mock-up TV commercials. Working with Newcastle ad agencies, Laraine was getting plenty of work for herself and her models.

She had two diametrically opposed lives: the model and businesswoman, on one hand; the outdoors girl, travelling all over the countryside, on the other. She was good at both, but it took some juggling to fit it all in.

Laraine ended up buying and converting a commercial building. It had a front shop where she operated as a certified beautician; it also contained a well-equipped makeup room for up to sixteen students, plus a hall complete with stage, lighting, catwalk and seating for an audience of 60.

On top of all this, Laraine was a wonderful mother, and Carmen was a delight.

•

Mike and I took several trips each year to Channel 8 in Orange to convert our films to videotape. On one trip

I complained that the image quality didn't look as good as usual, but I was assured the equipment was set up properly.

We put together eight episodes on that occasion and soon we were off again, filming more shows. While we were away, I got an urgent message to call Len.

'That last batch of shows was no good,' he explained. 'Our engineers rejected them. All the shadows are too dark or something.'

'Oh! I thought it didn't look quite right. Don't worry, I'll contact Channel 8 and we'll redo it all as soon as possible.'

'We know what's wrong!' he exploded. 'Our engineer called their general manager and he said it wasn't anything to do with them, as you were using 8mm home movie film and we couldn't expect anything better.'

Bugger! The cat was out of the bag, but still the quality shouldn't have changed. Something was definitely wrong.

'Well?' he demanded. 'Is it true? Have you switched film?' I started to explain, but he quickly interrupted me. 'Why the hell would you do that in the middle of such a successful run? This could spoil everything.'

I had to explain everything. He could hardly believe it. In the end he tried to insist that we revert to 16mm equipment or there would be no more contracts.

I dug my heels in and refused. The cost would have blown the show out of the water, and anyhow, the ratings were what mattered. It was one of the highest-rating shows they had and won its timeslot every week. I added that to change to 16mm film would add a lot to their licence fee. Was he prepared to triple it? I knew they were getting a cheap, successful show, and he knew it too, of course.

In the end we reprocessed the faulty episodes. The problem had resulted from someone interfering with the projector at Channel 8. Lots of apologies all round and everything was forgotten. Business as usual.

We produced hundreds of hours of TV using 8mm film and, as far as I know, it's a world record. I'm proud of our success with this experiment.

Only one in ten feature films make a profit, but we never made a show that we couldn't sell: we made a profit on all of them. *Open Boat to Adventure* did eventually break even, after we sold it to Nippon TV and German television.

Not bad for a couple of pommy imports.

18

High Hopes,
High Ratings

Our filmmaking was earning us good money at last. Laraine and I paid off our mortgage by my 30th birthday and soon invested in 12 hectares at Coomba Park on the shores of Wallis Lake near Forster, north of Newcastle. Here we had a modest three-bedroom log home built, which became a weekender for Laraine and me. I wanted to start writing novels and thought it would be a quiet place to escape the pace of TV production.

Sadly, it didn't work out. Our lives were too busy. Whenever we organised a few days off work, we'd find that the weeds had grown thick or that the driveway needed grading. Most visits turned into working bees.

I began to toy with the idea of growing our own food, and started reading all kinds of books and magazines on self-sufficiency. The idea of living on a small farm in the country was my dream, not Laraine's. She was living her dream. Her agency was training about ten groups each year; she was running huge fundraising fashion shows and loving the success of what she'd built up.

•

Dick Smith, the highly successful 'Electronic Dick', as he billed himself, offered Mike and me the job of shooting some documentaries for him to sell to TV. He would fly around in his helicopter and call the series *Dick Smith Adventurer*. He made us a very generous offer.

'Name your price,' he said. 'I can afford it. I want the best and I consider you two to be the best.'

Dick said he loved the way we made our shows with our families; he liked our way of doing things. He dropped in by helicopter at our weekender, and he and his wife, Pip, joined Laraine and me in a lamb spit-roast.

Naturally Mike and I were flattered, but we declined on the grounds that we were building our own reputation on television. If we interrupted that for a few years, we might never regain our momentum when Dick's project came to an end.

However, we spent some time with him, discussing how he could film his shows and explaining our use of 8mm cameras. I suggested that he find a couple of filmmakers in Sydney and employ them, as anyone with experience could do a professional job. In the end he did exactly that.

•

On the 25th November 1979, I returned home to find Laraine looking perplexed and mischievous.

'What's going on?' I asked.

'This came in the mail,' she replied, handing me an envelope with a government crest on it and the words:

PERSONAL AND CONFIDENTIAL. For the eyes of Malcolm Leyland only.

Looking a little guilty, Laraine then produced another large buff envelope. 'It was inside this one,' she said quietly. 'Sorry.'

This envelope was addressed to me and marked confidential too, but she'd opened it. As I unfolded the letter, I wondered what it could be. It was headed 'Government House, Sydney', and I was astounded to read:

His Excellency the Governor has received advice that Her Majesty The Queen will be pleased to confer upon you the award of a Member of the Most Excellent Order of the British Empire (MBE) for services rendered. His Excellency desires to know whether you will accept this honour. Would you kindly telegraph me at Government House, as a matter of urgency, saying one word 'Yes' if accepted, 'No' if refused. The telegram should be addressed to Wills, Official Secretary, Government House Sydney.

You will appreciate, of course, that this information is strictly confidential and must be divulged to no one prior to the announcement of the New

Year Honours on Tuesday, 1st January 1980. I would emphasise that, in accordance with the practice adopted by the Foreign and Commonwealth Office, London, recipients should not accede to requests by representatives of the media or grant interviews or discuss the award prior to publication on the morning of Tuesday, 1st January 1980.

RNA Wills, Official Secretary

Needless to say, I sent off the 'Yes' telegram immediately. When I rang Mike, I learnt he'd received an identical letter.

Laraine and I invited my parents to spend the New Year weekend at our house on Wallis Lake. On New Year's Day we woke early and put the radio on high volume. The ABC news came on. When our names were read out as recipients of the MBE, Mum and Dad were overjoyed. It was one of the best surprises we could have managed. They were both very proud.

They accompanied us to Government House in Sydney on the 2nd May 1980, where Mike and I had our awards pinned on our chests by the governor-general. We were among some very worthy recipients and felt humble in their presence.

The most moving part of the day occurred when everyone spilled out onto the lawn. Hundreds of people, all dressed in their finery, were milling about and sipping drinks. The press took pictures for the weekend papers and the Royal Australian Navy brass band played music under the shade of some large fig trees.

When Mike and I emerged from the building where the ceremony had taken place, the band went quiet for a few seconds and then burst into a brass rendition of our *Ask the Leyland Brothers* theme song. They'd been rehearsing for weeks.

The dignitaries, recipients and their families gave a mighty cheer and applauded in appreciation when the band finished. It was one of the most moving moments of my life. Mum shed a tear, as did Laraine and I. Dad had a grin from ear to ear.

I turned to Mike. 'Never reckoned on anything like this, eh? When we were kids. Running around with your home movie camera.'

'Hard to believe, isn't it?' he replied with an emotional quiver in his voice.

It was the first time in the history of the order that two brothers had simultaneously received an honour.

•

Given my desire to try a self-sufficient lifestyle and Laraine's wish to continue her career in the city, we compromised and bought a property of 10 hectares at Seaham on the Williams River. This was close enough to Newcastle for Laraine to commute to her studio, while I could play at being a farmer. We sold the place on Wallis Lake and bought a small two-bedroom flat in the heart of Newcastle as our city home.

Our shows were continuing to rate well. However, although all the rights to *Off the Beaten Track* had reverted back to us, two episodes were still being broadcast all over the place by the Nine Network. The first time this occurred, Len Mauger apologised; he promised it wouldn't happen again and so we let it go; but it did happen again. Because I couldn't get hold of Len, who was travelling overseas, I spoke to the station manager at TCN–9 in Sydney.

'Don't worry, mate, it won't happen again,' he assured me.

'Heard that one before. Too late for that. You've run out of second chances.'

'Oh come on, Mal. It's an honest mistake.'

I then reminded him of something he himself had said to me ten years earlier. When the network refused to increase our licence fee for three episodes of *Off the Beaten Track*, he'd told me, 'A deal is a deal.' I asked him if he remembered that.

'That was different. This is just some idiot scheduling your show and not knowing it was out of contract.'

I wouldn't have a bar of that. I told him if they weren't willing to pay up, we would take legal action. I enjoyed that moment and the opportunity to remind him that 'a deal is a deal'. The chickens had come home to roost at last. A letter was sent from our solicitor to Channel Nine.

Soon afterwards, Len returned and we settled on additional broadcast rights for $28,000. In total, the series was aired nine times.

•

Dick Smith contacted us again and said he had something to discuss in Sydney. Could we meet him at a North Shore restaurant? He refused to elaborate, but insisted it could be to our advantage. A curious but irresistible invitation.

Dick led us to a private table. We sat down and joined one other guest.

'I'd like you to meet Glen Kinging,' Dick said, 'the network programme buyer for the Seven Network.'

Seven Network? What is this? We all said our greetings, and then Dick excused himself and left us to dine with our new acquaintance.

'I understand from Dick that you two aren't too happy with Nine and could be in the market to switch networks. Is that so?' Kinging asked without any ceremony.

'We've had a few differences of late, but I don't know about changing networks,' I responded.

'We'll make it worth your while.'

'You'd have to. We've been with Nine for sixteen years.'

'Yes, but Dick tells me you only have a year-by-year contract arrangement, so there's no reason why you couldn't change, is there?'

'Loyalty,' I responded quickly.

'They haven't shown too much loyalty to you, as I understand it.'

Dick had obviously believed this could be to our advantage because by now he'd sold several shows to Seven and they'd paid him about four times the fee we were getting from Nine. He'd previously told me we were selling our programmes too cheap; there was no doubt he was a much more astute businessman than us.

Our lunch went well enough. By the time we were ready to wrap up, Kinging outlined the offer he had in mind. They would pay us about five times the amount we were receiving from Nine for each show, plus sign a three-year contract to make eight one-hour episodes per year. With a rise clause annually, this brought the total for the three-year deal to just under one million dollars.

Holy shit! This was serious money. I'd always suspected we were being poorly paid by Nine, but had never imagined that this kind of money might be available.

'There are a couple of conditions, though,' Kinging added.

Aha! Here we go.

'I need an answer here today,' he said, 'and I don't want you to go back to Nine and see if they'll match this deal. I'm not getting into an auction. If you agree, we don't want you to tell Nine anything. We'll make the announcement when we're ready to do so.'

I felt that this was a little harsh. How would he have felt if one of his highest-rating programme producers had done this to him?

'This is showbiz, boys,' he said. 'It happens all the time and those are my terms. You can't say the offer isn't a good one.'

The offer was not only good: it was astounding! We agreed we wouldn't get into an auction war, but we asked if we could have until the next day to think it over and let him know. He reluctantly agreed.

I felt a strong loyalty to Nine, and suggested to Mike we should discuss it with Len Mauger. I reckoned we should give the network a chance to match Seven's offer, but Mike reminded me of the undertaking we had given to Kinging.

Our discussion became lively, but Mike won the day. I agreed not to contact Nine and to accept the deal. However, I never felt right about it; it smacked of greed and betrayal. I ended up justifying it to myself by remembering how cavalier and off-hand Nine had been in using our shows out of contract. I could also console my conscience with the incredible size of the deal.

Our shows were now to be used as part of *The World Around Us*, a regular Sunday night documentary spot on Seven following the news. They didn't want *Ask the Leyland Brothers,* but needed one-hour shows under a new title. We came up with *The Leyland Brothers' Great Outdoors.*

•

In keeping with our promise to tell Nine nothing, we ended up being used by Seven to shock and humiliate the network.

Seven asked us to come to Sydney, dress up in our dinner suits and present an award for the best documentary at a live national broadcast. It was a Night of Nights award show for the TV industry's stars, presenters and producers. The commercial networks took it in turns to broadcast the awards each year, and this was Seven's turn. Mike and I were nervous, as the key executives from all the networks were there.

We were kept out of sight backstage until Roger Climpson, the compere, announced the best documentary category. He introduced 'two blokes who are well known to us all. They have travelled all over the countryside, but tonight they have travelled just two clicks on the dial of your TV set.' Then he called our names. 'Please welcome Mike and Mal Leyland, The Leyland Brothers, who have now joined the Seven Network.'

Mike and I felt a prod in our backs and we were pushed forward, through the curtain and into the spotlight. An enormous cheer went up from the Seven contingent seated on one side of the auditorium. A murmur of discontent rippled through the equally large Nine party. We staggered out like stunned mullets to the podium. I held the envelope containing the name of the award winner.

I could see the Nine people getting up from their seats. Len was there, shaking his head from side to side, as he too left the auditorium in disgust. I felt ashamed, but we went ahead and did our bit by reading out the winner.

Then we made a quick exit from the stage, leaving Roger Climpson to pick up his microphone and move the show along. This was the most embarrassing moment of my business career. I felt like a traitor.

The next morning Mike and I were driven around in a stretch limousine to have breakfast with a journalist. We were interviewed for a major newspaper piece. The resulting article, along with many others in the next few days, made a big issue of our defection. I felt that the extent of the publicity was humiliating for Nine, but at least we had a guaranteed future for three years.

A few days later I had Len on the phone. 'This is unheard of in the industry,' he told me. 'How could you do this after our long association?'

I pointed out that we did have all those shows run out of contract. Besides, we'd been offered considerably more money, and that made us feel we had previously been taken advantage of by Nine.

'If you think that supporting you when you started out and sticking with you for all this time is taking advantage of you,' he said, 'I'm afraid I don't understand. We would have matched whatever they paid you.'

I said I was sorry about the live broadcast, but we had been ambushed on that one and felt a bit used. I also reminded him that he'd never previously offered to pay us more. Every year, when we'd needed to bargain for a little more, he'd given us the impression that Nine's coffers were almost dry and that we had no hope of a significantly better deal.

'Is it locked up?' he asked. 'Is it too late for us to make a better offer?'

'Yes, it's a watertight contract.'

'How long are you contracted for? I don't think they want you on Seven. They just want you off Nine, because our ratings are killing them.'

I told him it was for three years.

He was disappointed by this news. 'This is devastating. I hope for your sakes that I'm wrong, but a change like this could ruin your popularity. I've seen it before. Will you promise me that, when this contract is due to run out, you won't renew with Seven until you talk to me? Give us a chance to better their offer.'

I readily agreed. I felt we owed him that much. Despite our legitimate disappointment with some aspects of our relationship with Nine, he'd been like a father to us in the industry.

Two days later, at about 3 a.m., Laraine and I were woken by the shrill ring of our telephone. I staggered out of bed, into the hall. Who the hell could it be at this time of night? Had something gone wrong? An emergency? Mum or Dad?

'Hello,' I uttered into the handpiece.

'You fucking bastard!' shouted a drunken voice. 'You and your brother are bastards! You've abandoned us when we did so much for you.'

'Who the hell are you, arsehole?'

'It's Sam Chisholm, you prick,' came the slurred reply. 'What you did is unforgivable, so go and get fucked!'

Sam was the new TCN–9 station manager in Sydney. Although I'd met him a few times, I hardly knew the nuggetty little man, who looked like James Cagney.

'You're drunk, Sam. Now piss off and go to bed.'

He hung up without another word.

This was one of many such calls he made in the weeks that followed, always in the middle of the night or early morning, always after he'd been drinking. Most of them were simple two-word conversations: 'Get fucked!'

I told him he was acting like a schoolboy; that this wasn't the way a so-called executive of a television network should behave. But the calls kept coming and mostly they ended with him slamming the phone down. Eventually he gave up trying to intimidate me, and my family's nights became peaceful once more.

The calls were infuriating and stupid, but they confirmed one thing: we'd contributed a lot to Nine's ratings and their profits. They missed our show.

19

Nothing Succeeds
Like Success

Life settled into the rhythm of hard work again. We organised filming trips, built better editing facilities at our homes, and found an improved way to convert our 8mm film to video. The money was great, but the one-hour format for *The World Around Us* required a different approach. While the material we were providing was as strong as ever, the appeal to viewers of us meeting their requests was gone.

We'd originally expected Seven to schedule our shows weekly, but they were aired spasmodically throughout the year and almost got lost among other shows from all over the world. Once the ballyhoo died down over our change to Seven, there was hardly a word of publicity. It was obvious that the motivation behind the whole exercise was indeed to snatch us off Nine.

Of course, we were making good profits. Our homes were all paid for and so we sunk much of our money into property investments. Plenty of spending money if we needed it, and no worries.

I was keeping a small flock of sheep on the farm, and Laraine would spin and knit garments from them when she had a spare moment, which wasn't often. She was simply loving her life. She spent a lot of time dashing back and forth to her studio, a trip of about 30 minutes. Most of her commitments were at night. She organised all kinds of antics on the catwalk, some involving complex dance routines and comedy sketches. From a camera-shy young woman, she'd become the epitome of glamour and sophistication. Our love for each other grew even stronger.

•

At the end of 1983 we'd fulfilled our obligations to Seven, so I made the promised call to Len Mauger. Within days we were seated around a conference table at TCN–9 in Artarmon.

'We would need to have an incentive to return to Nine,' I stated.

'Naturally,' Len responded. 'So what would that amount to?'

'We'd like to make more of *Ask the Leyland Brothers*. We propose a flexible commitment of, say, thirteen episodes a year with a maximum of eighteen.'

'Anything else?'

'A three-year contract and a rise clause for fees based on the Consumer Price Index for Sydney.'

'How much?'

'It would need to be in excess of Seven's deal, or we may as well stay where we are.'

'Fair enough.'

'Our three-year contract with Seven amounted to almost one million dollars over the three years, as you would have read in the newspapers. So we reckon about 10 per cent more than that would do the trick.'

Len scribbled on a piece of paper for no more than 20 seconds before stating, 'Very well, we've got a deal. Are you happy? No back and forth with Seven?'

'We'll need to let you know in a few days,' I said.

We all shook hands, and Mike and I drove back to Newcastle.

'Why the hell didn't you agree then and there?' my brother asked.

'Because only you and I know that Seven don't want us anymore. If they did, this is exactly how we would negotiate.'

I'd been playing poker with a dead hand, but within two weeks we were back in Sydney signing the contract. Smiles all round. Len was there and so too was Sam Chisholm. The dead-of-night abusive phone calls were a very distant memory. The station photographer was rustled up and we had our picture taken with Sam in the middle, between Mike and me, his arms around us.

As the photographer was fiddling with his camera settings, Sam turned to me and whispered, 'No hard feelings, eh boys? It's just show business. Glad to have you back.' Mike and I turned to the camera and forced ourselves to smile.

Nine got a lot of publicity in the print media and on their own evening news, making a big deal of our return. It was, as everyone said, just show business.

•

At the same time as all this was going on, things were happening on the personal front. Mike called me at home one evening and wanted to meet. I joined him in the city for what I thought would be a quick chat. It turned out to be more than that.

Mike looked nervous and was obviously uncomfortable.

'Spit it out, Mike. Whatever it is. Or we'll be here all day.'

'You know that things haven't been too good with Pat and me.'

I nodded.

'Well, I've had enough of her moods. Our marriage isn't working anymore and I want to call it quits.'

Great, here we go again. I'd heard it all before. 'Give it a few days and it'll blow over,' I assured him.

'I don't want it to, because I've found someone else.'

Ah . . . now *this* was different. Perhaps it would really happen this time.

'Go on,' I urged him.

'It's someone you know very well.'

'Who?'

Mike wriggled in his seat. It was as if he were about to admit to some horrific crime. 'It's Margaret,' he blurted out.

I couldn't think of any Margaret.

He explained that I'd met 'Margie' once, for a few minutes, when we filmed a TV commercial using her front lawn as a backdrop. I couldn't remember what she looked like, but I'd heard of her because Mike and Pat were best friends with Margie and her husband.

For the next hour Mike bashed my ears about how it had blossomed over the years from a friendship into a full-blown affair.

'What do you think? Am I doing the right thing? Perhaps our TV careers will suffer. Well . . .?' he pleaded.

I didn't want to take sides. I told Mike to do what he thought was best for him; that I wouldn't condemn him or commend him, whatever he decided.

He looked relieved, but what he really wanted was for me to reassure him that it was okay. 'It could affect the business,' he suggested.

I said I didn't think it would but in the end, he was my brother and I would always support him. He thanked me for that with genuine relief.

In time he did leave Pat and married Margie. It had no effect on the popularity of our films.

•

We'd had a clause added to all our contracts that called for cash on delivery (COD). This had been considered a bit of joke, that the boys from the bush had such an arrangement, but it suited us just fine.

One time, however, there was no cheque ready when we delivered a batch of six master videotapes to TCN-9, so Mike and I walked out of the station, carrying our tapes back to the car.

'No! No! Don't do that,' pleaded the new station manager. 'One of these episodes is scheduled to air on Sunday night. Just leave them. We'll put the cheque in the mail. There's no one here to sign it right now.'

'Sorry, but the contract is COD,' I replied.

'Don't go, please! Have lunch on us and I'll see what I can do.'

We were driven to a nearby upmarket restaurant where we had a three-course meal, killing a couple of hours.

When we arrived back at the TV station, miraculously the cheque was ready and fully signed, in spite of the fact that we'd been assured there was no one available on that day to sign it. Amazing, and rather funny really.

Another odd clause in our contract stated that our shows shouldn't be too sophisticated or slick. Probably the only clause in the history of Australian TV insisting that material be produced to a slow, amateurish, folksy standard!

•

There are so many stories from these times that I could write two more books just relating them. One of the most memorable occurred on the other side of the Ditch and involved my mother.

Ask the Leyland Brothers embraced New Zealand and our subjects there ranged from Maori crafts and culture to exotic wildlife and the sensational scenery. Mum and Dad came along with Laraine and me on one of our three-week filming trips, mostly to act as babysitters.

On the South Island we filmed the famous Franz Josef Glacier. We trekked up its icy tongue, through narrow ice caves and across astonishing flows of cracked weather-worn ice formations as big as cars.

It was good footage, but I felt we needed a different perspective, so I hired a small helicopter with a highly experienced pilot to fly me over the rugged terrain of the upper glacier.

Laraine dislikes being in any kind of aircraft so, since we had a spare seat, Mum happily took her place. With the door removed, we took to the air, rugged up in our jackets. The glacier looked like a frozen rippled blanket, stretching down from the clouds that concealed the highest of the surrounding mountains.

I asked the pilot if he could land me somewhere in the upper reaches of the glacier. There the blocks of ice were the size of houses.

'Not on the ice,' he responded, 'but I'll find something.'

He soon spotted an outcrop of barren, moss-covered rock, protruding above the ice like a finger reaching skyward. It had sheer sides and was shaped almost like a column. Its top wasn't wide enough for him to land on, but he rested one skid on its precipitous edge.

I leapt out with the camera and tripod. Then, to my surprise, Mum jumped out too!

The chopper took off. I wanted shots of it flying over the ice, to show how massive the glacier is. The pilot carried out my instructions, flying up and down the glacier several times.

Then a huge, fluffy white cloud rolled off the cliffs behind us, as though a giant was creeping across the barren landscape and enveloping all in its path, including us. The cloud rolled on down the valley to shroud the glacier completely.

Within about a minute, our tiny outcrop was consumed. Although we could hear the chopper, we could no longer see it. In fact, Mum and I could barely see each other, even though we were just a metre apart.

The sound of the chopper faded as the pilot flew off, avoiding the thick fog. We were about 2000 metres above sea level and I knew the chopper could only go to 2500. There was no wind. Dead stillness. We had no water, no food and inadequate clothing. We were freezing. Oddly, a kea, a spectacular, brightly coloured parrot, was grounded too. He sat on the far edge of our pinnacle.

Bugger! If the cloud didn't lift and the chopper didn't return soon, we'd be out of light. The sun was due to set shortly and, if that happened, we'd have to spend the night on this damned rock. There was no way we'd survive. I knew the pilot would attempt to rescue us, but only if the cloud moved off.

Already we were both shivering uncontrollably. I removed my jacket and gave it to Mum. Our conversation was somewhat stilted as we both knew how dire our situation was. We tended to avoid the elephant in the room for some time until Mum told me not to worry about her as she'd had a good life. She told me I had to make it through the night for Laraine and Carmen.

I shed a few tears as she spoke. Mothers always put their children first. The helplessness of our predicament angered me. This was my fault! The thought I may never see Laraine and Carmen again was almost unbearable. It's not supposed to end like this!

After about an hour, the cloud began to break up a little. It was on the move, swirling and twisting as it slid slowly down the glacial valley. The kea took off and disappeared down the valley too. Where were our wings?

I heard the faint sound of the chopper's rotors, but visibility was still low. It was somewhere in the cloud around us. Suddenly an opening developed right in front of us and, out over the white, the helicopter made an appearance. Like a small insect against the giant, jagged teeth of the ice flow, it flew directly towards us.

Within seconds the skid rested on the edge of the precipitous pinnacle and we scrambled on board. As the pilot took off, the cloud rolled in again and closed the gap he'd flown through. The valley and the glacier were quickly shrouded in thick water vapour once more. It was almost dark when we touched down and stepped onto flat ground.

Our pilot explained that when he'd left us behind, he'd had no choice: it was a white-out with zero visibility. He hung around as long as he could, but he had to return to the airport because he was chewing up fuel fast at that altitude. Once he refuelled, the glacier was sheathed in cloud and he was forced to wait nervously, hoping for an opening to appear.

He begged us not to tell anyone or he would lose his licence. So please don't tell a soul, okay?

•

Back home we were having a dream run. The shows were turning out well. The travel costs and overheads had trebled, but the money was good and the letters kept rolling in from viewers.

Nine however didn't schedule the episodes well. They ran them in short bursts and moved the timeslot about. The ratings were waning.

I reckoned it couldn't go on forever and one day we'd wake up to find that television no longer wanted us. We needed to plan for that day.

Laraine and I had invested most of our spare money in property, so our future income was secure. Mike, having now left Pat, expected that in the fullness of time he would lose a considerable share of his assets. He wasn't so secure and he wanted to try something new. He turned to me for support.

Mike told me he wanted to build an Australiana theme park. He was now living with Margie, and she seemed just as enthusiastic as him about this idea. She was amiable and supportive, and left him to do the talking.

In the end Mike and I made the decision to give the theme park a go, provided we could find the right piece of land. To be successful, it needed to be visible on a busy highway. It would need rides, entertainment, good food options and enough variety to amuse a family for a full day's outing.

We reckoned on calling it Leyland Brothers World.

20

Leyland Brothers World: the Dream

In 1986, after much investigation, Mike and I bought three 40-hectare blocks along the Pacific Highway north of Newcastle, near Karuah. We'd use one for the theme park; one for a new home for Laraine and me; and one for Mike and Margie to build on.

While Mike's financial settlement with Pat hadn't been resolved, Margie had some money from her divorce. Laraine and I had no available cash but plenty of investments, so we decided to sell some of them. As a result, we not only bought our block of land but also the equipment needed to create our venture: backhoes, tip trucks, tractors, pumps, and all manner of tools and equipment. We lent money to the new company, expecting to have it repaid in the future when sufficient cash flow was generated.

One of the three blocks was rezoned for tourist development. The plan that was approved was for a theme park involving a train, a lake, a cinema and a larger central wooden building to be called the Bullockies Rest, which would be used as a roadhouse, food outlet and museum.

We still had some episodes of *Ask the Leyland Brothers* to complete. This was providing us with cash flow, but we needed more money. I reckoned we should try to get a new programme up and running however, Nine wasn't interested.

Between us, Mike and I came up with an idea to make a quiz show using our extensive library of Australiana footage. We'd show short film clips, featuring all sorts of subjects, to two teams: each would be a family of Mum, Dad and one child. Then Mike and I, as the hosts, would ask a series of questions. First in with the buzzer and a correct answer would score points in the form of kilometres on a large illuminated map of Australia. The aim was to accumulate enough kilometres to complete a circuit of this map.

We intended to make five episodes per week, to be aired at 5.30 p.m. prior to the news. In all, 130 episodes per year, totalling a licence fee of $1.3 million. This was the biggest deal we'd ever proposed. We called it *Travel Trivia* and set about making a presentation tape to show to Network Seven.

Glen Kinging was dubious at first, but he finally agreed that, if the pilot episodes were good enough, they'd proceed with full production.

Great. It looked like we had a show.

We'd decided to use NBN Channel 3's facilities in Newcastle, rather than ATN-7's studios in Sydney, because they were closer to home and more affordable. When I got down to fine-tuning the costs, it looked as though the only real winner would be the studio providers.

I then made the radical suggestion that we take the money for the pilots and build our own studio facilities on the edge of our development site for Leyland Brothers World. We could construct the set, buy the cameras and editing gear, and meet all the costs. If the show wasn't taken up, we'd still have the studio and all this equipment ready for other projects. This was better than wasting our budget on hiring facilities. Mike agreed, so that is what we did.

In due course the contract arrived from Seven. It was so thick that I thought it must be a book manuscript! It was heavily biased towards the network.

A specialist lawyer in Sydney advised us that the contract would take a lot of untangling in court, if it was ever tested, and that we should be aware that, if we signed it, Seven would own the show whether they proceeded with it or not.

The now-infamous Christopher Skase had just acquired the network and all kinds of changes were occurring. Apparently long, indecipherable contracts were part of his way of doing business. Could he be trusted? We had no idea. Better to have loved and lost than never to have loved at all, eh? Well, the same applies to the risks of business: better to have tried and failed, than never to have tried at all.

Self-doubt scuttles more plans and dreams than failure ever has. We had always trusted our instincts, and so we boldly reasoned that this would be no different. We signed the contract, confident that they would love the show.

•

Construction of the studio started and we had a big team of people on the job. It was a very busy time. The theme park was also moving along, a bit at a time.

One day Mike told me that our Bullockies Rest was the wrong idea. He thought we should make an Ayers Rock-shaped building. It would be the park's central feature, and every food outlet and main attraction would be inside it.

'Think about all the successful man-made tourist attractions we've filmed over the years, 'Mike argued. 'The ones with big things work best: the Big Pineapple, the Giant Rocking Horse, the Big Banana.'

We were now well down the track and I was anxious about changing our plans. Mike was worried that the whole thing wouldn't work without something big enough to have the most important parts of our park under cover in case of foul weather. This made sense: wet weather was a serious concern.

As usual, we were soon engaged in a lively debate. I was concerned about the increase in costs, but Mike had made up his mind and wasn't budging. I gave in to his demands and we abandoned the Bullockies Rest. It would be a 1:32 scale model of Ayers Rock and visible from the highway. No one could possibly miss it.

Building such an object isn't straightforward. Most people think that holding a building up is the main concern, but in fact holding it down can present a bigger challenge. Strong winds can lift a building clear off its foundations and throw it around like a toy.

Using aerial photographs of the real thing, Mike built a balsawood model of the skeletal frame and a friend of ours made a fibreglass model of the finished product. Armed with this, we flew to Melbourne and met with an engineer who designed prefabricated trusses for large buildings.

He ended up gaining access to wind-tunnel tests conducted by the Soviet Union when they were planning to construct dwellings on Mars. Winds on Mars are extreme! The shape the Russians had settled on was very similar to that of our Ayers Rock model. Their test results indicated that we needed a long slit in the roof, so that high winds slipping across the surface wouldn't create sufficient lift to cause damage. In effect, our odd shape would act like an aeroplane wing if we didn't have this relief valve in the roof.

Our intention was to build the frame from steel girders and lightweight trusses; to crisscross it with thousands of metres of reinforcing rods, bent into shape; and then to weld the structure together like a massive spider's web. This steel mesh would be draped with a cheesecloth-like fabric and sprayed with an expanding foam cladding, similar to that used to make surfboards. This would be coated with a plastic seal and painted. Simple idea, really, but to carry it out was a huge task.

•

Laraine and I were selling off our assets to free up more money, but all we had was being consumed fast. The biggest blow occurred when Seven advised that they were not proceeding with *Travel Trivia*. All our commitments to complete our massive theme park were in place. We started thinking that if we couldn't fund it with our television earnings, we might have to borrow money.

We'd been drawing on another source of income: our Bush Camp, the first construction we'd completed, with a large octagonal meeting hall, permanent tents on concrete pads for accommodation, and ablutions blocks. It was an expansion of our School Screening Service, offering heaps of educational and fun activities for groups of schoolchildren.

The children came by bus, stayed for a week and participated in all kinds of outdoor activities. We had a fleet of twelve Canadian canoes to explore the tidal creek, cooked three-course meals for all the guests and showed some of our films at night. In all it was a huge success, making profits from day one.

This had been running alongside the construction of the theme park, and it had provided us with considerable cash flow. However, it wasn't enough.

•

Soon our TV production facility was completed and we set out to get some work for it. Even though we proposed several programmes to the networks, none were interested. They had lots of our material and plenty of repeat runs to use up: they didn't need any new shows when the old ones rated just as well.

We decided we'd have to take out a loan to get our park going.

Our bank wasn't interested in lending us money, so we shopped around and moved banks. Our new bankers spent a lot of time going over the extensive proposition that had been prepared by our accountants, and in the end offered us more than we had asked for. They reckoned we might have underestimated the costs.

We entered into a huge lending agreement. About a million dollars from the bank and an additional two million from the development bank. In return, the bank required security over all the company assets, and a personal guarantee from Mike and me. We signed the agreement and our cash flow problem was solved.

Before approaching the bank, Laraine and I had gone through a property settlement as if we were being divorced. An order was issued by the Family Law Court transferring our home and several other investment assets to Laraine. Mike had entered into a similar agreement with Margie.

We explained to the bank that we'd done this to protect personal assets in the event of a disaster. They understood this and had no problem with it. The Family Law Court overrides the Equity Court, where commercial disputes are settled.

At about the same time, we got a repeat programme idea sold to the Seven Network for a series with the same name as our park, *Leyland Brothers World*. It would use re-edited material from everything we'd made. We were to create 104 episodes over three years. At last our TV production facility had some work to do!

Mike and I supervised the construction of the theme park while recutting our life's work into this new format. We really needed a project manager, but we took it all on ourselves and muddled through. It was a crazy, hectic, worrying and exciting time. Our lives were busier than ever! I was convinced that building the park would be more of a thrill than running it.

•

One night Carmen asked Laraine and me if we thought students going overseas on exchange was a good idea.

Yes, we said, we thought it was a great, mind-broadening exercise for young people to undertake.

'Okay,' she said, 'will you sign this consent form please?'

She handed us a four-page application for her to join a group shortly going to the United States. It was a very cunning ambush.

Three months later we found ourselves at Sydney Airport, bidding our daughter farewell for twelve months. Two days earlier she'd turned fifteen, the minimum age to participate.

•

Money was flying out the door as the theme park took shape, but the construction period of two years was dragging on because of some of the wettest summers on record. Lake Ivan, the huge dam we created, took only one day to fill, and that was the only good thing about the endless rains.

By now we had a mini train in operation and our Video World demonstration studio was finished. Here visitors could go through a museum of all our filming equipment, from our earliest gear to our latest, and then move into the studio, where we used a mock-up Jeep in a set to show how a chase could be filmed. Two volunteers from the audience acted as driver and passenger.

At this stage coach groups would come for a day out. There was the train, the museum, the Jeep ride experience and a full roast dinner with all the trimmings. Laraine and Margie organised the food, and we used the studio as a dining hall.

The coach groups and the Bush Camp were providing us with a good living. By January 1990 we were still spending up big as we got everything ready for the grand opening and the closer we got, the higher the interest rates on our massive loan climbed. When we'd taken out the loan, the interest was about 11 per cent. By the time we were ready to open the doors, it had risen to 20 per cent. Within a year, it would rise to 28.

How the hell could we survive? We needed to make a profit of about $2000 a day to meet our interest payments alone. Could we do it?

21

Leyland Brothers World:
the Nightmare

In 1988 Laraine closed her modelling school so she could work full-time helping with the LBW venture. Given that construction of the park was taking a lot longer than we'd planned, she and Margie attended craft classes in Newcastle, where they learnt how to make decorated caneware, baskets, ornaments and wall hangings.

This soon led to a new business venture between them. They called it Bloom 'N' Nuts and, in the three years leading up to the opening of LBW, it became a thriving wholesale business. They bought imported caneware from the Philippines, Macau and other Asian countries, using Laraine's old modelling studio premises as their warehouse.

The enterprise grew rapidly and they soon set up a party-plan marketing arm. Laraine began recruiting people to organise parties in people's homes, just like she'd been doing with jewellery when we first met.

Bloom 'N' Nuts was providing much-needed income for Mike and Margie while his divorce and property settlement were still being sorted out. But there was one problem: Mike hated it. I don't think he could live with the idea that he wasn't the breadwinner.

•

Mum and Dad had been visiting our families regularly during this hectic, wildly ambitious time, and they were keen to move closer. Mike and I decided to build a home for them on the 40-hectare block that also had Mike's house on it. After they moved in, we sold their old home.

Dad took ill with emphysema, and was hospitalised on and off for a while. He used a breathing machine with a face mask to get some sleep. It was obvious that his time was nearing its end. Mum was kept busy looking after him.

One day Mike didn't turn up to work. Around 10 a.m. I found him at our parents' house, busy laying cement pavers up to the verandah.

I asked what was going on.

'Just helping Dad!' he burst out angrily. 'Building a ramp. He can't handle the steps too well, you know.'

'Hey, calm down,' I said. 'I was only asking.'

'Of course you wouldn't care, would you?' He accused me of only caring about the 'bloody' business and that 'stupid' Bloom 'N' Nuts. He said he never saw Margie anymore.

I reasoned with him. The girls were earning money and we needed that. Plus, they loved their work.

'It's all about Laraine,' Mike said. 'She's obsessed with the business.'

I was staggered. As he continued to let fly at me, I tried to let him get it out of his system, but it seemed as though that wasn't going to happen any time soon.

Finally Mum came out from the house and pleaded with us to stop shouting.

'He doesn't care about you or Dad,' Mike said to her. 'He's just like Laraine, only interested in money.'

After that outburst, he continued putting the pavers down. He refused to speak to me, pushing me aside and telling me to piss off. I pointed out that if he'd wanted me to help provide a ramp for Dad, then all he'd have needed to do was ask and we could have fixed things up together. He ignored me.

By criticising my wife, he'd overstepped the mark. He thought Laraine was obsessed with her work. Bloody hell, she put her heart and soul into everything she did! He was confusing enthusiasm with obsession.

That day I knew my relationship with Mike was rapidly falling apart, but we had so much money wrapped up in Leyland Brothers World that it was too late to pull out. We were on a treadmill that was moving ever faster. All we could do was run and try not to stumble.

Mike's temper was getting shorter and shorter. Could I control mine?

•

The closer we got to the grand opening, the more terrifying it all became. The adrenaline was running high. Then, when the big day was just two weeks off, the bank pulled a despicable stunt.

The manager and one of his assistants turned up at the theme park and met us in our offices. They were withholding the clearance of $36,000 worth of cheques, claiming we had overdrawn our agreed borrowing limit.

I was furious. I'd been monitoring our spending very carefully.

'Here are the figures,' the manager said, handing me the list of our expenditure. On it was an amount of $50,000 for an electricity contingent liability.

'What's this?' I asked.

He said that, when we first started having the power connected, the electricity company had wanted either a security deposit of $50,000 or a bank guarantee. We had decided on the guarantee.

'That was a guarantee only,' I protested. 'You've charged us fees every month for that, but it's only a contingency. We've always paid our power bills and that is only to be called upon by the power company if we don't.'

'That's true,' he said, 'but as far as we're concerned, it's the same as lending you $50,000. Therefore, you'll exceed the agreed limit if we honour these cheques for $36,000.'

'Pity you didn't tell us earlier. Why now, when we're about to open the doors?'

He shrugged his shoulders dismissively.

I couldn't believe what we were hearing. How could we open in two weeks?

'This is a lot of crap!' I shouted. 'We've never used that money and the bank has never provided it to us, so you can't include that in the total of our borrowings.'

'Yes we can, and we are. But there's a simple solution. Sign over some more security and we can extend the limit.'

I explained that we didn't have any additional security. They already had the lot on first mortgage. He pointed out that there was still my home and Mike's.

'No way!' I exclaimed. 'Laraine and Margie own them, and they're not borrowing any money from your bank.'

The manager gave us a simple choice. If our wives signed a mortgage document, his bank would honour our cheques and we could open our park. If they didn't sign, we wouldn't open.

What a pack of bastards! They'd known all along that our homes were in our wives' names. Now they had us over a barrel.

I could have throttled the manager on the spot, but instead I told him to remain where he was. I returned to my office and faxed copies of the paperwork off to our lawyer. He advised us that if Laraine and Margie signed the mortgage they were guaranteeing the entire debt. If we struck out the unlimited part of the clause, it would limit the debt to the value of the homes and so, if the bank did foreclose, it could only take the two houses, which were worth about $400,000 each. All this was to cover a debt of $36,000.

I explained the situation to Laraine. At first she refused to sign, saying, 'The whole idea of putting the home in my name was to protect it.'

I pleaded with her, arguing that it would only be for a short while, until we reduced the debt a bit, when this mortgage could be released. We were so close to opening the place, what else could we do?

'Tell him to piss off!' she shouted at me.

I tried to convince her to sign. Margie had agreed already, but Laraine continued to be unwilling. She predicted, 'If I sign this, I know we'll lose our home. Everything we've worked for.'

However, in the end she accompanied me to the office where the bank manager and his underling were waiting.

Laraine picked up the documents and the manager handed her his pen.

'I'm signing this under duress,' she stated flatly. 'This is nothing but blackmail.'

'Oh no it isn't,' he insisted in a condescending tone. 'There's no duress.'

Laraine scribbled her signature. She then threw the pen at the manager and screamed, 'You've just stolen my house!' Before he could respond, she stomped out of the office, down the corridor and into her own office.

I followed her, but by the time I got there she was in tears. I gave her a big hug and she sobbed in my ear, 'They stole our house, Mal. It's gone. You'll see.'

I felt like a traitor, although all indications were for a great opening. The publicity surrounding the theme park was huge: we'd advertised on TV and radio, and placed big press ads in Sydney and Newcastle. The park had to work! Soon we wouldn't need the bloody bank.

Hard as I tried, I couldn't console my beloved Laraine. She cried for ages and I was feeling like shit. I loved her as much as life itself, and yet I'd convinced her to do something against her will. At that moment I hated myself. I couldn't believe it could end badly, but that didn't do anything to make me or Laraine feel better.

The bank showed how ruthless they could be that day. I will never forgive myself for talking Laraine into signing that rotten piece of paper.

•

The big day arrived in mid-December, and the crowds during the first few weeks were even bigger than predicted. The school holiday attendances filled the 1000-capacity car park and overflowed onto some of our adjacent undeveloped land. We had to refine our operating procedures quickly to cope. When Boxing Day arrived, we were absolutely overwhelmed.

Our rides were working well, although the mini train continually derailed. Its passengers (capacity of 80) regarded this as a great joke and would jump off while we heaved it back onto the rails with crowbars. They thought it was all part of the entertainment. Meanwhile, a six-wheel-drive bush-basher truck provided an intentional thrill ride. It went through a metre-deep water crossing and climbed down steep hillsides.

We had a huge collection of Aboriginal art and artefacts, including hundreds of pictures from the Arunta school of art in Central Australia. Four of them had been painted by Albert Namatjira. The display was a hit with the patrons. We wanted it valued, but the curators from the Australian Museum and the National Gallery stated that it was priceless. Without a doubt, it was the biggest collection of its kind in the world. The valuation agreed on for insurance purposes was $1 million.

The ice-cream parlour was busy all day. However, our cafeteria was inadequate for the task, and so overnight we installed a second one.

By the end of January 1991, our theme park had grossed more than $600,000. Not bad for five weeks' trading. During this hectic introduction to the world of tourism, we'd made no provisions for taking away the mountains of cash we were generating. Laraine, as an experienced cashier, balanced all nine registers every night and counted up the money before locking it in a safe.

I thought it amusing that we'd set off in the family sedan with a brown paper bag under the seat containing up to $130,000. A bit like the Keystone Cops running a security service, really.

There was no reason to think that anything could go wrong, but our overriding concern was making the payments to the bank. Now that the interest rate had risen to an incredible 28 per cent, I spent a lot of my time tabulating the takings and outgoing costs on a spreadsheet. This information was forwarded to the bank within three days of the end of each month.

Our bank manager, the one who'd so generously encouraged us to borrow more than we needed, was now breathing down our necks. With every addition to the park and every advertising dollar spent, he wanted to be privy to the details. I, on the other hand, wanted to be left alone to get on with greeting people and making sure our staff were all doing their jobs properly.

It became a nightmare. A hugely profitable one, but a nightmare nonetheless.

Carmen was still in the United States, so Laraine and I were able to focus all our attention on running the show. Bloom 'N' Nuts now had a manager running it, so Laraine was busy every day at the park. The long-term intention was for Laraine and me to be one management team and for Mike and Margie to be a second team. For now, however, we all ran the show together.

Our first year's turnover was looking like it was going to top $3.6 million. This would result in about a million dollars net profit. All of that, however, was going to the bank to meet the interest on our $3 million loan. We weren't whittling away at the principal at all, thanks to that shocking 28 per cent interest.

All through this time, the tension between Mike and me was mounting. At least we were receiving a wage, but soon it became obvious that any unneeded plant and equipment should be sold off to assist with the cash flow. Then the takings fell, but only slightly. The honeymoon was over and the revenue had stabilised, now that all the ballyhoo of the opening had passed.

While Mike and Margie took an around-the-world trip, including a visit to Hitchin, Laraine and I made some changes. We switched ice-cream suppliers and saved $34,000 in the first month. We reorganised the staff rosters and altered the cafeteria menu. We retained our most popular meals though: the Mike Burger and the Mal Burger (the Mal was almost twice the size of the Mike!). We also cut staff back a bit, not too drastically.

Our Bush Camp was still running along smoothly and we hired an experienced restaurant manager to take the load off us. She was brilliant at her job and knew all about controlling meal portions to keep costs under control.

With these changes, although we weren't turning over as much as during the first six months, we were still making the same profits.

•

Dad's health took a downward turn and he went into a nursing hospital. He could barely breathe without the use of an oxygen mask. His body weight halved and he couldn't even muster the strength to get out of bed. He needed around-the-clock nursing care. Every day Mum and I were driving the 30-minute run to the hospital.

Although the end was obviously near, Dad was hanging on. I think he was hoping to see Carmen when she returned from the United States. He'd always felt proud of her for deciding to spend a year overseas.

On Father's Day 1991, Mum and I called in to see Dad with a box of his favourite soft jubes. He was on the oxygen and a bit out of it, when he began to cough and splutter, as he often did. Then he simply stopped.

The monitor on the wall started screaming and I pressed the emergency call button. Two nurses were there in seconds and they tried valiantly to revive him, using the electric paddles.

Nothing. He was dead. His bladder muscles relaxed and urine flowed from the bed. I'd seen that before.

Mum was distraught and I tried to comfort her. The nurses quickly pulled a curtain around the bed and apologised that they could do no more. They were now waiting for a doctor to declare my father deceased.

Mum and I were still hugging when a coughing and spluttering came from within the enveloping curtains. The nurse ripped them aside to reveal Dad sitting up, trying to clear his throat. He was breathing again, but was a pallid grey.

The doctor turned up and, after conducting several tests, announced that Dad was alive. Unfortunately, he was like a vegetable. He'd been out for ten to twelve minutes; he spoke nothing but rubbish, and didn't seem to know who we were. By late afternoon there was no improvement and so we returned home.

Next day Dad was sitting up with a good colour to his face and no mask to be seen. He was as chirpy and lucid as I've ever known him.

'I believe I gave you a bit of a scare yesterday,' he said.

'Yes,' I replied, astonished, 'you could say that.'

'Sorry, out of my control, but I'm feeling great now!'

He had no recollection of our visit the day before and we talked for hours.

When Mum slipped off for a few minutes to use the toilet, he whispered to me, 'Mal. Get a piece of paper. I want you to write down a few things.'

'What things?'

'Don't argue. Do it now, while Frankie is away.'

I dutifully wrote down what he told me. It was a wish list for his funeral, from the church he wanted to the service in detail, including the playing of 'Amazing Grace' as his coffin was carried out.

'By the way,' he added, 'tell Mike not to interrupt his overseas trip for a funeral. No point in wasting money to come back here to see a bloody body.'

'Dad,' I protested, 'you're not dead yet, so don't worry about that stuff.'

'Well, I will be soon. Have you got it all down?'

I nodded and showed him the paper.

'Now listen to me carefully,' he said. 'I died yesterday, so they tell me, but don't you worry. I know now where I'm going and I'm happy about that. So promise me you'll look after Mum. Okay?'

I reassured him on that count, but I asked him what he meant when he said he knew where he was going.

'I went there yesterday. It's all right. I'll be fine. There's nothing to fear.'

'Dad. You're not dead yet. You could live for ages. You don't know.'

'I do know. I'll be checking out any day now. Probably even tomorrow, but that's okay. I just want to make sure you know how I want the send-off. That's all, son.'

Mum then returned to the room and he never mentioned the subject again. We spent all day there for a treasured few hours. For the first time in his life, Dad spoke to me as an equal and not down to me, as if I were still a little boy. I didn't tell Mum of our conversation.

Next morning we were up early. Laraine was going to run things while Mum and I went back to the hospital.

About six-thirty, the phone rang. No one rings at that time. I knew what it would be. The head nurse advised me that Dad had died just ten minutes earlier.

I already knew. I'd just felt it. I told Laraine, and then we went over to Mum's house. We let ourselves in and could hear the shower running. It stopped and we started down the hallway to the bathroom.

'Mum? You dressed yet?' I called.

She came out with a dressing-gown wrapped around her. I was about to tell her the news, but she beat me to it.

'Why are you here early?' she asked. Then her expression turned to one of realisation. 'He's gone, hasn't he?' she said with a quiver in her voice.

I rushed up and grabbed her. Just as well I did, as her legs almost gave out.

She hugged me tight and we all three shed a few tears. I told her then of my talk with Dad the day before.

Before I began organising the funeral, I telephoned Mike in England. He was staying with Mum's brother, our uncle Ron. Mike was upset, but not surprised. When I told him of Dad's wish that he shouldn't interrupt his big trip, he decided to carry on to the United States as planned.

The send-off was a sad but inevitable day. I've often contemplated Dad's words, 'I know now where I'm going and I'm happy about that.'

22

Stop the Treadmill!
I Want to Get Off!

Our first year's trading with Leyland Brothers' World did indeed reach expectations. We took more than $3.6 million. It was a heady time of huge crowds and high expectations. We had truly arrived. We'd made a success-ful theme park!

If not for that 28 per cent interest and our massive debt, we would have been laughing. We paid almost all our profits to the bank in interest, and we knew they'd hang on to our home mortgages until we started reducing the principal.

When Mike and Margie returned from their trip, they seemed uninterested in the business. They did their duty, but the spark was no longer there. I could tell Mike's heart wasn't in it. Margie was managing all the banking, but Laraine and I were up to our ears in the day-to-day running of things. Mike didn't tell me this at the time, but years later, when he became very sick, he admitted that he'd come to the conclusion that Laraine and I were too obsessed with the business. On his 50th birthday overseas, he'd experienced a change and had concluded that life was passing him by. He'd let us do the worrying and carry the burden of management, while he and Margie went along for the ride. I wasn't aware of all this, but I knew things weren't right. Our disagreements were even more frequent.

•

One morning when I arrived at the roadhouse for work, I greeted our staff with my usual cheery 'Good morning,' but got a cool response. Almost everyone ignored me. This attitude persisted all day, so I called them together to get to the bottom of it.

After close questioning, I found out there was a rumour going around that I was having an affair with one of our managers. They were all so disgusted that I could do this to Laraine, they'd chosen not to talk to me.

When I told her, Laraine laughed it off and asked how I managed to get the time to do it, let alone the energy.

I discovered the cause of the rumour was that I'd been seen sitting with this manager over lunch. I frequently discussed the figures with her and how we might reduce our overheads: it was convenient to do this over lunch, because things were so hectic. Besides, if I was going to have an affair with someone on the staff, did they really think I'd flaunt it in front of everyone, including Laraine?

Thinking about it a bit more, everyone agreed it was very unlikely. I'm always amazed by how quickly people are willing to believe the worst of others and not mind their own business, just for the sake of a bit of gossip.

•

My 29-year business partnership with Mike continued to crumble from within. When doubt feeds on rumour, mistrust flourishes. The next mini-crisis was that Mike accused Laraine and me of stealing from the company.

He insisted he could prove it and drove home to get a three-page list of small personal transactions he reckoned we had chalked up to the company. It included the processing and printing of films with Kodak, but the biggest item was the travel expenses, including airfares, associated with a trip to Ayers Rock we'd taken with Carmen before her journey to the United States.

It turned out that Mike's list went back years. I couldn't believe my eyes.

'What about the other side of the ledger, Mike?'

'What are you talking about?'

His list must have taken ages to compile, but it only showed that we'd used a travel agency in Newcastle to book our trips. What he hadn't taken into account was that we scrupulously repaid all that money to the company at the end of each month. Every time the Kodak account came in, I'd work out what we'd put on it, write a cheque for that amount and deposit it in the business account.

This was easy to confirm. 'Just ask the secretary,' I told him. 'Yvonne knows. We do it every month. I assumed you were doing the same thing, since you use the same accounts for personal purchases.'

I was really hurt that he'd believe I could have done this to him, after all the money and assistance Laraine and I had provided to him when we'd decided to get Leyland Brothers World off the ground.

It turned out that Margie had compiled the list. Mike wouldn't back down from his accusations, even when I showed him our chequebook, which clearly revealed how we'd repaid the company each month. If he'd taken the slightest interest in the financial end of the business and watched the figures, he would have known this.

Now it was too late! Trust had flown out the window.

We never resolved the differences that came to a head that day. In the interests of the staff, we went back to work and pretended nothing had happened. The loss of good faith and the honest, unconditional trust I had in Mike evaporated, leaving a pain I could barely live with.

•

When the figures from our second year of trading were completed, so that they could be compared with the first year, it was obvious that things were taking a downhill turn. I prepared forecasts for the next few months; if the trend continued, we'd be in trouble continuing to make our massive interest payments. Winter was approaching and winter trading is always worse than summer.

I took my forecasts to our accountant, who suggested we get an equity partner: someone with enough money to buy a share in our company, so we could use this injection of cash to retire our debt.

We had a valuation done. It came out at $12 million. Our profits were good and indications were that they would grow over the years. We'd need to sell half the company to achieve what we had in mind.

However, when our accountant suggested we sell to a tobacco company and have their logos and name all over the park, I steadfastly refused. Mike was willing, but I wasn't. I've always regarded tobacco as a scourge of modern society. It had sent our father to an early grave and, even if it did save us from financial oblivion, I wasn't prepared to prostitute myself for money.

After some heated discussions with Mike, I convinced him we should look into the idea of going public and floating on the stock market. This way, mums and dads all over the country could have an interest in our venture.

The advisers who had prepared the valuation now produced a draft prospectus to be used for the launch, but they suggested we wait until we had the summer trading figures so the business could be seen to be on a rising trend after winter.

This all took a lot of time. We'd now reduced our staff to about thirty. Everyone worked double shifts. The road-house was open 24 hours a day and coaches were dropping in from the highway on a regular basis. We just needed time, or for interest rates to come down.

Our accountants presented our proposal to the bank. We needed them to allow us to miss a couple of payments and to add that amount to the loan. In summer we'd float the company and, with an underwriter already lined up, it couldn't fail.

The bank didn't respond. The shit was ready to hit the fan.

We had $60,000 in the bank and we needed that much to pay our suppliers and staff. We also needed a further $60,000 to make a payment to the bank. We decided that we had to pay our staff and suppliers, otherwise we had no business.

I wrote to the bank manager and pointed out that we were still waiting for a response, and in the meantime we had no choice but to miss the payment. The result was silence. I phoned, but couldn't get him. He was supposedly always too busy or out of his office. I wrote a few letters. Nothing.

Finally, on the very day the next payment was due, about fifteen minutes before close of trade at the bank, the manager called me.

'Are you making that payment today or not?' he asked sternly.

'No. I've written to you explaining what we're planning to do. What's going on?'

'So you *will* be missing the payment due today? Is that correct?'

'Yes. How many times do I need to tell you?'

'Okay then,' he said solemnly.

'What now?' I asked.

'Nothing much. I just needed to be sure, that's all. Goodbye, Mal.'

He hung up. What a rude bastard. I called our accountants, but I was assured it was a technicality. The bank would need months to move on us; anyhow, we had the public company ready to go and by then it wouldn't matter.

Next morning I was over at the complex at about seven o'clock. The staff were getting ready for another day's trading when I received a call from one of our kitchen hands. A man was in the cafeteria asking to see me. I approached him from behind the serving counter.

'Are you Malcolm Rex Leyland, managing director of Leyland Brothers World Proprietary Limited?' The man who asked these questions was a giant. He stood at about 6-foot-4 and was huge across the shoulders.

'Yes. Who wants to know?'

'My name doesn't matter,' he stated bluntly and handed me an envelope. 'This is for you.'

'What is it?'

'Read it, mate. You've just been served.'

He turned and exited the building before I could ask any more questions.

Served? What the hell did that mean? I was all set to serve him breakfast!

The envelope contained a demand from the bank, advising that we were in default with our payment arrangements and that we had seven days to pay either the missed payment or repay the full amount of the loan.

Fan and shit had now collided.

Our accountants suggested it was just a formality, so that the time and date of our notice was on the record. We were now in default, but not to worry: the bank couldn't do anything without going through a court hearing, and that would take months.

Seven days! Could they actually act in seven days?

•

On the seventh day we were nervous from the time the park opened. We were planning to close an hour early, with everyone cleared out by four. Any patrons still in the park could get a refund on their entry fees if they wanted.

Mike and I moved our vehicles off the property onto the adjacent block of land where Laraine and I had our home. We then locked up all the outbuildings and rides. We were still doing this when four o'clock rolled around.

Laraine and Margie came running across to tell us that some men in black suits had just arrived. One of them said he was a receiver appointed by the bank, and he wanted to talk to me and Mike.

We approached him: a tall bloke in an immaculate jet-black suit. He introduced himself and handed us a letter from the bank. It advised that he'd been appointed as receiver for our company and that we should co-operate with him.

I asked him to wait, as I needed to check a few things with our solicitor. I then went to my office, phoned our solicitor and faxed him a copy of the letter.

After that, I asked the receiver to come to my office. I told him our legal advice was that although his letter has no legal standing, we should co-operate with him in whatever way we could.

'Good. Pleased to hear it,' he said coolly, then turned to one of his hangers-on and whispered something to him.

The subordinate left quickly, leaving the receiver and a massive bloke who looked like a gorilla. I'm sure his size was meant to intimidate.

'Now what can I do to help?' I asked. 'We want this to be as smooth as possible.'

'Leave immediately!' the receiver shot back. 'I want you out of here in fifteen minutes.'

'But there's so much you need to know! How to run the water treatment plant. Where the cash room is. The combination to the safe. How the cash register's central computer works. All sorts of things.'

'Oh! I have plenty of experts to help me and unlimited money to do it, so just go. You now have ten minutes.'

Unlimited money? The bank wouldn't even let us capitalise a couple of monthly payments to give us time to launch our public company!

I picked up my briefcase and placed it on my desk.

'What are you doing?' he asked.

'Collecting a few personal items.' I picked up a framed photograph of Laraine that was facing me.

'What's that?'

'A picture of my wife,' I said, raising my voice.

'Okay. You can take that,' he said. He turned to the gorilla and instructed him to write it down on the clipboard he was carrying. I was surprised the bloke could even write.

I then went to pick up a good-quality, expensive pen.

'Leave that! That's company property,' the receiver said forcefully.

'Bullshit!' I exclaimed. 'This is mine. See—here's my name engraved on it. It was a present from my mother. It's not company property!'

'Write that all down,' he instructed the gorilla. Then he looked at me again. 'Mr Leyland,' he said in a soft, menacing manner, 'I've got news for you. What was once yours is now mine! Now pick up your bag, leave that pen, and go away and cogitate on your problems for the rest of your life.'

Cogitate? What the hell did that mean? I'm not a violent person; I reckon reason and calm persuasion can resolve most disputes. There's a time for action, however. I picked up Mum's gift and placed it slowly in my shirt pocket.

The anger in my eyes must have done the trick, because he backed off. I grabbed my briefcase and briskly walked through the main office to Laraine's, leaving the two men behind.

Laraine was locked out and crying because she couldn't get in to retrieve her handbag. A locksmith, one of about six running around the complex, was standing there with his toolbox, having just replaced the lock.

'Open the door,' I instructed him. 'My wife needs her handbag from her desk.'

'Sorry, mate,' the locksmith said, sounding sympathetic, 'but I can't do that for anyone, other than that gentleman in the black suit.'

'Okay. Have it your way.' I rushed across the room, Rambo-style, and smashed into the door. It fell inwards and crashed to the floor. I scrambled over the splintered wood, grabbed the handbag and handed it to Laraine.

She gave a little laugh between the tears and we hurriedly exited the building.

We'd always had trouble with that door, and the only thing holding the hinges in place were a few matchsticks I'd stuffed into the screw holes. Of course, my rage was up, so even a perfectly good door might have caved in that day! It was the only light moment in the worst day of our lives. The day our world collapsed.

•

Laraine and I moved out of our 40-hectare property next to the theme park and into our terrace house in the heart of Newcastle. The house was Laraine's, one of the assets assigned to her by our deed of assignment. We owed some money on it, but the bank couldn't touch it.

All my life I'd had a peculiar birthmark on my left temple. I'd always combed my hair over it. In the few months before our eviction from LBW, it had turned a bright red and started to weep, and now it was getting much worse.

A plastic surgeon in Newcastle operated on it, and tests were being carried out to see if it was malignant or benign. I felt like I'd had a facelift: the skin was tight and I had a bandage wrapped around my head.

I was still wearing it when Mike and I were granted an audience with our once-friendly bank manager. When we entered his sanctum, I handed him a written proposal, then we sat in chairs positioned a few metres from his desk.

When the manager had finished reading, I launched into my carefully rehearsed presentation. We proposed to raise sufficient money from the public to repay our debt to the bank. Our idea was to run TV ads nationally on the Nine Network, encouraging viewers to buy family passes to our park that would give them unlimited access for three years.

Nine had agreed to run saturation advertising without any money upfront; they'd get 10 per cent of the funds collected. They were confident we could raise between three and four million dollars. Our idea was that people could take their money to the nearest branch of the bank and deposit it into the Leyland Brothers World Fund in exchange for their tickets.

The money would be available for us to repay our debt and to use as operating capital. We would expect that an independent manager would be appointed, who would run things and report to the bank. With the bank's approval, we could get the whole thing off the ground in about two weeks. For us to honour our deal with those who bought family passes, we needed to know that the park would remain open for three years.

It would look like the bank had helped save the Leyland brothers, rather than that they'd ruined us. Everyone would be a winner.

After I'd finished my presentation, there was a long silence.

Then the manager raised his eyes from the folder I'd handed him. 'Just who do you think you are, coming in here like this with this ridiculous idea? With your head all bandaged up in a theatrical stunt to try and get some sympathy! I'm not falling for that. No way!'

I rose from my seat. My head was pounding from the operation of just a few days earlier. I strode towards the man, hating him with a vengeance.

'You have no idea what you've done to us, do you?' I said. 'This bandage is from a recent operation.' By now I was almost at his desk and ready to punch him in the face. 'We just want some courtesy out of you, but that's not likely to happen, is it?'

He looked blankly at me and then pointed to the door. 'Get out!' he ordered.

I felt Mike grab my arm. I turned to see that he too was seething with anger. 'He's not worth it, Mal,' he urged. 'Besides,' he added with a laugh, 'you'll only get shit on your fist. He's full of it.'

Although my relationship with Mike was never going to be the same, and the grim circumstances we were dealing with were extreme, this moment of unity sparked some of our old spirit. We were facing an impossible obstacle but, momentarily at least, together once more.

Financial tribulations were proving more difficult than Simpson Desert sand dunes.

•

Our home phone kept ringing with enquiries from the coach companies that were now calling in every day to LBW. The receivers were telling them we were away on some trip. Half the rides and equipment weren't working.

At the Pink Elephant Markets in Newcastle, we found a bloke selling our Leyland Brothers T-shirts for $1 and $2. They'd cost us $12 to have made and we had sold them for up to $30. When we quizzed the stallholder, he said word had got out that the manager in charge at LBW was selling off everything for about $70 a trailer load: fill it up with whatever you could fit in, and hand over the cash. Our good name was being ruined by the actions and statements of others.

We contacted the Nine Network programme *60 Minutes* and arranged for their host Mike Munro to visit us. We explained our side of the story and they ran an eight-minute segment one Sunday night in prime time.

The next morning, I drove past the local bank and there was a queue of people stretching all the way down the block. A friend worked in the bank and told us that loyal fans of ours were closing their accounts all day, out of disgust at the way we'd been treated. Our viewers felt for us. It helped a lot to know this.

Armed with the fee we received from *60 Minutes* and a small amount of money we'd set aside, we consulted a barrister in Sydney who specialised in equity cases, to see if we had any chance of getting our homes out of the bank's clutches. He looked at the paperwork, listened to the full story and scrutinised a copy of the mortgage documents. Then he told us how it would probably go.

'You have a 50 per cent chance of success if you go to court. Laraine, you have a better chance because of your reluctance to sign.'

We listened grimly to the advice, which was costing us about $600.

'How much is all this going to cost?' I asked.

'Thousands of dollars a day if it gets to court. Even if you win, the bank will take it to the next highest court and will continue to do so until it reaches the top.'

'Are they really that vindictive?' Mike asked.

'It's a matter of principle for them. They've never lost a case and they have unlimited funds to fight you. They can drag it out for years. They have all the time in the world. They'll send you broke and wear you down until you give up. I know, because that's what I usually do for them.'

'Great! So we're buggered,' I said.

'Perhaps not. But you're paying me for my advice, and my advice is to walk away and try to put it behind you. I've seen so many people fight the impossible fight and destroy themselves in the process. Forget it. Start a new life.'

This made sense. Time to let the house go. Laraine's prophetic words came back to haunt me: *They stole our house, Mal. It's gone. You'll see.*

•

Around this time I received the good news that my skin growth wasn't a malignant cancer. Laraine and I were suffering from depression, however.

Our local GP spoke to me privately one day. 'Get away from here as far as you can and don't look back,' he suggested. 'Your wife's heart took a beating with Carmen's birth. This kind of stress could prove too much.'

So we sold up our terrace house, packed up all our furniture and personal stuff, and in September 1992 we moved to a heavily mortgaged property on the Gold Coast. We'd been renting it out and it had just become vacant.

Mike and I split up, never to go into business together again. Laraine and I had a new life before us. Carmen, now in her late teens, would come with us. Would it prove to be a good move?

23

Bankruptcy and Bloody
TV Reporters

There is a place I go to in my mind where nothing from the real world can touch me. A kind of retreat that is comforting, relaxing and private. Even though I can go there when the weight of reality is overwhelming, it's a delusion. I can't stay forever. No matter how heavy reality may be, it has to be faced.

I've lived my life honestly and never wavered from hitting a problem head-on, but in the weeks and months after the bank turned our lives upside down, I felt the need to retreat into my private place more often. I knew it wasn't healthy, but I had to cope with my huge sense of guilt. I'd lost our home and most of our assets. I had, for the first time in my life, failed my beautiful wife and our precious daughter.

Laraine, to her great credit, remained supportive and never stopped loving me. Our bond grew stronger the more difficult our lives became. They could take everything, but we still had each other. I felt we would succeed, not succumb.

So on the Gold Coast we began to assemble a new life. The house was nice, but we needed to earn a living and pay our mortgage. With money from the sale of the terrace house in Newcastle, we shopped around for a new business venture.

We considered video rental shops, but the owners couldn't show us audited figures. Much of the turnover was cash under the counter, they said, with a nod and a wink. Bloody tax evaders.

We looked at an upmarket hairdressing salon, but this depended on their senior qualified hairdresser remaining on staff. Too risky. Laraine was a beautician, not a hairdresser.

In the end we settled on a one-hour processing laboratory. We believed that the amount of business it was doing would be directly proportionate to the amount of consumable chemicals and printing paper being purchased from its suppliers. At least we could be confident we were buying an honest business, couldn't we?

I was the one who really wanted it, not Laraine. I felt a compelling need to make up for my failures. I also desperately wanted to be with my wife as much as possible. We could work together every day, and that was something I cherished.

Laraine bought the business and owned it. I worked for her but, damn it, she only paid me a pittance!

She ran the processing machines and I built up a second arm to the business by offering a photography service to the many real estate agents on the Gold Coast.

Carmen drove our small courier car. At first, she'd pick up the unprocessed films taken by the estate agents, and we'd return them in the afternoon of the same day. The sales staff were certainly not photographers so, when we offered them our complete service: photography and processing for just $35 per listing, we gradually trebled the lab's turnover.

Laraine was a whiz at colour correction and graded every single print we put out. Largely due to her skills and attention to detail, we had a reputation for high quality. We made a good team and the business grew.

It needed to. In spite of our best efforts to investigate the business, we'd been sold a belt without a buckle. The equipment was rundown and the figures we'd been shown were false. I'd reckoned that, by analysing the amount of chemicals and materials used in the lab, I could figure out the turnover. I was wrong. The previous owners had been processing plenty of film for family and friends free of charge. We were suckers and they saw us coming.

I got to know a lot of the estate agents and quickly learnt why there are no sharks off the Gold Coast. They're all on land, many selling real estate. Obviously, some were selling businesses.

Life soon settled into a Monday-to-Saturday routine that was so unfamiliar to me. I missed the freedom we'd enjoyed with our TV work. At least our new jobs kept my mind off the events that had led up to this, and it was a living. Just. Profits were minimal and we still had a big mortgage to feed.

We were struggling partly because to bring the processing lab up to the latest industry standards, we'd replaced all the equipment with brand-new gear. Plus the business was on a long-term rental lease and meeting those costs drained much of the profits. It would take a few years for things to improve.

I vividly remember one very painful occasion when our situation hit home hard. Carmen, Laraine and I were walking down a street in Surfers Paradise when Carmen suggested we buy some KFC. She didn't know her parents simply couldn't afford it. We had virtually no money to spend on 'luxuries'. All our meals were basic and homemade.

Carmen couldn't understand. All her life we'd been able to spend money as we wanted to. We lived in a beautiful home, but had never explained to her fully how dire our financial circumstances were. She was just starting her life as an adult, and we'd felt we could protect her from our anguish and stress.

It was time to enlighten her. The three of us sat down and I explained how we'd ended up like this. When our daughter realised just how dramatically our lives had changed, I felt about as disheartened as I could get. We all cried together.

•

I received a phone call from the executive producer of the Nine Network show *A Current Affair*. They were putting together a story alleging that Mike and I had stolen money and equipment from our own company; the receivers had provided them with interviews and so-called facts. I listened in disbelief to their accusations.

The purpose of his call was to invite Mike and me to go on the show and answer the allegations. I insisted on knowing what the details were. He refused to provide them, but said he could send a film crew and journalist up to the Gold Coast to put questions to me.

I called Mike. He reckoned we should refuse, as it was obviously a hatchet job. I agreed that this would be their aim, then suggested that we should agree anyway, provided it was live in their studio. Mike said no to that, but I called the executive producer and gave him my terms.

I would need to see all their pre-edited footage prior to responding, so I would know exactly what it was all about. The telecast would have to be live in a studio. No cuts. No edits. My answers would have to go to air in full.

'You're kidding, Mal,' the producer said with a laugh. 'TV doesn't work like that. This is entertainment. We'd have no control over what you said.'

'So what? I'd have no control over what you're accusing us of. Seems fair to me.'

'I have to tell you that these reporters have been working on this for some time and the charges are serious,' he came back.

'Charges! Who do you think you are? The police?!'

'Of course not. But we've invested a lot of time and money putting this together, so we'll use it with or without your response. You still don't want to respond?'

I told him I was happy to answer his allegations, but it must be live in the studio or not at all.

In the end I talked him into giving me considerable details about the story, but it was mostly a pack of lies. After I'd explained to him its many errors, I said that he surely now realised it was a total beat-up.

'All the more reason for you to come on the show,' he replied.

'Well, if you know it's rubbish, why not scrap the story?'

'A bit of controversy is good for ratings. Besides, we've spent too much money on it to drop it. We use it tomorrow night with or without you. Your choice!'

'Use it and we'll sue you!' I boldly declared.

'That's your privilege. But, before you do, you should know we have several QCs on permanent retainer and I have an enormous fund to defend such lawsuits. We have the freedom of the press on our side. This is in the public interest. How many QCs can *you* afford?'

What bullshit! The only interest being served by the airing of this rubbish would be the egos of those involved in its production.

'You know it's untrue,' I said, 'but you want to use it anyhow. How do you sleep at night?'

'I don't have any trouble. Do you?' He hung up.

Get away from here as far as you can and don't look back. Our doctor's advice had been sound, but now the task was impossible to accomplish. Our problems, thanks to the self-serving arrogance of TV journalists, had followed us.

True to their threat, *A Current Affair* aired the story. They even fronted it with a statement that Mike and I had been invited to answer the allegations on the show, but had refused to make any comment. They'd filmed a huge building in Newcastle that belonged to W.D. and H.O. Wills, the tobacco giants, and claimed that it belonged to Laraine. They had tried to film our house on the Gold Coast from across the canal, but wrongly identified it and filmed a huge two-storey property next door with a voice-over saying, 'Who owns this? Laraine Leyland.'

They inferred that Laraine owned plenty of properties and she'd somehow taken money from the company to buy them. It was a lot of crap and infuriating.

Luckily the episode aired during the summer holiday season and only attracted a small audience. We chose to ignore it and let it die off naturally. As our barrister had advised, never fight the impossible fight. All we wanted was to be left alone and get on with our lives.

When I spoke to Mike afterwards, I was horrified to learn that he'd paid for a title search to be carried out on Laraine. He should have known she had no such properties, yet he was still so mistrusting of us that he'd decided to check it out.

As a result of his actions, our relationship was at rock bottom. No trust left. No respect.

•

Laraine and I couldn't keep making mortgage payments on our Gold Coast house, so we put it up for sale. It took a year to sell. We walked away from our $350,000 home, after paying the agents' fees and all the advertising costs, with $4000.

Just before the house was sold, I received a notice in the mail advising that the bank was now demanding a payment for $3.4 million within 28 days, or they would proceed to have me bankrupted to recover what they could. This sum apparently comprised the original debt plus the accumulated costs of receivers and managers during the last two years.

How ridiculous! There was no way I could pay that or anything like it. What was left of our assets were all Laraine's, and they were diminishing fast.

The letter came from a law firm in Sydney acting for the bank. I phoned the letter's signatory and was told I couldn't talk to him. Only my legal representative could do that.

'I'm my own legal representative!' I assured the frosty female voice on the other end of the line.

'Are you a lawyer?'

'No.'

'Then you can't talk to him. Only your lawyer can do that.'

'I demand to talk to him! Now put me through immediately!'

She did so. As soon as I had the lawyer on the phone, I informed him I had no money for a legal representative and he had no choice but to talk to me in person. I explained my financial position, then offered to come to Sydney and show him all the paperwork to prove it.

I pleaded that there was no point in bankrupting me as it would yield nothing.

'I have no doubt we'll find nothing,' he replied. 'I've been warned how clever you are. Everything will be well and truly untouchable. All safely hidden in your wife's name, no doubt.'

'Where do you get your information? Off the TV?'

'In part, yes,' he responded blandly. 'But most of it comes from the report from the receivers, and they have no doubt you've squirrelled away huge amounts of company money. I may not be able to find it, but we will bankrupt you.'

'If I can show you that your information is wrong, what's the point?' I asked, trying to control my temper.

'The point is to make an example of you and deter others from trying to take the bank on. Those are my instructions so, unless you can come up with the money, we will proceed to bankruptcy within the 28-day period.'

I found a solicitor on the Gold Coast who advised that I should declare myself bankrupt before the bank could act. It would be less painful and put the whole thing behind me forever. We could then get on with our lives.

I called Mike and advised him what I intended to do. Up to now, he hadn't been pursued by the bank as relentlessly as me. As the former managing director of our company, I'd been deemed the one who needed to be made an example of. In spite of our differences, we decided it would be best to act together.

Mike completed his paperwork at home and mailed it for me to submit. Within two weeks I walked into a big government building in Brisbane. I was so ashamed while filling out my forms that I nearly didn't go through with it.

I sat down with the woman who was to become my government-appointed trustee and she explained the consequences of declaring myself bankrupt. I expected to lose everything that was in my name, but I soon found out that I could keep my clothes and my watch, as it wasn't very valuable. I couldn't own a car unless it was under a certain value.

Any money I earned was to be handed to her and she would send any excess, above my basic living costs, to the bank. This was to persist for three years, at which time I would be automatically discharged from bankruptcy.

I knew all this was simply a result of circumstances, but I still felt like a failure. It was excruciatingly shameful. My sense of self-worth was at its lowest ebb. The lady on the other side of the table was very helpful and compassionate, and she reassured me it was nothing to be ashamed of.

Bankrupting me was of no benefit to the bank.

•

Our photo processing lab was still running along smoothly and it had now grown into a decent little business. Laraine, however, had grown bored with the work.

Out of the blue, we received a call to say that Betty, her mother, had collapsed at the lawn bowls club and been taken to hospital in Newcastle. The message was that the doctors had inserted a pacemaker and she was expected to be fine. When we phoned the hospital that night, we were told the situation was very serious and we should get down there straight away.

In the dark, Laraine and I set off to drive right through to Newcastle. We took no breaks and, for the first time in my life, I drove as fast as the vehicle could handle the road.

At 8 a.m. Laraine's brother, Dennis, called on the mobile phone to tell us that Betty had died a few minutes before. We hadn't made it.

This was devastating for Laraine, she'd been so close to her mother and had desperately wanted to be with her at the end. Unfortunately the seriousness of the situation hadn't been conveyed in the first place.

Soon afterwards we sold the photo lab, and Laraine and I moved into a rented house in Loganlea, a suburb of Brisbane. Carmen was in a relationship with Robert Scott, an RAAF airframe fitter, and they moved into a house they'd bought in another Brisbane suburb.

•

Laraine and Carmen decided to start up a business together, so we searched for something suitable. We found a small coffee shop in Ipswich. It wasn't any great shakes as a business, but we all felt confident we could build it up.

We renamed it Sweet Seduction and bought a proper cappuccino machine. Carmen and Laraine were in their element, coming up with exciting lunchtime treats to put on the menu, but just as we were all gearing up for the big takeover day, I suffered a severe strain.

I'd carried a heavy second-hand commercial oven from the garage and set it up on the kitchen table for Laraine to use. Fifteen minutes later, I was shocked when I passed blood instead of urine. I captured a sample in a spotlessly clean washed-up Vegemite jar to take to a nearby suburban surgery.

When I presented my sample, Dr Alex Dowland showed serious professional interest, but he informed me the sample would be of no use. He needed a fresh one in a sterilised specimen jar, which I provided for him. About a week later he had the results, but he suggested that I should have further investigative tests. I hadn't realised so many tests existed!

Eventually I turned up to hear the results.

'Everything's come back negative,' he told me.

I smiled. 'That's great!'

'No, it isn't,' he said grimly. 'We must have missed something. I think we need an ultrasound of your abdomen.'

About four weeks after I'd first walked into his surgery, Dr Dowland sat with me and explained that the tests had shown I had a growth inside my bladder. It was about the size of a golf ball, and it would have to be surgically removed and tested. The chances were it was a malignant growth.

I was stunned. *Cancer!*

He made a couple of phone calls. Within ten minutes he said, 'I can get you into the Mater Hospital tomorrow or the Princess Alexandra Hospital in six weeks. Do you have a preference?'

'No. If you were me, where would you prefer to go?'

'The PA,' he replied. 'I used to work with the head urology surgeon there, Dr Peter Heathcote. He's possibly the best in his field in this country.' I was still taking this all in when my doctor spoke again. 'I don't think the six-week wait is all that much of a risk. After all, this growth has possibly been there for a long time. A few weeks shouldn't be that much of a concern. Your choice.'

'I'll take the PA and Dr Heathcote if he's as good as you say he is.'

Dr Dowland booked me in.

I was thankful that I hadn't ignored the blood in the first place and that I'd encountered an experienced doctor who cared. With some, the tests would have been enough for them to take it no further. Dr Dowland had surgical experience in urology and that was just a stroke of luck. On the other hand, I felt like the blade of a guillotine was being slowly raised above my neck.

While I was driving home from the appointment, Dr Dowland rang Laraine. He warned her that I would possibly be depressed and she should try to maintain an upbeat attitude. I didn't know about this call until years later. Apparently severe depression is common when patients find they are likely to have cancer.

I was simply astonished. After all the anguish from banks, TV reporters and the bankruptcy, now cancer had come calling! Could it get any worse?

24

The Big 'C'

Carmen and Robert were married on the 2nd of September 1995. We were delighted, even if we both thought she should have waited a few more years. She was only just twenty. Laraine had kept a few thousand dollars aside to pay for Carmen's big day and now we were glad she had. We gave our daughter the best we could afford.

The wedding went well with lots of dancing and laughter. I couldn't have been more proud of our little girl as I whisked her around the floor.

Carmen told me many years later that she was worried I wouldn't survive long enough to give her away. No way was I going to die and stuff up her wedding day!

A month before this, Dr Peter Heathcote had operated on me. I'd woken up with plastic pipes all over the place. One emerged from my penis and ran to a plastic bag, half full of blood. I had an intravenous tube connected to my arm dripping saline fluid into my system and another one on the other arm for administering drugs. I felt an aching abdominal pain and generally like I'd been hit by a car.

At our post-operative meeting, Dr Heathcote told me that they'd removed a large tumour by cutting it into small pieces. It was one of the biggest they'd taken out in this way. However, there are several types of cancer that can occur in the bladder, and this was one of the most aggressive.

'You managed to remove it all, didn't you?' I asked anxiously.

Dr Heathcote assured me he had, but said that normally these things regrow quite quickly. He would need to monitor my progress closely; I would have to come back in three months' time so he could have another look.

'What's the long-term prognosis?' I asked.

'I have to be honest with you. We can slow it up a bit but you most likely have about eighteen months to live. So my advice is to make the most of it.'

Holy shit! Eighteen months. This hit me like a Mack truck.

'Bear in mind,' he added quickly, 'that's based on averages. Your general health is above average for your age. We may be able to extend your life further but, if there's anything you really want to do, you'd better get on with it.'

I told him that I respected his professionalism, but I was determined to live longer than eighteen months. I sounded as confident as I could.

'That's excellent news,' he responded, a smile on his face for the first time since our meeting had begun.

He observed that very often when patients receive news like this, they throw in the towel. He felt that, with my positive attitude and general good health, I could well prove him wrong about my life expectancy. Often attitude could do more than a scalpel or drugs. He predicted that, with luck, my life could be extended to five years. Time would tell.

I asked him what might have caused this cancer. When he heard that I'd never smoked, which is the most common cause, he asked if I'd ever worked in the rubber or petrol industries.

'No,' I replied. But what about photographic chemicals?

'Never been any connection shown to exist there,' he informed me. 'How about stress? Have you been under any great stress in the last few years?'

'Well, yes,' I replied, 'I lost our entire $6 million savings and went bankrupt.'

'That'll do it,' he said. 'Stress is probably the biggest killer in the modern world. How about now? Are you still living a stressful life?'

'Apart from this news, I've had little to stress about. When you have no money, worrying is reduced. All we have is a rusty old F100 truck and a slide-on camper. Nothing much of value to lose anymore.'

'Well, live as stress-free as possible. Just remember to enjoy your remaining life. Decide what's important to you and make sure you do it now.'

Oddly enough, the thought of dying wasn't so frightening. I'd faced it before and it held no dread. I'd been lucky and had achieved more than some people do in a lifetime, but to check out now would be a fizzle. An uneventful fade to black.

It was disappointing that I wouldn't get my full three-score years and ten, but my biggest concern was for Laraine. We had so very little to show for our life together, and that was due to my willingness to embark on that damned theme park venture with Mike. I didn't want to fail her again; I hated the idea of leaving her almost penniless. This was an extreme low point. Depression was difficult to avoid.

•

Back at our rented house, Laraine asked me if there was anything I really wanted to do. Of course there were plenty of things. I was only 50 and I'd expected to have at least another 25 years ahead of me.

'I'd like to go right around Australia,' I said. In all our travels, we'd never done that. We'd always gone to places like the Kimberley, North Queensland or Tasmania to film, and then come straight back.

'Okay, if that's what you want, we'll do it,' Laraine said. My beautiful upbeat girl. Always cheerful. Always happy.

Of course we had one big problem: we had next to no money. Also, we had the coffee shop with Carmen. Laraine insisted we could go away and our daughter could run the business. She'd just need to pay an assistant.

I suggested that I take photographs and write magazine articles while we were travelling. That was what I did best and perhaps I could bring in enough to meet our travel costs. 'When I'm dead, you'll have a good collection of photos from all around Australia. Maybe you can bring out a memorial picture book. I don't have anything else to leave you. What do you reckon?'

She thought this sounded like a good idea. 'Now get moving and find some magazines that'll buy your stuff!'

I thought that, to begin with, we should dig up a couple of stories within a few days' drive of Brisbane and see how I went with those.

I wrote to the editor of the *Australasian Post*—the *Aussie Post*—a tits-and-bums weekly that had been around for years. It was trying to reinvent itself and to shake off the trashy image some people had of it. I offered my services as a freelance writer and suggested I could do a travel feature from anywhere in Australia. The editor was interested, but he wanted to see samples of my writing and pictures.

So we set off on a few local-area trips with the truck and camper, and I dug up some reasonable stories and sent them off to him. He liked them, ran them and paid for them. The money wasn't much, about $280 to $300 per article. With the cost of travel, film and processing, I thought, we might just survive on our around-Australia trip if we could place one per week.

In the meantime I was spending a lot of time at the cafe helping Carmen and Laraine. The business was building slowly and they were loving it. The idea of taking off and dragging Laraine away seemed cruel, but they both felt we should go. It was expected to be my last trip. That axe was hanging ominously over my neck.

•

On Sundays Laraine and I would get up around 3 a.m. and drive our F100 to the Mount Gravatt markets, where we were trying to sell off any surplus bits and pieces we had, including second-hand shoes, clothes and all kinds of household items. We were downsizing, a necessity to make ends meet. Sometimes we would take $120, and occasionally $300. The fee for our space was $12.

We'd park the truck outside the showground and set up our tables in the dark. I would pitch a small camping tent. When we were set up, I'd dash off to check out what other folks were selling at the car-boot market. With my torch, I'd have a quick look at any newcomer's goods; if I liked what I saw, I'd make an offer.

'Twenty-five dollars for the lot,' I'd say, for example. 'You can go home and have breakfast with your family. What do you reckon?' Occasionally they accepted.

I'd also buy some individual objects if I thought the price was low enough. I'd return to Laraine with all my purchases and spend the next week cleaning them, often with toothbrushes. After pricing them, we'd take them back the next Sunday.

The markets finished about noon, but we usually stayed until one o'clock and often made a few last-minute sales. As I was driving out of the showground, Laraine would count the money. If we had enough, we'd fill the tank with fuel on the way back, but more often than not we only had enough for a half-tank. We kept $25 aside to pay for the week's groceries.

We met some great people at the markets, mostly other traders. I would front up to the fruit-and-vegetable man and buy his seconds. He had some big shops in Brisbane, but anything that was getting a bit too old he sold cheaply. After I'd been one of his regulars for a few months, he said to me, with his strong Italian accent, 'I see you here every week, mate, and you always buy my cheapest stuff.'

'Yes, well, we don't have much money, so I have to restrict myself to about $10.'

'It's just that I recognise you. You're one of the Leyland brothers, aren't you?'

'Yes. I'm Mal.'

'Pleased to meet you, Mal,' he said, extending his hand to shake. 'I used to watch your shows all the time. Why are you here every week?'

'Long story but we went broke, so we do this to get by. That's all. No different to a lot of other people, really.'

He apologised for asking; I told him I didn't take offence. But the following week and every week thereafter, when I went to buy fruit and vegies, he'd see me coming and he'd greet me like this:

'G'day, Mal. How much you got today, eh?'

'Eight dollars today.'

'That's all right. I got you some good stuff.' He'd produce a big paper bag filled with fruit.

'That's too much for eight bucks, mate.'

'Not to worry. Here, have a pineapple! I got plenty.'

It turned out that when they'd first come to Australia, he and his brother had watched our shows. He reckoned they had helped him learn about his new country and to talk 'Australian' better. He simply wanted to thank me for that.

Although I felt a little humiliated, I knew it was heart-felt. I'd pay as much as we could, but always got at least twice as much as I should have. Such overwhelming generosity was so moving and unexpected. A big lift to our spirits.

•

Our shakedown trip in the old slide-on camper high-lighted a few issues. The worst was that the refrigerator had stopped working. I pulled it apart and discovered that the thermo-coupler had failed. This is the device that adjusts the gas to keep the fridge at its regulated setting.

I was advised to call Bruce Binns in Sydney: he'd made the old Freeway slide-ons and we hoped he might be able to fix me up with some parts. Mr Binns said he could no longer get parts for such an old fridge and I'd need to replace it. I told him that I couldn't afford a new fridge. I just wanted a thermo-coupler.

He knew I was planning to travel around Australia writing magazine articles, and he was intrigued that I couldn't afford a fridge. 'What makes you think you can sell your articles to magazines? I'm sure it's not as easy as that.'

'Well, I'm a professional photographer and I've worked for newspapers and the *National Geographic*,' I said. Besides, the editor of the *Aussie Post* had agreed to take my stuff.

'Has he?' Mr Binns was even more curious now. 'Why would he do that? What's your name?'

'Mal Leyland of the Leyland brothers,' I replied. 'You may have seen some of our shows on TV over the years.'

'Of course I have. Now I understand. Why didn't you say so in the first place?'

'I didn't think it was relevant to buying a small part for a fridge.'

All of a sudden the direction of our conversation changed. He was an avid fan of our work and was shocked to find that we'd lost everything. He suggested that, if I could do something for him in the way of a story or similar, he could possibly fix up the old Freeway in exchange.

As soon as we hung up, I phoned the editor of the *Aussie Post* and asked if it would be possible for me to give credits in my articles to a couple of supporters, like Fuji Film and Freeway vans. He agreed. So I called Fuji and they agreed to provide the film, but I would need to pay for the processing myself.

I then wrote a letter to Bruce Binns outlining all my problems with the slide-on. I told him about my arrangements with the *Aussie Post* editor and Fuji Film. I said that I'd be most grateful if he could fix up the van. As a cheeky sign-off, I wrote, 'If you're feeling really generous, you could always supply us with a new one.'

Three days later, Mr Binns phoned me. He said he'd read my letter and, yes, he was going to do as I asked.

'That's great!' I was ecstatic. 'There's a problem, though. We'd need to get down to your factory in Sydney. How long do you need our slide-on to fix everything up?'

'Oh! I'm not going to fix up your Freeway. I've thought about your proposal and I'm going to make you a new one.'

Now I was a little anxious. I knew I could only provide him with so much in the way of publicity and exposure. Was he sure this was okay?

'Yes, I'm sure. But there's just one provision.'

Aha! Here it comes. 'What's that?'

'I want you to have a Winnebago, not a Freeway. I haven't made a slide-on for years, but I believe there's going to be a resurgence in them soon and I expect to be making them under my other brand, which is Winnebago. Is that okay with you?'

Okay? Crikey, it was overwhelming!

'Sure, no problem at all. How long can I have it? We'll be away for up to eighteen months.'

Mr Binns didn't intend it to be a loan. It would be ours to keep, a $23,000 Winnebago! He wanted to do this as a 'thank you' for all the years of enjoyment the Leyland brothers had provided to him. The Winnebago would be made in Sydney, but he asked us to go to his Brisbane dealer and select the colour scheme Laraine and I wanted. 'And, by the way, call me Bruce.'

We thought it was a real hoot that we were almost penniless and yet we were ordering a brand-new Winnebago. After a couple of months it was ready and so we drove south with our old Freeway on the back of the truck.

At Winnebago's Sydney headquarters Bruce took us on a full tour of the factory, where an assembly line of bus-sized motorhomes looked like a traffic jam. Bruce proudly explained all the details of the manufacturing process until we reached a unit with a rear door.

We stepped inside, just as we'd done with several of the

others. Bruce had an enormous grin on his face as he said, 'This one's yours.'

It was a fantastic brand-new motorhome. Laraine burst out crying tears of joy. We hugged each other and could hardly believe the generosity of this man we'd only just met.

'By the way,' Bruce said, pointing to the ceiling, 'I got some additional support from Camec, and they've supplied that air-conditioner for you.'

'Air-conditioner?!' I said, still staggered by the quality and finish of the unit.

Bruce just smiled. He seemed as happy as we were.

To this day I believe Bruce Binns was largely responsible for turning our lives around. We were on the bottom rung of a very long ladder when his generosity touched our hearts and gave us new hope. We promised ourselves that we'd make sure he never regretted his decision. Amazing to think that the failure of a small component in a fridge had led to this astonishing change of fortune.

On the 14th of July 1996, Laraine and I set off with our sparkling new Winnebago slide-on camper on the back of our old F100 to drive right around Australia.

I counted my blessings. I had my camera, my tripod, the truck, the Winnebago, a whole country to explore, and my beautiful and, as always, loving Laraine beside me. I expected the rest of my life to be short, but I felt it was going to be fantastic. The best part yet. Meaning and hope had returned.

25

Determination:
the Long Hard Battle

I stood on top of a magnificent outcrop of weathered sand-stone in the Keep River National Park, near the Northern Territory border with Western Australia. It was late in the afternoon and the yellow-red glow of the approaching sunset illuminated the outcrops of ancient stone like a beacon. A timeless light show that I captured with my camera. I knew it was a good shot. I was in my element, doing what I loved.

Laraine was walking along the barely discernible track. My favourite model was in one of nature's most amazing settings, with the light perfect. I took a second shot, then packed up the camera into my backpack.

I glanced at my watch, only to be reminded that the hands hadn't moved for most of the day. The battery had run out. As Laraine came closer, I ripped the watch from my wrist and prepared to hurl it over the precipitous drop in front of me.

'What are you doing?' she asked.

'Chucking this away. The damn thing hasn't been keeping proper time for days, and now it's stopped.'

'Don't throw it away!' she pleaded. 'It'll just need a new battery.'

I knew that, but this wasn't about the battery. I loved being in places like this, on days like this, doing what I liked doing most, and doing it with my darling wife. I knew I didn't have a lot of time left, and so I no longer wanted to measure time in seconds, minutes and hours. I no longer needed a watch.

Laraine agreed but, practical as ever, she told me not to chuck it. We could sell it at a market and, besides, it would be pollution if I threw it away there. I was persuaded, but from that day on I have never worn a wristwatch.

•

We were on the Top End run of our around Australia odyssey. Even though *Aussie Post* was paying me pretty poorly for my stories, we were travelling in luxury thanks to the Winnebago. We camped out almost all the time, only using caravan parks when we were in big towns and needed a few days to restock, have film processed and mail off despatches to Graham Johnson, the editor.

In Darwin I dropped the film at a lab while Laraine and I did some shopping with the last of our cash. But when I went to an ATM to get some money to pay for the processing, I was horrified to find we had no funds. We scraped together the coins in Laraine's purse and used a public phone to call Graham.

We relied on the *Aussie Post*'s usually regular payments to get by. We had no spare money at all. What had gone wrong?

'Sorry about the delay,' Graham explained. 'Our accountant is on annual leave for four weeks and he's the only one who does the payments. Don't worry—he'll be back in three more weeks. He'll make one big payment to catch up.'

Crikey! This was a serious problem, I explained, we had no money at all. We couldn't even pay for the film processing or the caravan park fees.

'Just how close to the wind are you sailing, Mal?' he asked incredulously.

'Very close.' Without some money from him, we'd be unable to move on from Darwin, let alone keep up our supply of stories.

'I'll see what I can do. Call me back in half an hour.'

'Okay, but I'm almost out of coins for this bloody phone.'

'Shit, is it really that tight?'

'Yep, sure is. I'll call in 30 minutes.'

Half an hour later I was relieved to hear that when Graham had explained our dilemma to the hard-nosed journalists that worked in his office, they'd generously organised a whip-round, dug deep and came up with $500 cash between them. The office receptionist had run down the street to the nearest bank and deposited the money into our account. We were flush with funds once more.

Our fly-by-the-seat-of-the-pants approach to travel writing had given them all a big laugh and, it seems, a bit of a shock. Even so, they were great friends to have, even though we hadn't met any of them at this stage.

About eight months later, when Laraine and I wandered into their office in Melbourne, we were greeted fondly and all of us had a good laugh. We were able to express our gratitude in person.

•

Life on the road was relaxing, as if there were no worries at all. Every two weeks I would type out my stories on a small early-model clunker of a laptop, select the best slides from those I'd taken and send off a despatch. In spite of breaking down several times and getting bogged in a sandy creek in the Gulf of Carpentaria, the trip was trouble free.

In Karijini National Park in Western Australia, we pulled up at one of the big gorges. Red cliffs, rich with iron ore, were carpeted with yellow spinifex and speckled with stands of clean white snappy gums. The well-weathered course of an ancient river had carved deep trenches into the sun-bathed landscape.

Laraine and I had packed our water bottles, cameras and a cut lunch for a full day's walking along these sensational canyons, when I noticed oil running from the left-hand front wheel and pooling in the red dust. Time for an inspection. I found that the left brake line had been ripped off completely, probably by rocks that had been thrown up. What I was looking at wasn't oil, it was brake fluid!

'Can you fix it?' Laraine asked.

'Not really. I haven't got any spares for the brakes.'

'What should we do then?'

'Leave it here and enjoy our walk. The light's just perfect for photography. We can look at it later. Something will turn up. It always does.'

We set off and took almost four hours to get some of the best pictures ever of the gorge. When we returned to the truck I stood looking at the useless brake on the left wheel and considered what to do. I started removing the wheel.

Another visitor saw me and asked if he could help. I explained the problem and he looked worried. 'What are you going to do?' he asked.

'Don't know yet,' I said. 'You never know the next bloke to stop off here may be a mechanic.'

He smiled and started to walk away when a Ford ute pulled up next to us. I was still staring at the front wheel, which I'd now removed. I had my toolbox out, but no idea what to do next. Laraine was inside the camper making a cup of tea.

The driver of the ute walked over, stared at the wheel and glanced at my tools.

'Got a problem, mate?' he asked.

'Yes,' I said glumly. 'The brake line is broken.'

He stooped down and inspected the damage. 'I'm a mechanic working in the mines,' he said, and offered to make a temporary fix.

He selected a hammer and a small pair of vise-grips from my toolbox, and went to work. He bent the metal pipe over and hammered it flat, sealing it off, and then used the vise-grips to flatten the flexible pipe, leaving it in place to hang under the wheel arch.

'That'll get you out of trouble, but you only have one front brake, so it'll pull heavily to the right. Take it easy and pick up some parts as soon as you can.'

'Thanks mate,' I said. 'Want a cuppa? Laraine's just made a fresh pot.'

'Glad to help, mate, but I want to reach the bottom of the gorge for sunset, so I'll give the cuppa a miss. Drive carefully, okay?'

He set off briskly along the walking track.

The first bloke was still standing next to the truck. 'You knew he was coming, didn't you?' he asked.

'No, but things just work out sometimes. Good timing, eh?'

He hopped into his car, shaking his head.

What a bloody fluke! No stress was what the doctor had ordered, so we took it in our stride and drove away slowly, using the brakes sparingly.

Our trip around Australia took four months, and I'd driven all the way back to Broken Hill before we'd saved enough for the spare parts we needed. I fitted them on the side of the road one afternoon, just before we hit the congested towns and cities. I reckoned we needed good brakes for that.

•

At the Princess Alexandra Hospital I had an operation every three months, the same procedure that they'd used to cut out my first tumour. Every time I had small regrowth tumours removed.

In between, Laraine and I continued to travel, and I wrote more magazine stories. I loved the writing but felt a little unfulfilled. The cancer growths were a frequent reminder of how tenuous my grip on life was.

I was reading a lot of Australian novels. Most, I thought, must have been written by people who'd never seen the outback or visited a cattle station.

'These are laughable,' I complained to Laraine. 'The image these authors have of the outback is a load of rubbish.'

'Well, stop whinging and start writing,' she urged. 'You always wanted to write fiction. So get on with it.'

I did. I even wrote post-operatively, while sitting up in my hospital bed. It took almost a year. I had a finished manuscript, but no publisher. I called it *Gold Fever*, and it was a mystery involving stolen gold in the outback.

I outlived my eighteen-month prognosis. Time was marching along and I started to think I could beat this thing. The operations continued. One time I had 21 small tumours removed; on other occasions, just one or two. Sometimes none. The good news was that cancer wasn't running rampant through my system as predicted.

'What are you doing with your life?' asked Dr Heathcote.

'Just travelling, writing and avoiding stress, like you suggested.'

'Well, keep it up. You're doing well. Keep those stress levels down.'

•

The magazine articles weren't bringing in enough money and the coffee shop in Ipswich had died. The town was full of empty shops. I contacted the Nine Network and proposed a new series, depicting our family, Laraine and me, Carmen and Robert, travelling around Australia by caravan. We would start in Brisbane, make an around-the-country tour and produce up to 26 one-hour episodes. Each would depict a new leg of the odyssey.

We called it *Leyland's Australia* and Nine jumped at the proposal but they needed to see a pilot. Could we produce the first episode?

We had no production equipment. None at all. I borrowed a professional tripod, a broadcast TV camera from Sony and the use of some editing equipment. I contacted Ron Chapman from the Caravan Industry Association in Brisbane: we needed a caravan on loan for the pilot. He secured it and also helped with some of the production costs. I made contact with Ford and borrowed a 4WD Explorer.

Carmen and Robert would use the caravan, and Laraine and I would take the Winnebago. This way we reckoned the show would appeal to a wider audience: our traditional supporters with my wife and me, and a younger demographic with our daughter and son-in-law. Robert's contract with the RAAF was ending and he had no intention of staying in for a further five years.

Our lives became hectic once more as we set off to film the pilot. It was a great eight weeks and we ended up cutting the film down into two episodes. Of course, in that time we had to return to the city for my operations. On top of everything, we started doing seminars at the Brisbane Caravan Show.

In 1999, when we had six episodes finished, Nine scheduled our series to commence on a Sunday night in our old *Ask the Leyland Brothers* timeslot.

Mike, unbeknown to me, had also set himself up to film some more travel documentaries. He now had a contract with the Seven Network. As is typical of the networks, they scheduled our programme debuts almost back-to-back on the same weekend: Mike's show on the Saturday, ours on the Sunday.

The TV critics had a field day. The *Newcastle Herald* ran a double-page spread with a big rip down the page: Mike on one side, me on the other. James Joyce, its TV critic, had viewed both episodes prior to them going to air, and reckoned we were fighting each other on rival channels. He concluded that Mike's show was more professional and better made than ours.

The day after the ratings came out, Joyce ran a follow-up story declaring that the winner was our *Leyland's Australia*, but that it was a mystery to him how our programme had attracted 1.4 million viewers and Mike's hadn't. He even criticised a brief cooking sequence that featured Laraine making a fast on-the-road meal.

He claimed that no one wanted to see cooking hints and recipes on prime-time TV.

I felt good when I read his assessment because, in my opinion, the critics always get it wrong. If they don't like it, the show is most probably a hit.

What I didn't like was the fact that Mike, during an interview with Joyce, said that he resented me for making a documentary. He even claimed I was hanging onto his shirt tails, that he was the true filmmaker in the family.

Fortunately I'd always been the business negotiator; as a result, I made a better deal and Nine pulled a much bigger audience. It did feel good to achieve that, but I was left painfully hurt that my own brother had such a low opinion of me. Or was it just a high opinion of himself?

Even though our series had performed well, Nine only used those first six episodes. Then the programme manager was replaced by a new bloke who didn't want our show. So we took it to Network Ten, and they aired the entire series as each episode became available. Our production time amounted to three years and the series achieved high ratings for our new network.

We travelled all around Australia with Carmen and Robert, and visited some of the most exciting wild places our great country has to offer. Many of the subjects and locations were familiar to Laraine and me, but it was all new to Carmen and Robert. I felt a fantastic sense of achievement and pride to be able to give our daughter a chance to enjoy Australia as I'd done at her age. Seeing it through young and fresh eyes also revitalised our enthusiasm for travel and for our nation.

•

My book, *Gold Fever*, had been read by several folks I trusted and respected. They liked it, so we decided to self-publish. It was a risk but by backing it with personal appearances, radio interviews and press reviews we sold about 50 per cent of our print run. A fair result, considering we had no experience in publishing fiction. My desire to write more novels had passed the first test.

Laraine now appeared regularly on TV, demonstrating campfire and on-the-road cooking. This brought in lots of mail from viewers wanting her recipes, so we self-published a cookbook, *Food for the Road*. She wrote it and I photographed the food. It sold well, outperforming my novel by a factor of about five.

Our biggest publishing venture, however, was a quarterly travel magazine: a glossy production with lots of photographs and details about destinations around Australia. We gave it the title of our TV series, *Leyland's Australia*. It was a huge success, but we were naive when it came to the magazine business. Like the film business, it's full of rogues and smooth-talking executives who are only too willing to take advantage of the unwary.

We used a national distributor to get it out to the newsagents while promoting it ourselves as best we could. Sales started off at about 5000 for the first edition and slowly climbed from there. The newsagents returned unsold copies, and we were charged for both the distribution and the returns.

We didn't get paid until six months after each issue went on sale, so in the meantime we had to find the money to print two more editions. Our profit margin was very small and we didn't have much financial backing.

By the time we got to our sixth edition, we had no money to pay the printer. Sadly, we were forced to abandon the magazine.

•

During the filming of the series we'd been on the lookout for a place to settle down. Living in a caravan for three years is great, but we needed a base. A home. We were open-minded about where it could be, but we certainly didn't want to live in a big city. We wanted a country town; not too big, but big enough to offer an interesting choice of shops. Carmen was heavily pregnant, so she too was in nesting mode.

One day we found ourselves at Glen Innes in New South Wales. We were about to leave the town when Robert and Carmen's starter motor broke down.

During the 24 hours it took to fix it, Laraine and Carmen went shopping, and returned with more than the groceries. They'd spotted a big brick house for sale on a corner block along the New England Highway. We arranged an inspection with the real estate agent and put in an offer.

Laraine and I liked the size of the place, because we wanted both to live in it and use it for a photography gallery and a tearoom/restaurant. We also intended to convert the large extra space upstairs into four bedrooms and open it as bed-and-breakfast accommodation.

Our offer was accepted, and Carmen and Robert bought the house next door. It was a modest three-bedroom place, but very convenient. We intended to run the new business together.

We were now getting near to the end of the TV contract and there was no guarantee of any further work. We needed an alternative income, partly because we'd had to take out huge mortgages to buy these houses.

26

Tough, Sad and
Exciting Challenges

Although the TV series had been paying quite well, the costs were high and our profits small. We paid Carmen and Robert a wage for their work, and Laraine and I took just enough to get by. A large part of the profit went into paying off our lease on the $140,000 or so worth of broadcast production equipment.

We sank every spare dollar into restoring the big old house in Glen Innes and creating the rooms for the B&B, but we still didn't have enough to complete the job. Money was extremely tight.

Then, on the 18th of January 2002, Carmen gave birth to our grandson, Rex, at the Glen Innes Hospital. She had a quick and trouble-free delivery without any pain killers. Laraine and I became proud grandparents; a role we thoroughly enjoyed.

With several shows yet to film, we took off to the Gulf of Carpentaria in our four-wheel drives. We planned to do a circuit run into rugged country not really suitable for caravans, and to make three episodes. Baby Rex travelled well and, of course, we had Laraine, a doting grandmother, to help with the extra chores.

When we arrived at Mataranka Springs in the Northern Territory late one afternoon, our phone came into range and among our missed calls were a few from Laraine's brother, Dennis. When we called him, we discovered that her father had died five days earlier, and Dennis had already organised the funeral. It was to take place the next morning. Of course, it was impossible for us to get back in time, so we sent a message to be read out at the send-off ceremony.

Several months later, when we were back in Glen Innes editing the shows and still carrying out renovations, Laraine received her inheritance. Most of it went into upmarket furnishings and building materials so we could complete the B&B, gallery and restaurant. We decided to call the place Leyland House.

•

I was still having my three-monthly operations at the Princess Alexandra Hospital for the removal of cancerous regrowth in my bladder. While the cancer was sort of under control, the large number of procedures was taking its toll: my recovery time from each one had extended to several weeks. The total number of tumours removed had now exceeded a hundred.

We opened the gallery and restaurant, placed large signs on the highway leading into town and printed brochures to be handed out at the Visitor Information Centre.

Highway travellers started dropping in, and it was soon producing a nice little income. Unfortunately, not enough to sustain our large mortgages. Some days I'd sell two or three of my framed photographs, but then we could wait weeks for the next sale. The regular income came from Devonshire teas, coffees and meals.

It was a full-on family business, with Carmen working alongside Laraine and me in the gallery and kitchen. Robert would often meet and greet the customers, and he was also busy helping me with the renovations to complete the B&B rooms.

We worked hard at it for a full year, building up the business, but it reached a point where it couldn't expand any further.

•

In late December 2002, Laraine suffered a collapse while walking back from the shops. Our local doctor examined her and within days we were in the Prince Charles Hospital in Brisbane.

Tests revealed that her damaged heart valve, the one that had been such a big concern 28 years earlier, when she'd given birth to Carmen, was now seriously damaged. It was so torn and covered with scar tissue that about 70 per cent of the blood pumped into her heart with each beat was leaking back out again. One side of her heart had enlarged to twice its normal size to compensate. If she didn't have the valve replaced with a mechanical one as soon as possible, her heart was sure to fail.

Dr Peter Tesar, the heart specialist, showed us a mechanical valve. It was made of titanium, with diamonds as fulcrum hinges, and worth more than $10,000, but the entire procedure would be covered by Medicare.

This operation involves placing the patient on a heart–lung machine while their heart is removed from their chest. The damaged valve is surgically excised and the mechanical one sewn into place. The heart is then stitched back in and restarted with an electrical shock. If all goes well, the machine is turned off and the heart resumes its normal role. The chest is closed up and the body has a big job repairing the damage. Full recovery takes about six to ten months.

We listened to these terrifying details.

'Have you done many of these?' I then asked stupidly.

'Oh! One or two, but I'm getting better at it,' Dr Tesar replied with a laugh.

We laughed along with him. In fact, he is one of the leading open heart surgeons in the country, and the Prince Charles Hospital carries out thousands of heart operations every year.

'What happens if the heart doesn't restart?' I asked.

'We keep trying but, if it fails, I'm afraid there's nothing we can do but turn the machine off.'

'Does that happen often?'

'No. It's extremely rare. But that's the risk you must understand you're taking when you agree to the surgery.'

'If I don't have the operation,' Laraine said, 'what will happen to me?'

'Your heart will fail and you will die. Probably within six months.'

Laraine and I were grateful to be in the hands of such an experienced surgeon. She agreed to the operation and it was carried out on the 12th February 2003.

I was with her all that morning. At noon she was wheeled along the corridors to the operating theatre. I was allowed to accompany her. I walked briskly alongside the trolley, holding her hand the whole way. She was looking up at me with those beautiful dark eyes, forcing a smile.

When we reached the theatre doors, we paused. The nurse disappeared for a few moments. Trying to hold back the tears, I told my wife that I loved her. 'See you when you come around.'

'I love you too,' she whispered with a slight slur. The oral medication she'd been given to calm her nerves was taking effect.

We gazed into each other's eyes. No more words, but plenty of love flowing between us.

The door opened. Dr Tesar in full surgical gown and mask came in, and they wheeled Laraine away.

I walked slowly back along the hospital corridors. Everything was a blur and I shed more than a few tears on that long walk to a waiting area staffed by the Red Cross. If this was one of those rare times when it went wrong, I would never see my beautiful Laraine again. Statistically she should be fine, I told myself, but one needs always to remember that occasionally the worst does happen.

The Red Cross people plied me with tea, and suggested I go home and await the results. No way was I going anywhere, and certainly not back to the caravan park where we had our van.

I tried to read a book, but kept rereading the same paragraph, taking none of it in. Four hours passed slowly.

A phone call came through: Laraine had survived the operation and was now heading off to intensive care for the recovery process!

Another hour and I was allowed to enter intensive care's recovery ward. There were rows and rows of patients, each with a huge array of electronic monitoring devices attached to them, and with their own nurse.

I stood next to Laraine. My darling lay like a corpse. She was ashen grey with a breathing tube taped to her mouth, and myriad cables and tubes running in all directions. The male nurse attending to her was taking continuous readings from the instruments and writing the results on a clipboard.

I touched her hand and it felt cold. Very cold. The nurse informed me that her body temperature had been lowered as far as possible for the operation and it was now slowly being raised back to normal. I stayed with her for about half an hour, and then left as I'd been told she wouldn't be brought around until mid-morning.

After a restless night in the van, I returned and was relieved to find Laraine in bed with her full colour back and most of the monitoring equipment disconnected. She still had a few wires here and there, and she was drowsy, drifting in and out of consciousness all day.

I spent the next ten days at her side. Soon she was up and shuffling around the corridors until she was discharged. The operation had been a complete success.

•

Six months later, Laraine was her old self. In fact, she was better than ever. Her enlarged heart gradually shrank back to its normal size.

All was well with our business, but the mortgage debt was still a worry. Luckily the last of our TV broadcast rights came in and kept us afloat.

On the 24th November 2004, Carmen gave birth to twin girls, Jasmine and Samantha. We had known for some time that twins were on the way of course but when they were on their way we quickly rushed her to Armidale Hospital just over an hour's drive south of Glen Innes. She gave birth naturally. No drugs and no mechanical devices and no painkillers. They were the first twins the staff had seen that had arrived without drug assistance. Such an oddity was this that most of the hospital staff dropped by to have a look at the remarkable woman who had given birth to twins naturally. Twenty-four hours after the happy event, Carmen was home.

She and Robert moved out of their house next door and into Leyland House. This made sense because handling young Rex and the twins was a huge job, made easier with extra help at hand.

My own operations were continuing every three months, but in 2005 the nature of the cancer altered. It became more aggressive. It was now doing what had been predicted at the start. Left unchecked, the prognosis was for it to become invasive and eventually fatal.

'How come it's taken off now, after so long?' I asked Dr Heathcote.

'Have you increased your stress levels recently?'

'I suppose so,' I confessed, and explained our situation with the mortgages.

'I did warn you,' the surgeon reminded me.

My options were limited: leave it alone and hope for the best; continue with the cystoscopy checks; or have my bladder surgically removed and a new one made from part of my intestines. This would require radical surgery, and if replacing my bladder didn't prove possible, I would have a urostomy bag.

I opted for the operation to remove my bladder. Dr Heathcote advised me of the high risk of dying on the table, but reckoned that, as a very fit 60-year-old, I had a better-than-average chance of coming through it for someone my age.

The seven-hour operation went to plan, although I did end up with the bag. In all, I'd undergone 36 operations and had 130 tumours removed by the time I lost my bladder. Since then I've had a clean and clear check-up every year. It appears that I've beaten it.

Dr Heathcote refers to me as the patient who refused to die. It's a title I'm proud to have, but in all honesty the credit goes to the marvellous staff and the talented surgeon and his team at the Princess Alexandra Hospital.

I'm also grateful for our remarkable public health system. Laraine and I owe our lives to the medical experts available to us all for free. I wouldn't want to live anywhere else on earth. Australia is certainly the lucky country.

•

Keeping in mind the advice to reduce my stress levels, Laraine and I were forced to accept that we couldn't hold onto Leyland House. It just wasn't earning enough to diminish its debt.

We sold it, walking away with only a fraction more than $60,000, a car and a small caravan. Carmen and Robert sold their house too. They had less than us.

Together we moved on to a 10-hectare block in Mount Mitchell, 40 kilometres or so from Glen Innes. We bought three 12-metre-long shipping containers, stacked our possessions into them and set out to build ourselves a new life in the bush.

We wanted to create a self-sufficient lifestyle: to grow our own food, have a solar power system and build a decent home. With Laraine, me, Carmen, Robert and the three grandchildren, we almost had a commune.

The block was original eucalypt forest. A hectare-sized patch had been cleared some ten years earlier and was now sprouting saplings all over, and here we set up our camp. We had a creek and carted buckets of water from it.

Life was going to be rough for a few years, but we had little choice. If we were to round a bend in our journey, we had to knuckle down to hard work. We needed to claw our way back once more, and I made myself a promise that I would do it.

I owed that to my loyal and loving Laraine.

27

A Self-Sufficient Life

The fourth of July 2006 was a big day for us. Laraine and I moved onto the vacant block of land and spent our first night sleeping in our 4-metre caravan. News of our move was so important that the whole of the United States celebrated with us!

The mercury plummeted to minus 12 degrees Celsius. A water-filled plastic bucket on the floor of the van froze solid. I dived out of bed, lit a small gas heater designed for camping, and dived back under the sleeping bag to snuggle up and wait for the van to warm a little.

What had we done? Until we could create a home, this was how we'd need to live. The setting was superb, but there was no time to muck about, we had a lot of work to do, and the van wasn't suitable for the freezing winter conditions.

We were equipped with our three shipping containers. One was full of furniture and precious belongings, including my life's work in still photographs. The second was crammed with tools and more belongings, including Carmen's furniture and some of our old films, which were buried deep under a mountain of personal items.

We insulated the third container with fibreglass batts. This was to be the living quarters for Carmen, Robert and our grandchildren, who joined us two weeks later.

Our block of land was a valley in itself. It sloped down to a small creek that was heavily overgrown with tea-tree scrub. We were collecting all the water we needed from the creek, in jerry cans and buckets. Our shower consisted of a canvas bucket in the open air. Even in the evenings, after a full day's work, the temperature was usually hovering around minus four, so showers were short and invigorating.

Eventually we used a pump to push water up the hill to a storage tank. Later on, we added a gutter and downpipe to catch rainwater. It came together slowly.

At first, our living conditions were primitive but functional. We had a large open fire in the ground, a steel tripod to suspend billycans and a small two-burner gas camp stove. Really, we were camping.

For the first year our electrical power came from a small generator that charged up a set of batteries. A small inverter attached to those batteries provided us with 240-volt power in the evenings for about three hours.

With money from the sale of Leyland House, we bought a brand-new portable sawmill. It had long rails and was capable of cutting 8-metre-long logs, enabling us to convert large stringybark trees into timber of any dimension we needed: weatherboards, framing timber or tiny tomato stakes.

Off the side of one of the containers, Robert and I built a carport, which at the time served as an outdoor kitchen. We nailed tarpaulins around its sides, and that kept the wind and rain out.

I was delighted that we had three generations together. It was going to be a steep learning curve, but a shared experience.

•

Our decision to live at Mount Mitchell was based on an ideal of self-sufficient living, and our first challenge was the soil. Granite soils, which have spent most of their time supporting native forest, are notoriously difficult because they are saturated with eucalypt oils from fallen leaves; but we persevered, using all the knowledge we could acquire from our self-sufficiency books. We bought a tractor with a rotary hoe, grader blade and slasher to be our workhorse.

I clearly remember the first time we planted something. I'd run the rotary hoe through the soil, creating a bed about 5 by 3 metres. Carmen and I laboured away all day, cleaning the patch up and removing all the grassroots, before raking it over and planting all kinds of seeds. It was dark by the time we completed the job in the headlights on our car. This was a special moment. We gave each other a hug. Our first step on the long road to growing all our own food.

•

I was welding brackets onto the side of a shipping container when Carmen asked me, as she walked by, 'Why is the steel container black, Dad?'

Black? It's not black.

I took my helmet off and felt intense heat radiating from the container's steel wall. The paint was turning black and peeling off. Tiny wisps of smoke were curling from these charred flakes of paint.

Hell! There must be a fire inside the container!

I hurried to the container door. It was slightly ajar. When I opened it, a rush of air surged inside and a massive swirling fireball roared into life, swallowing our personal items. Boxes vanished and our furniture went up in flames.

Since I had protective clothing on, I crawled into the inferno to try and reach my boxes of slides. My life's work was in there.

The heat was unbearable and toxic smoke burned my lungs. I had no choice but to retreat to the door.

By the time I emerged, clutching a few items, coughing and spluttering, Robert had arrived. His first reaction, when he saw the fireball roaring around like a mini tornado, was to slam the door. 'That'll starve it of oxygen,' he yelled.

Robert had firefighting training with the Air Force that kicked in straight away. I hadn't even considered shutting the door. I was expecting to try and extinguish the fire with buckets of water. Robert's quick thinking saved us from experiencing a total catastrophe. Because shipping containers are airtight, the crackling sounds inside subsided quickly.

We had a satellite phone provided by Telstra as a temporary measure until they could lay the landline along the last kilometre of road. Carmen had made a triple-0 call and the rural fire service arrived within fifteen minutes. We'll always be very grateful for their fast response and the advice they gave us.

Laraine started crying when we opened the doors. Almost everything was lost: nearly all of our furniture and a great many personal items. They weren't insured.

I tried to comfort Laraine, but she was devastated. My turn to try and be strong. I did my best. We hugged each other so tightly I never wanted to let her go. She was sobbing. Our few remaining things were all but gone. Our new dream had been shattered before it could begin.

Within a few hours the ground around the container was strewn with charred and smoke-damaged items that mostly couldn't be identified. We lost our lounge, dining and kitchen furniture: about $15,000 worth. Other things were irreplaceable. Fortunately, although the precious boxes of slides came out charred on the outside, their contents were mostly undamaged.

At the time it seemed that we might not stay after such a setback. So much for reducing stress. After the initial shock, though, we took stock of our financial situation and decided that we were in no position to move elsewhere anyhow, so we stoically gritted our teeth and resumed the project.

•

We dug stump holes, laid bearers and joists, and built a platform between two shipping containers set 6 metres apart. I drew up the plans and slowly our first building took shape.

Carmen and Robert decided to pull out shortly after Rex started school, and they moved into a rented house in Glen Innes. Laraine and I felt abandoned, but continued to build and to work the garden, using an old pot-belly stove to cook up our food in the carport.

To replace our furniture we shopped around in Glen Innes. The local furniture store allowed us to lay-by a dining setting and a lounge, and we paid small amounts for six months until we could finally bring them home. That's the good thing about small country towns; the staff were happy for us to take as long as we needed to pay off the debt. Country folks are friendly folks.

We planted 62 fruit trees, including apples, pears, nectarines, plums, peaches, almonds and apricots, and a large number of berry vines. The plots were laid out between the fruit trees with meandering grass pathways. Our vegie gardens eventually covered roughly a quarter of a hectare. Bordering everything was a fence to keep the friendly kangaroos and wallabies at bay.

With hard work we avoided chemicals and pesticides. To make it productive, the soil needed huge amounts of organic compost and dolomite to free up its 'locked-in' nutrients. We also removed many eucalypts, which are selfish trees: they shed their oil-filled leaves in the summer and the oil discourages almost all other plants from growing.

We paid to have a half-million-litre dam built. It was fed by a spur off our small creek. We pumped the water to a tank on a high hill among huge granite rocks, and from there it gravity-fed the entire property. An underground loop pipe fed twelve sprinkler heads. This way we could water the entire garden and orchard in about half an hour with the equivalent of an inch of rain. Water was plentiful, as our creek and river never ran dry.

Back when we turned the first sod on the land, we found a solitary earthworm within the entire garden area. Today, the turn of a fork anywhere would reveal vibrant living soil, full of humus and worms.

•

As we developed the gardens and built runs and accommodation for the chooks, the construction work on our home advanced slowly; one small piece at a time, as money allowed. Over five years I used our portable mill to cut all the stringybark timber needed to build our two-storey house.

Once our old friends Dick and Pip Smith dropped in to say hello: they were travelling in their new motorhome. Laraine and I were living in the shipping container at the time, as the house was still in its early stages. We all sat down together, ate fresh scones from the woodstove and had a cuppa. It was good to catch up. Laraine and I didn't get too many visitors.

About a week later, when I visited our roadside mailbox, there was a letter from Dick. He expressed how much he admired our spirit to get on with things, even though we didn't have much to work with, and he praised our obvious love for each other.

It was nice to receive such a thoughtful sentiment, but even more surprising and equally wonderful was the enclosed cheque for $10,000 to 'Help with your project'. Such generosity was utterly overwhelming. With our second winter approaching, it couldn't have come at a better time.

We used the money to buy a first-class, modern, slow-burning wood heater and flue to install in the open-plan living area. Thank you, Dick and Pip, your timing was perfect.

•

One day Laraine was in the carport preparing lunch and I was sanding down some old window frames when we heard a vehicle pull up. So we both wandered over.

'Hello!' a woman's voice called out. We looked up to see Margie approaching. An old man, partly stooped over, shuffled along behind her. Who was he?

It was Mike. I could hardly believe my eyes. He'd aged so much he reminded me of our father towards the end of his life.

We had no idea they were coming to visit, and were both surprised and bewildered. We hadn't been in touch since Mum's funeral two years earlier. Our old wounds had mostly healed, but they still lingered. The pain of mistrust never goes, it just gradually fades. Their desire to re-connect had brought Mike and Margie here.

They'd brought along a cut lunch, which we all ate while seated at our outdoor table under an umbrella. Mike was obviously unwell.

'I wanted to catch up, Mal,' he said after lunch, as we walked together around the property, having a chat. He shuffled along slowly, but managed to make it through our extensive garden plot and down to the creek. I showed him the pump, where Laraine and I pulled our water, and we perched at the end of a deep pool.

After that, we wandered around. He said he'd felt a need to see me, to see that we were all right, and he hoped that our past differences were now out of the way. He didn't want to discuss it in any detail. As he was talking and I was responding, it became obvious to me that his brain wasn't functioning properly.

On the way back to the house camp, where Laraine and Margie were still sitting under the umbrella, we strolled past the pump again.

'What's this here for?' Mike asked.

I couldn't believe it! 'That's the pump we use to pull water up to the camp,' I explained. 'Don't you remember? I showed it to you ten minutes ago.'

Mike didn't answer. He just stopped and stared at the pipes and the pump. He looked vacantly ahead. He obviously had a serious memory problem.

When we returned to the girls, Margie explained that Mike had been diagnosed with Parkinson's disease. It's a rapid degenerative brain condition that has no cure. He was on medication to control the symptoms, but the condition was expected to accelerate, with death inevitable. The big question was how long would it take.

This was devastating news. In spite of his poor posture, slightly frozen facial muscles and the lapses in his short-term memory, my brother's ability to converse about old times seemed normal.

They left in the afternoon and Mike seemed contented that he'd caught up with us. I felt he'd wanted to reassure himself that I wasn't at death's door too, and that we were coping with our difficult circumstances.

•

By incorporating the two shipping containers into the outer walls of the building, I improved its structural integrity. The construction was a conventional stud frame, but I took extra care with the insulation: the walls and ceiling are crammed full of fibreglass batts. For the outer cladding I used timber weatherboards.

Erecting the roof trusses without a crane was tricky. They spanned just over 6 metres and I'd made them from hardwood milled on the property, bolted together with steel plates at the apex. The roof has a 42 degree pitch, so each one was quite heavy. To erect them 10.5 metres from the ground, I constructed a vertical post and, using a chain block, hauled them one by one into position. It was a slow process. I needed ropes everywhere to control the heavy trusses and keep the work safe. It was a major achievement and I felt proud of my effort.

Laraine and I kept cooking in the carport until I had a roof over the building. We bought an Australian-made woodstove with a wet back on which we cooked all our meals and which provided our hot water, which was stored in a 360-litre tank.

Our stove was the heart of a highly productive kitchen. It burned all year round, night and day, fuelled with wood from the property. The kettle's always on at our place and the huge walk-in pantry was full of Laraine's preserved fruits and vegetables, and our stock of bulk staples. We'd buy organic wheat, use a small stone mill to make flour, and Laraine would bake bread every few days.

In order to have money to live on and to build our dream, we started selling at as many local markets as possible. We'd take any excess produce from the garden, and Laraine's baked bread, cakes and biscuits. We ran our stall at festivals in the region too. If we had a good day at the weekend markets, we'd pay a bit off our lay-by for the furniture on Monday.

•

Mike and Margie paid us a second visit several months after their first, and it was depressing to see how much Mike's condition had deteriorated. He seemed sad and his ability to walk was highly restricted. He did, however, manage to make it up the flight of stairs to see the progress I'd made on the bedroom. He hardly spoke, but seemed pleased with the chance to see us again.

I have a photograph of Mike and me together, taken on that day. His drooping face and the lack of sparkle in his eyes are evident, but it was the last time I saw him when we could still communicate. Not much, but a little.

In July 2009, Margie phoned. She suggested Laraine and I might like to drive down to their home at Lake

Macquarie and see him. His condition had worsened and the end couldn't be far off.

We immediately drove to their place and stayed for a couple of days. Mike could just manage to feed himself with a shaky, unsteady hand. It took him about an hour to eat what we consumed in six or seven minutes. It was painful to watch.

He sat in his chair for most of our visit, staring vacantly into the room. He could say Margie's name when he needed her help and his eyes still had a bit of a sparkle.

He was wearing nappies 24 hours a day as he couldn't control his bowels. On one occasion I led him across the room to the toilet, where I helped him undress. His whole body vibrated with a trembling shake. It was unnerving and depressing, but I kept up some cheerful chatter all the time. There was no response. This must have been embarrassing for him. I felt sure he knew what I was saying, but he simply couldn't talk back. I wondered if he had a functioning brain locked in limbo.

The time came when Laraine and I needed to return to our block in the bush. She and Margie went out to the car.

I looked at my brother and tried to retain my composure. He'd been my closest friend for so long. I bent forward, so we were face to face as he sat in his chair, and I asked him, 'How would you like to do one more trip, Mike?'

For the first time in two days, his face brightened. One side of his mouth lifted in an attempt to smile, and he slowly uttered two words. 'One more.'

I felt very moved, but it was time to go.

I walked a few metres from him, and then turned and said, 'I've got to leave you now, mate. I have to go.'

He stared straight back at me. Nothing happening. Was anybody home? Then I raised my hand in a thumbs up gesture, just like we'd done on our shows. A flicker of recognition flashed across his face. He tried to raise his hand and, although it was curled up like a claw, he made an attempt to give the thumbs up.

My heart was thumping. I just knew this would be the last time I'd see him alive. I struggled to remain composed as I spoke my last words to him, 'Goodbye, Mike, it's time to go.'

It took me fifteen minutes sitting in the front seat of our car before I'd regained my composure enough to drive home.

That was indeed the last time I saw him. He died three months later, on the 14th September 2009. Ten days after his 68th birthday.

I was the only survivor from our original quartet of pommy bastards. Mum had died at the age of 93 in June 2006.

•

Back at Mount Mitchell, Laraine and I resumed our task of creating a place to live, using next to no money.

What matters in life has nothing to do with money. We have enough to get by but, more importantly, we have each other. Our health, although challenged, is holding out. I value every day. Mike's passing only reinforces that philosophy.

Our electricity is now coming from a solar power system that uses battery storage and a large inverter. We aren't connected to the power grid, so if we have four overcast days in a row, we run our generator for three hours to top up the batteries. Our cost for power amounts to about four jerry cans of petrol a year.

We can run any gadgets we like, but we have to be careful with motors and appliances that use large heating elements. Laraine uses the hairdryer about three times a week and the vacuum cleaner once a week; we have two deep freezers (for storing summer excess to get us through winter); and, of course, we use lights, computers and kitchen appliances, although our main fridge is run on LP gas. I built the house with what I call 'zone lighting': we have lights everywhere where we need them, but only use those in the zone we're in at the time.

The upstairs part of our three-bedroom home is a huge space, 12 by 6 metres. The master bedroom has an ensuite bathroom with a washbasin and toilet, and a large walk-in wardrobe. There's also an upstairs craft area where Laraine makes dichroic glass jewellery for the markets. In the cool winter months, heat rises from the slow-burning woodstove downstairs, keeping the master bedroom and craft area at a comfortable 18 degrees Celsius, even when the outside temperature drops as low as minus six. It's very pleasant to wake up in such comfort and gaze out the window at a light snowfall or dusting of frost.

Nothing compares with sitting down to a meal and knowing that everything on your plate came off the farm.

Not just the vegetables, but also the chicken from our highly productive brood.

I still have check-ups at the Princess Alexandra Hospital, but now they amount to a few scans and blood tests. Ever since we changed to our alternative, self-sufficient way of life, my checks have been clear. My doctor actually told me I could legitimately call myself a cancer survivor now!

Laraine has biannual checks to see how her heart is going. Her little metal miracle clicks with each beat. I can hear it if I'm close and in a quiet place, such as lying next to her in bed. I like to think it clicks a bit faster as I give her a hug. Her check-ups have also been excellent. In fact, we're both convinced that our present sense of wellbeing is a direct result of our lifestyle.

We grow everything organically, our cost of living is low and our carbon footprint is about as small as is possible in the modern world. We've just reached our seventies and have no more building work to complete. We live on the aged pension and that's enough for us. We're enjoying the benefits from the hard work, love and tears that we've lavished on this piece of heaven, which we call Lara's Valley.

We love this way of living: the rooster crowing, the beautiful king parrots greeting us on our verandah for a handful of seed, and the peace and tranquillity of the Australian bush.

How things have changed. We feel very contented with what we've managed to achieve on our small property. The warm fuzzy feeling that you get when seated in front of a glowing fire on a winter's night, knowing that you're surrounded by something of your own making, is very hard to beat. To awaken to the sound of magpies singing in the trees just makes the day.

We'll continue to go to the markets, to travel with our caravan into the fantastic outdoors this wonderful country has to offer, and to enjoy each other's loving company. Laraine will make her jewellery and I'll keep writing, for I have many fictional stories yet to tell.

Many people reckon we're odd. Our life has been unconventional, that's true. We've taken on numerous challenges and, in some cases, created our own. I'm glad we chose to be different. We're smitten with wanderlust, the desire to move around and taste the variety of life. Some people pity us because we're different; I pity them because they are all the same.

Our lives have been full of ups and downs, but it's been a grand ride. I consider that I've had a fortunate life. I have lived every bit of it as an adventure.

When I wake up in the morning, I'm thankful for the start of another day. I have a roof over my head, healthy food, my beautiful daughter, the grandchildren, and I have my loving Laraine to share it with.

I may not have much money, but I have the memories of a life well lived. In that respect, I'm the wealthiest man in the world.

Keep watching this space—I've no intention of checking out just yet!

Epilogue

Since writing this book, Laraine and I have sold our farm in the bush at Mount Mitchell and moved north to Maleny in Queensland. This was not an easy decision. We put so much into creating our own special self-sufficient home in the bush, but we wanted to be closer to our daughter and grandchildren.

Also, Laraine recently suffered two mild strokes, and this made us realise that the manual labour we had to do to tend the animals and our huge orchard may, in time, become too much for just two people approaching their later years.

Our move has given us more freedom. We can take off and travel whenever we like without having to think of the animals or relying on neighbours to look after them. Laraine is keen to set up a food business with Carmen as a partner and I can pursue my ambitions to write more books. I have lots of historical fiction yarns to tell.

Our new home is conventional and modern and part of a community of over-fifties semi-retired folks. It's a far cry from Mount Mitchell, but it is an easier life with medical assistance at our fingertips and a short stroll to the main shopping street.

On reflection, I like to think that we had a part to play in awakening Australians to what a great country we have. It is indeed the lucky country and we're continually delighted and amazed at how many people we meet who credit us with arousing their own curiosity to get out and see it. If that is true then it's been an unexpected and wonderful result of our lives so far.

Acknowledgements

I would like to acknowledge the innumerable and wonderful people of the outback who have helped me along my way through a lifetime of travel across their country and who, on so many occasions, gave us their encouragement and assistance. Outback hospitality never ceases to impress me.

I would also like to acknowledge the wonderful team of editorial staff at Allen & Unwin who moulded and shaped my huge manuscript into a manageable volume, and Dick Smith who helped us along the way and brought me together with my publishers.

Other publications by Mal Leyland

Non Fiction
(Co-authored with Mike Leyland)

Great Ugly River
Where Dead Men Lie
Untamed Coast
Off the Beaten Track
Further Off the Beaten Track
Leyland Brothers Trekabout
Leyland Brothers Australian Animals A to Z
Leyland Brothers Australian Wildlife
Discovering Australia
Leyland Brothers Australia

Children's Fiction

Kerry's Lost Dog
Gypsy Goes to the Country
Gypsy's Animal Alphabet

Adult Fiction

Gold Fever